STATE TROOPER

HIGHWAY PATROL OFFICER/STATE TRAFFIC OFFICER

Macmillan•USA

STATE TROOPER

HIGHWAY PATROL OFFICER/STATE TRAFFIC OFFICER

HY HAMMER
EDWARD SCHEINKMAN

Macmillan•USA

Twelfth Edition

Macmillan General Reference
A Simon & Schuster Macmillan Company
1633 Broadway
New York, NY 10019-6785

An ARCO Book

Library of Congress Number 97-070043

ISBN: 0-02-861523-9

Manufactured in the United States of America
10 9 8 7 6 5 4 3 2 1

CONTENTS

PART THREE

Skill Building

What This Book Will Do for You

You want to become a state police officer, state trooper, or highway patrol officer. That's great. Every state needs qualified and enthusiastic new recruits to maintain staffing at full level and to cover all parts of the state and all functions. You have made a good start toward joining a state police force by buying this book.

This book has been carefully researched and has been written to help you through the application and screening process. The information in this book will prepare you for the written exam, forewarn you as to the physical skills on which you must concentrate, and give you valuable tips for your interview and psychological screening.

It is important that you allow the book to help you. Read it carefully. Do not skip over any information. Information about police work itself should help psych you for the job. You should get more and more excited about the work as you read about all the possible assignments. The information about the screening process itself should calm you and help to allay your fears. Taken step by step the process is not so frightening. Each step has a purpose. There is a way to handle each one. Once you know what to expect, half the battle is won. Thorough preparation for the written exam should win the other half of the battle. If you are prepared, you can feel self-confident. If you feel confident, you can answer questions quickly and decisively, finish the exam, and earn a high score.

So make a study schedule. Assign yourself a period of each day to devote to preparation for the police-screening process. A regular time is best, but the important thing is daily study. Choose a quiet, well-lighted spot with as few distractions as possible. Try to arrange not to be interrupted.

Begin at the beginning of the book. Read. Underline points that you consider significant. Make marginal notes. Flag the pages that you think are especially important with little sticky notes.

The bulk of this book consists of model examinations for practice. These are not real examinations, but they are examinations that we have created using questions that have appeared on many state police and city police examinations over the years. The questions that come from city police exams may describe situations that occur only in cities, but the thinking required to answer them is the same thinking required of state police officers. The formats of the model exams are based on actual exams given at different times in a number of states.

The last part of the book is composed of a number of chapters that should help you with answering police exam questions. The chapters give instruction and practice with reading comprehension, observation and memory, and police judgment questions. You may want to read through the last part of the book and answer the exercise questions before you tackle the exams in the middle of the book. Or, you may take one model exam and then turn to Part Three before trying other exams. The skill-building chapters should help you improve your performance from one model exam to the next. You can return to these chapters for targeted practice in your areas of weakness.

Try to answer an entire exam in one sitting; you want your practice to prepare you for the demands of the real exam. If you must divide your time, divide into no more than two sessions per exam. When you take the exams, treat them with respect. Time yourself accurately and do not peek at the correct answers. Remember, you are taking these for practice; they will not be scored; they do not count. So learn from them. Learn to think; learn to reason like a state police officer; learn to pace yourself so that you can answer all the questions. Then learn from the explanations. Study all explanations, even explanations to questions that you answered correctly. An explanation may bring out points that had not occurred to you.

IMPORTANT: Do not memorize questions and answers. Any question that has been released will not be used again. You may run into questions that are very similar, but you will not be tested with any of these exact questions. These questions will give you good practice, but they will not give you the answers to any of the questions on your exam.

With all of this emphasis on time, you may be wondering if it is wise to guess. The best policy is, of course, to pace yourself so that you can read and consider each question. Sometimes this does not work. Most civil service exam scores are based only on the number of questions answered correctly. This means that a wild guess is better than a blank space. There is no penalty for a wrong answer, and you just might guess right. If you see that time is about to run out, mark all the remaining spaces with the same answer. By the law of averages, some will be right.

Far better than a wild guess is an educated guess. You make this kind of guess not when you are pressed for time but when you are not sure of the correct answer. Usually, one or two of the choices are obviously wrong. Eliminate the obviously wrong answers and try to reason among those remaining. Then, if necessary, guess from the smaller field. The odds of a right answer increase if you guess from a field of two instead of from a field of four. When you make an educated guess or a wild guess in the course of the exam, you might want to make a note next to the question number in the test booklet. Then, if there is time, you can go back for a second look.

Your exam probably will be machine scored. You will mark your answers on a separate answer sheet. Each exam in this book has its own answer sheet so that you can practice marking all of your answers in the right way. Tear out the answer sheet before you begin each exam. Do not try to flip pages back and forth. Since your answer sheet will be machine scored, you must fill it out clearly and correctly. You cannot give any explanations to the machine. This means:

1. Blacken your answer space firmly and completely. ● is the only correct way to mark the answer sheet. ◐, ⊗, ⊘, and ∅ are all unacceptable. The machine might not read them at all.

2. Mark only one answer for each question. If you mark more than one answer you will be considered wrong even if one of the answers is correct.

3. If you change your mind, you must erase your mark. Attempting to cross out an incorrect answer like this ✸ will not work. You must erase any incorrect answer completely. An incomplete erasure might be read as a second answer.

4. All of your answering should be in the form of blackened spaces. The machine cannot read English. Do not write any notes in the margins. If you have done any figuring in the margins of the test booklet itself, be sure to mark the letter of your answer on the answer sheet. Correct answers in the test booklet do not count. Only the answer sheet is scored.

5. MOST IMPORTANT: Answer each question in the right place. Question 1 must be answered in space 1; question 52 in space 52. If you should skip an answer space and mark a series of answers in the wrong places, you must erase all those answers and do the questions over, marking your answers in the proper places. You cannot afford to use the limited time in this way. Therefore, as you answer *each* question, look at its number and check that you are marking your answer in the space with the same number.

6. In general, because of the risk of getting out of line on the answer sheet, we recommend that you answer every question in order, even if you have to guess. Make an educated guess if you can. If not, make it a wild guess. Just mark the question number in the test booklet so that you can try again if there is time.

On the examination day assigned to you, allow the test itself to be the main event of the day. Do not squeeze it in between other activities. Arrive rested, relaxed, and on time. In fact, plan to arrive early. Leave plenty of time for traffic tie-ups or other complications that might upset you and interfere with your test performance.

In the test room, the examiner will hand out forms for you to fill out. He or she will give you the instructions that you must follow in taking the examination. The examiner will tell you how to fill in the grids on the forms. Time limits and timing signals will be explained. If you do not understand any of the examiner's instructions, ASK QUESTIONS. Make sure that you know exactly what to do.

At the examination, you must follow instructions exactly. Fill in the grids on the forms carefully and accurately. Filling in the wrong grid may lead to loss of veterans' credits to which you may be entitled or to an incorrect address for your test results. Do not begin until you are told to begin. Stop as soon as the examiner tells you to stop. Do not turn pages until you are told to. Do not go back to parts you have already completed. Any infraction of the rules is considered cheating. If you cheat, your test paper will not be scored and you will not be eligible for appointment.

Once the signal has been given and you begin the exam, read every word of every question. Be alert for exclusionary words that might affect your answer: words like "not," "most," "least," "all," "every," and "except."

Read all the choices before you mark your answer. It is statistically true that most errors are made when the last choice is the correct answer. Too many people mark the first answer that seems correct without reading through all the choices to find out which answer is *best*.

If you happen to finish before time is up, return to difficult questions that you marked in the booklet and try them again. There is no bonus for finishing early, so use all your time to perfect your exam paper.

PART ONE

Learning About the Job and Preparing to Apply for It

State Police Officer

DUTIES OF THE JOB

State police officers provide police services to the public by patrolling state and interstate highways, turnpikes, and freeways and by enforcing motor vehicle and criminal laws. Powers of the state police vary widely among the states. Some forces have full police powers throughout the state, while others are restricted to highway patrol and traffic regulation. Regardless of these variations, the officers perform a vital service in ensuring the safety of all citizens. The following are typical work activities of state police officers.

In most cases, state police units are organized into posts or troops within specified geographic areas. Each troop or post is housed in a headquarters building that contains a communications center, barracks, lockup, crime laboratory, pistol range, and motor pool. The workday begins at the headquarters location where state police officers report daily for roll call, inspection, and duty assignment. The vast majority of these officers use specially equipped patrol cars in performing their assignments, but there are a small number who use motorcycles or fly helicopters or light, fixed-wing aircraft on special duty. When patrolling assigned sectors, state police officers carefully observe conditions, strictly enforce motor vehicle codes and criminal laws, watch for traffic violations, and issue warnings or citations to offenders. Where justified, arrests are made for violations of motor vehicle regulations and safe driving practices, and offenders are escorted to headquarters for detainment.

Other duties include monitoring traffic to detect vehicles reported as stolen and arresting drivers whose ownership credentials are lacking or questionable. Often, state police officers provide assistance to motorists on the highway, furnish road information and directions to drivers, and may give details about restaurants, lodging, or tourist attractions in the area. At accident scenes, or where vehicles are disabled, state police officers radio for emergency equipment, such as ambulances or towing vehicles, and give first aid to injured parties until help arrives. They prevent further accidents, damage, or injuries by directing traffic around the accident, using road flares at night, and by removing debris and vehicles from the roadway. They investigate the causes of each accident and prepare detailed written reports including information such as names and addresses of parties involved, scale drawings of the scene, road and weather conditions at the time of the accident, description of damage, and estimated speed of the vehicle or vehicles involved in the accident. This report is legal evidence that the officer may be called upon to present in court.

State police officers are also responsible for providing help to victims of fires, floods, or other disasters, and for controlling traffic in such circumstances. In some states, job duties include weighing commercial vehicles, stopping vehicles for spot check of drivers' licenses, and conducting driver-training sessions in public schools. State police officers may also test applicants for drivers' licenses, inspect motor vehicles for safety, and, on occasion, serve as escorts for parades, military convoys, and funeral processions.

In many states, besides being involved with highway activities, state police officers have responsibilities similar to those of municipal and county police, particularly in areas that do not have local police forces. In such cases, these activities include investigation of burglaries, robberies, assaults, domestic disturbances, drug traffic, and liquor violations; taking part in roadblocks to apprehend suspects or escaped criminals; and helping city and county police agencies in cases of riot or civil disturbance. They seize and arrest lawbreakers using physical force and/or firearms when the situation warrants, patrol business and residential areas, and check security of buildings in the district. Some state police officers are given special training and serve as radio dispatchers, instructors at police academies, or pilots of police aircraft. They also may work with canine and mounted units or may be assigned to protect governors and legislators. All state police officers are required to prepare written reports of their work activities and to maintain accurate police records and may be called upon to testify in court proceedings.

WORKING CONDITIONS

The conditions under which state police officers work vary according to assignment. For the most part, they work outdoors in all types of weather while patrolling highways and roads in their sectors. Officers work alone or with a partner and, *because of the nature of their duties, do not receive direct supervision.* They do, however, stay in constant touch with their communications centers to report to superior officers and to receive new or revised orders. Since the state police operate around the clock, officers are subject to rotating shifts, usually consisting of a 5-day, 40-hour workweek, including weekends and holidays. In addition, they are on call at all times and may work for extended periods during emergencies. *Certain aspects of this work are dangerous.* State Police Officers risk serious injury or death from high speed pursuits and from the apprehension of criminals who may be armed and dangerous.

Fringe benefits that state police officers receive usually include paid vacation, sick leave, and holidays; overtime pay; life, medical, and disability insurance; uniform allowances; tuition-refund program; and retirement pension.

TRAINING AND PROMOTION OPPORTUNITIES

As is the case with nearly all law enforcement positions, prospective state police officers do not achieve permanent status until they have successfully completed the probationary period that follows training. Probation may last from six months to a year, depending on the state. During the probationary period, the new officer gets valuable experience at the side of a veteran officer.

Advancement opportunities in state police agencies are based on merit, and promotional examinations are scheduled periodically. All qualified personnel can compete for promotional opportunities. The first level of advancement is to Sergeant. Thereafter, qualified officers may advance through experience and education to the positions of First Sergeant, Lieutenant, Captain, Major, Inspector, Deputy Superintendent, and Superintendent.

HOW TO QUALIFY

Candidates for the position of state police officer are selected according to civil service regulations that vary from state to state. Generally, applicants must be U.S. citizens between the ages of 21 and 35 at the time of appointment; service in the military may be deducted from the candidate's chronological age in meeting this requirement. As a rule, most state police agencies demand completion of high school or its equivalent, but persons with college training have a distinct advantage. In many states a certain number of college credits is required. Secondary and postsecondary courses considered useful in preparing for this work include government, English, psychology, geography, American history, physics, chemistry, and foreign languages. It is necessary to receive a passing mark on a written civil service examination as well as a qualifying rating on an interview conducted by a police board of examiners. The board evaluates candidates for such factors as verbal communication skills, tact, physical appearance, and the ability to exercise sound judgment. Each applicant must pass a comprehensive medical examination, and some state police agencies require candidates to undergo psychological and psychiatric testing to determine emotional stability and suitability for this work. In addition to meeting the physical requirements (including standards of height, weight, and vision), applicants are given performance tests designed to measure strength, agility, and stamina. A thorough background investigation is also made to determine general character, honesty, past history, and overall suitability for the job. Finally, possession of a valid driver's license is necessary prior to employment by the state police agency.

Candidates who meet all of the entry requirements of the state police agency are placed on a certified civil service list of eligibles and are selected from this list as vacancies occur. The annual number of openings for this work varies within each state and is dependent on such factors as budget limitations and legislative actions.

When a number of vacancies occur or appear to be imminent, a group of prospective state police officers is selected from the civil service list. These recruits enter training school on a probationary basis. They must complete an intensive training program of approximately 12 to 16 weeks. Instruction is given in a variety of subjects, such as criminal law; state motor vehicle codes; laws of evidence, arrest, search, and seizure; methods of patrol, surveillance, and communications; arrest, search, and seizure procedures; accident prevention and traffic control; crime prevention and criminal investigation methods; police ethics; pursuit and defensive driving; armed and unarmed defense tactics; use of various types of firearms; physical conditioning; safety education; first aid; community relations; photography; written and oral communications; and agency rules and regulations. Candidates who successfully conclude this training are assigned to duty on a probationary basis for a period ranging from six months to one year or longer, depending on state police policy. They work with experienced troopers until they are skillful enough to function independently and receive permanent employment status after completing a probationary period.

Some police agencies have cadet programs for high school graduates under the age of 21 who are interested in a law enforcement career. They work as civilian employees performing non-enforcement duties but also receive instruction in the various facets of police work. Some of these cadets attend colleges offering programs in law enforcement and criminal justice as preparation for a police career. Cadets who successfully complete this program may receive an appointment as state police officer upon reaching the age of 21.

Traits of a State Police Officer

State police work differs from city police work only in proportion of time spent at various duties. State police officers deal with traffic control and with helping motorists in distress. The traffic accidents to which state police are called tend to include more vehicles and more damage to persons and property. High-speed traffic presents problems quite different from heavy-congestion traffic. State police are more likely to deal with hijacking, drug traffic, and smuggling and are less likely to deal with domestic violence and burglary. The emphasis of the work may be different, but the traits desired in a police officer are the same regardless of the duties or the location.

1. **The police officer must be intelligent.** First of all, the recruit must be intelligent enough to make it through the policy academy or whatever training program that the particular department offers. The recruit must read well to comprehend written materials, must have good listening skills, and must remember what he or she has been taught. The recruit must be able to synthesize material, that is, be able to learn rules and then be able to apply them to hypothetical or actual situations. Remembering information is not enough. The candidate must convince the examiners that he or she can understand, interpret, and apply information in the field. The intelligent police officer can separate what is important from what is less important, can make quick judgments, and can express him- or herself well in speech and in writing. Most police departments begin the applicant screening process with a written test. Written tests require a minimum of administrative time. They can be administered to a large number of applicants at one sitting. Applicants who do not score well on the written test are dropped from consideration. There is no reason to spend time administering medical exams, physical performance tests, psychological exams or interviews to candidates who do not demonstrate the intelligence to learn the job and to serve as effective police officers.

2. **The police officer must be healthy and physically strong and agile.** Police work is physically taxing. The officer must be able to spend many hours on his or her feet or on the road, to move quickly, to see and hear accurately, and to lift, move, or carry as the emergency requires. Obviously, an officer who is often ill or who cannot perform all physical activities adequately is not acceptable. Police departments have strict medical standards so that they hire only recruits in excellent health. A great many medical conditions that are not so severe as to interfere with everyday life or with most occupations are disqualifying for the police officer. Likewise, police departments have carefully devised physical performance tests of strength, speed, and agility. The applicant who cannot qualify on the tests does not show great promise for success as a police officer. Medical and physical screening are important hurdles in the selection process.

6

3. **The police officer must be emotionally stable.** A police officer carries a gun. Obviously, anyone who is armed must be even-tempered, well-adjusted, and impartial. When it comes to dealing with firearms, there is no room for error. It is vital that the officer not become excited or fire too soon. The police officer must be able to size up a situation without fear or prejudice, then act appropriately. The police officer cannot be ruled by anger, at the same time, the officer cannot hesitate when prompt action is required. Police brutality, insult, and behavior on the basis of preconceived opinions have no place anywhere in the police force. Choosing the most stable recruits from among the applicants is one of the more difficult tasks for those in charge of hiring. Applicants who have done well on the written exam and who have passed medical examinations and physical fitness tests must often submit to psychological examinations. Psychological examinations are not always satisfactory, but police departments must rely on them to eliminate those candidates who appear to be less than perfectly well adjusted and stable. Because psychological testing tends to be inexact, the test results are often confirmed through interviews. Through a psychological test (often more than one) and interviews, each applicant who has reached this stage of the screening process must prove the stability required for responsible behavior in the police role.

4. **The police officer must be honest.** The person charged with upholding the law must have a clean record as a law-abiding citizen. Youthful infractions of the law must be few, of a minor nature, and explainable. Character flaws are unacceptable in any law enforcement officer. Every applicant must undergo a thorough background check before appointment to the training academy. Beyond merely acting with integrity, the prospective officer must demonstrate the sensitivity to avoid giving any appearance of impropriety. The interviewers are looking for the recruit who projects upright behavior as he or she performs according to the rules.

5. **The police officer must be self-confident and tactful.** These personality aspects are the final refinements upon which hiring decisions are based. These judgments are based upon interviews. The police officer must have the self-confidence to make quick decisions and to stick with them. Unwavering decisions and firm actions are vital in maintaining control. Tactful, gentle, but firm: these are the hallmarks of the effective, successful police officer. The interviewer hopes to choose the applicants who best display these qualities in a fine, delicate balance. The judgment cannot be entirely objective, but the interviewer does his or her best. The police officer candidate, in turn, can make a conscious effort to impress the interviewer as a tactful, thoughtful person who can communicate and take over effectively under pressure.

Sample Official
Announcements

STATE TROOPER

Job Elements

To perform the duties of a State Trooper you must have good judgment, thoroughness, conscientiousness, common sense, motivation, and enthusiasm for the job. You must be dependable and willing to get involved. You must be able to: assume responsibility; make decisions, often under pressure; work without supervision; take orders; function in physical danger; act under pressure; communicate well; and combine physical and mental resources.

Duties and Responsibilities

As a State Trooper, you will use these characteristics to perform duties involving patrol investigation, station duties, maintenance activities, and special assignments:

- In the course of your *patrol duties* you will direct traffic; assist lost, stranded, or disabled motorists; approach motorists on routine or nonroutine violations; and make arrests. You may be called upon to control crowds and support other Troopers in stress situations. Other patrol duties will include inspecting and safeguarding property, responding to bank alarms, chasing violators on foot, and checking buildings at night for break-ins.

- When you perform *investigative duties* your work will include interviewing complainants and witnesses; aiding people injured in highway, home, and industrial accidents; handling fatal accident and crime scenes; responding to complaints involving vicious animals; using deadly physical force or firearms; interrogating suspects; and executing search and arrest warrants.

- There are times when you will be expected to carry out *desk work*. You will send and receive radio and teletype messages; make entries in station records; and respond to telephone inquiries concerning weather and road conditions, locations, law, or other topics. You will also prepare written memoranda and reports.

- You will be required to maintain a *good personal appearance*. Your equipment, uniforms, and vehicle must be properly cared for. You also will assist in keeping your station clean and orderly.

- In the course of your career, you may be assigned to *special work*. These assignments may be varied and may include securing major disaster areas, policing areas during natural disasters, participating in community public relations programs, escorting VIPs presenting speeches or lectures, scuba diving, and recruit training or counseling. When the work schedule or special duty require, you will work weekends, holidays, irregular hours, overtime, and in inclement weather.

How to Apply

Application blanks are available at all State Police Stations. Candidates may also obtain the forms by mail.

You must file a completed written application in order to be eligible to take the written examination. You will then be advised of the time and place of the written examination and provided with an admission ticket to the test location most convenient to you.

Examination Locations

Examinations are usually conducted in the state capital and most large cities. Exact locations can be found on the latest announcements.

General Information

The number of candidates selected for appointment will depend on budget allocations. All appointments are probationary for a minimum period of one year following completion of the Academy Basic Course.

Examination Procedures

The selection process has been developed through analysis of the Trooper position. The complete selection process consists of six phases: Written Examination, Physical Performance Test, Medical Examination, Preemployment Interview, Psychological Examination, and an extensive Background Investigation that will include a polygraph test. The process is job related and competitive in nature and is designed to determine a candidate's potential for successful performance as a State Trooper. No prior police experience is required.

Candidates will be ranked in order of composite scores determined after completion of the written examination plus any applicable veteran's credit. Candidates will remain on the continuous eligible list for a maximum period of four years from the date of the most recent eligibility list to which their name is posted, unless otherwise deemed to be ineligible (e.g., overage). The eligible list will be continually updated by adding the names of those applicants who subsequently pass future written examinations, based on the scores they achieve. Examinations will be given periodically. Candidates may retake an examination no earlier than one year from their latest examination date; however, only the *latest* score achieved by an individual on any one examination will be retained and posted to the continuous eligible list. As new Trooper positions are authorized, sufficient candidates from the eligible list will be notified to appear for processing through the remaining phases of the testing procedure.

The Physical Performance Test will measure the candidate's ability to combine mental and physical resources. The candidate must perform physical tests that are evaluated on a pass-fail basis. Detailed description of the Physical Performance Test will be provided to the candidates when they are notified to appear for processing at Division Headquarters.

Those candidates successfully passing this phase will also be given a Preemployment Interview. This interview serves to acquaint the candidate with the job of Trooper and enables the State Police to develop information that will assist in completion of the background investigation.

The Psychological Examination consists of written tests completed by the candidate and a follow-up interview with a psychologist.

Character and Fitness

Each potential appointee will be the subject of a thorough background investigation, including a polygraph examination, to help determine character and fitness and also to verify information provided by the applicant. Applicants must authorize access to educational, financial, employment, criminal history, and mental health records. Family, neighbors, associates, and others will be interviewed. Derogatory information will be evaluated and may result in disqualification. Candidates who receive a satisfactory evaluation on the background investigation and meet all other administrative requirements will be considered eligible for appointment.

Administrative Requirements

In addition to completing the competitive examinations successfully, a candidate must meet administrative standards established by the Division of State Police:

Minimum Age

All candidates must be at least 20 years old on date of examination and at least 21 years old at date of appointment.

Maximum Age

Candidates without allowable military service must not have reached their 29th birthday on date of appointment. Candidates with active military duty, as defined in Section 243 of the Military Law, may use allowable service time to extend the age limit proportionately up to a maximum of six years.

Education

Candidates must have graduated from a senior high school or possess a State High School Equivalency Diploma prior to appointment. Military GED Certificates must be converted to State High School Equivalency Diplomas before appointment. In addition, all candidates must have completed a minimum of 60 credit hours at an accredited college or university at time of application. The Division may waive up to *30* credit hours *only* for individuals who:

a. have an Honorable Discharge from the United States Military after serving at least two full years of ACTIVE duty. A DD-214 (showing type of discharge) must be submitted with application.

   NOTE: Individuals who are currently on ACTIVE duty may apply without submitting a DD-214, providing they have completed at least two full years.

   OR

b. have completed a certified Basic POLICE OFFICER Training Course approved by or equivalent to a course approved by the Municipal Police Training Council. A certificate of completion of training must be submitted with application.

   NOTE: A certified PEACE OFFICER Training Course does *NOT* satisfy this requirement.

Residence

Only citizens of the United States are eligible to take the examination. State Law requires that any person appointed as a Trooper must be a resident of the State on the date of appointment and must maintain such residency as long as employment continues.

Driver's License

Candidates must have a current valid State driver's license on the date of appointment.

Criminal Record

Any felony conviction is an automatic disqualification. Conviction for any other crimes and offenses is subject to evaluation during a background investigation.

Medical Fitness

Sound health and physical condition are required of all candidates since the physical activities of the job often demand extreme exertion in emergency situations. A medical examination will be given prior to appointment during which vision, hearing, weight, dental condition, and general fitness will be determined. Visual acuity can be not worse than 20/40 in each eye uncorrected and must be correctable to 20/20. Color deficiency is disqualifying. There is no minimum or maximum height standard. Weight must be in proportion to height and build. Candidates must conform to weight standards for appointment. Potential appointees may be required to provide blood or urine samples for analysis to determine use of dangerous or illegal drugs. Any medical problems deemed by the Division Physician to be disqualifying for service as a Trooper shall be grounds for rejection.

On unannounced occasions while in the State Police Academy Basic School and during the probationary period following graduation from the Basic School, appointees MAY be required to provide urine samples for analysis to determine the presence of illegal drugs, controlled substances, and/or marijuana. Confirmed positive tests will be grounds for discharge from employment.

STATE TRAFFIC OFFICER CADET

Definition

Under close supervision, a Cadet participates in a basic traffic law enforcement training program in order to learn the work of a State Traffic Officer and does other related work as required.

Job Characteristics

The class of State Traffic Officer Cadets must successfully complete all academy courses, including academic classes, physical training, vehicle operation, and use of weapons in order to move to the class of State Traffic Officer. Failure in the Cadet class to qualify for movement to the class of State Traffic Officer within the prescribed training period will be cause for termination.

Typical Tasks

Receives instruction in the interpretation and application of the Vehicle Code and other laws affecting the operation of vehicles on public highways; receives instruction in basic criminal investigation processes and techniques including police ethics, witness interrogation, and collection of evidence; participates in firearms training; participates in the Emergency Vehicle Operations Course, which includes skid training, high-speed pursuit, defensive driving, and emergency driving; receives classroom instruction in enforcement psychology, enforcement tactics, effective writing, and effective speaking; learns radio operation and methods of traffic control; and participates in a physical training program.

Minimum Qualifications

- Education: Equivalent to completion of the twelfth grade.

- Knowledge and ability to: Learn rules and regulations; think clearly and logically and apply general rules to specific situations; observe and record events accurately and completely; operate or learn to operate a motorcycle; analyze situations accurately, think and act quickly in emergencies, and adopt an effective course of action; follow oral and written directions; write legibly, spell correctly, and prepare understandable reports.

- Special personal characteristics: Interest in law enforcement work; willingness to work throughout the State, at night, and at unusual hours; willingness to work under strict discipline; willingness to operate or learn to operate a motorcycle; satisfactory record as a law-abiding citizen; tact; reliability; communication skills; officer-like bearing; keenness of observation; neat personal appearance.

- Special physical characteristics: Good health, sound physical condition; freedom from any physical or mental condition that would interfere with the full performance of the essential duties of a State Traffic Officer; effective use of both hands; strength, endurance, and agility; normal hearing; normal visual function and visual acuity, not less than 20/40 in each eye without correction and corrected to 20/20 in each eye; normal color vision as assessed by the Farnsworth-Munsell D-15 test. Wearing an X-Chrome lens during vision testing is prohibited; height not more than 6'6"; weight proportional to age and height.

- Age limits for participation in examination: 20-31 years.

- Minimum age for appointment: 21 years.

- Felony disqualification: Existing law provides that persons convicted of a felony are disqualified from employment as peace officers. Such persons are not eligible to compete for, or be appointed to, positions in this class.

- Citizenship requirement: Existing law provides that no person shall be appointed as a member of the Highway Patrol who is not a U.S. citizen. Persons who are not citizens may compete in examinations for this class, but must show proof of citizenship before appointment can be made.

- Additional desirable qualifications: Education beyond the twelfth grade.

DEPARTMENT OF CIVIL SERVICE STATE POLICE TROOPER I EXAMINATION PROCESS

General Information

The State Police Trooper I Employment List will be established through a competitive examination process. This is an entry-level job classification.

The Departments of State Police and Civil Service are under a Federal Court order that stipulates hiring goals in regard to minorities and females for the State Police Trooper Training Schools. In order to ensure compliance with the Federal Court consent decree, the Department of Civil Service must maintain adequate sex/race representation on the Trooper Employment List. Adequate sex/race representation may require expedited processing of applications from minorities and females.

Positions in this job classification are located throughout the state.

Names of applicants who successfully complete the examination process will be combined with the current Employment List for the class.

When job vacancies occur, they are filled from the list. The Employment List will be continuously updated by adding the names of those applicants who subsequently pass the examination based on the score they achieved. Passing the test and having your name placed on the Employment List does not mean that you will be offered employment in this job classification. Appointment to this job classification will be dictated by departmental work force needs. Applicants who are appointed to positions must successfully complete one year of probationary training, which includes 16 weeks of State Police Trooper Training School conducted at the State Police Training Academy. An employee will be in pay status during the training period.

Policy on Taking the Examination Again

You may retake an examination and receive a new score. However, the Bureau of Selection policy requires that only the *latest* passing score achieved by an individual on any one examination will be retained on all Department of Civil Service records for that examination.

Conditions of Employment

The employee is required to work on a rotating shift basis, to be available for duty 24 hours a day, to work on state and national holidays, and to work and drive in inclement weather. The employee is subject to transfer on a temporary or permanent basis anywhere in the state. The employee must carry firearms and may be required to use them in the line of duty. The employee must maintain the capability to perform strenuous tasks requiring muscular strength and cardiovascular endurance.

Reallocation

After completion of one year of satisfactory service at the entry level classification, the employee will be appointed to the position of State Police Trooper II. Should an employee fail to meet the requirements for the position, the employee will be separated from the job.

Examples of Work

First-year employees receive training in the knowledge and skills required to function independently as law enforcement officers. The employee is initially assigned to residence in the State Police Trooper Training School for approximately 16 weeks where he or she completes a basic police training curriculum of law enforcement course work and physical training. Upon graduation from school, the employee is assigned to a State Police post as a probationary trooper. In the company of an experienced trooper, the employee patrols an area to detect or prevent traffic and criminal law violations, investigates complaints of law violations, and provides a variety of related services to the general public.

Minimum Qualifications

Citizenship

A citizen of the United States at the time of the written test.

Residence

A resident of the state for at least one year immediately prior to taking the written examination; or for four years between the ages of 17 and 35 years. State residents in the armed forces and students attending colleges or universities out of state for the past school year will be considered as meeting this requirement.

Age

At least 21 years of age at the time of the written examination and less than 36 years of age as of the date of hire.

Education

Graduation from high school or General Education Development Test (GED) results meeting Department of Education standards. (GED tests must have been taken at an official GED center. A standard score of 35 or above on each of the five tests *and* an average of 45 for the five tests must have been attained. GED results should be submitted at the time of application if they are not already on file with Civil Service.)

Driver's License

Possession of a valid operator's or chauffeur's license without restrictions applying to time, area, special mechanical control devices, or conditions (except corrective lenses).

Vision

At least 20/50 vision in each eye without lenses, corrected to 20/20 with lenses prior to appointment to a Training School. Must have adequate color and depth perception and a visual field of no less than 70 degrees in the horizontal meridian in each eye. Must have normal vertical and lateral muscle balance.

Hearing

Must have normal hearing in both ears. Hearing deficiency, if any, must not exceed 25 decibels (I.S.O.) in either ear in frequency ranges 500, 1000, 2000, 3000 cycles. Deficiencies in higher frequency ranges (4000–6000 cycles) must not exceed an average of 40 decibels.

Convictions of Law Violations or Civil Infractions

Conviction may serve as a basis for disqualification. The applicant's total record will be evaluated. The pattern of law violations, the seriousness, the surrounding circumstances, number, and recency will be considered. The convictions noted below will be cause for automatic disqualification:

1. Conviction of a felony.
2. Lost driving privilege through suspension or revocation of license due to an unsatisfactory driving record as defined by the state's driver's license point system.

EXCEPTION: Those who maintain a driving record free of license suspension or revocation and moving violation conviction/s or civil infraction determination/s in the two years previous to taking the written examination through appointment to a training school will be accepted.

In the four years previous to taking the written examination through appointment to a training school:

3. Conviction of driving while license was suspended or revoked.
4. Conviction of driving while under the influence of alcohol or drugs. (This includes driving while ability impaired.)
5. Two or more convictions of reckless driving.

In the two years previous to taking the written examination through appointment to a training school:

6. Accumulated eight or more points on the driving record.

7. Conviction or civil infraction determination of three or more moving violations.

8. A record of two or more traffic accidents, each resulting in a moving violation conviction or civil infraction determination.

Selection Process

Written Examination

A written test containing multiple-choice and true-false questions pertaining to accuracy of observation and memory and ability to read and comprehend reports, manuals, and laws will determine 40 percent of the final score.

The written test will be administered by the Department of Civil Service at various examination centers throughout the state.

Background Investigation

Applicants who pass the written test may be scheduled to participate in the remainder of the examination process (oral appraisal), based on departmental work force needs. The candidates will be subjected to a thorough background investigation designed to assist in measuring suitability for police work. The background investigation will include fingerprinting and a vision test. Evidence of unsuitability may serve as a basis for disqualification from the oral appraisal examination process. Applicants who are disqualified will receive notification of the disqualification by mail.

Oral Appraisal Examination

Applicants who pass the background investigation will be scheduled for the oral appraisal examination in which a board of examiners will assess their communication skills and personal fitness. Questions asked by the oral board will pertain to the applicant's background investigation and employment objectives. The oral appraisal examination will determine 60 percent of the final score.

Medical Examination

Applicants who are called to a training school must pass a medical examination. The applicant's physical condition must be adequate for performance of the work as determined by an examining physician. A hearing test, blood test, urinalysis, and blood pressure examination will be included. The applicant must be free from any chronic diseases, organic or functional conditions, or physical defects that may tend to impair efficient performance of a Trooper's duties. Failure to meet medical standards will result in removal from the Employment List for this job classification. Correction of a medical deficiency may result in a return to the Employment List.

Physical Performance Test

Prior to their hiring, applicants will be called to the Training School for a physical performance test. Failure to meet required standards will result in rejection of the applicant for the Training School.

There are six test parts designed to assess: strength to push, pull, drag, and lift; cardiorespiratory endurance for strenuous work and running; abdominal strength and spine flexibility to avoid low back pain, problems of strains, loss of mobility, and agility.

The physical performance test consists of the following:

1. *Push-ups:* This is a standard push-up where the back and legs are kept straight. The event starts in the up position and the count occurs when the applicant returns to the up position after having touched an audible beeper on the mat with his/her chest. The applicant is to do as many push-ups as possible in 60 seconds.

2. *Grip:* Using a hand grip dynamometer, the applicant squeezes the meter while keeping the arm extended parallel to the leg. Both right and left grips are tested and recorded in kilograms of pressure.

3. *Obstacle Course:* The total distance for this obstacle course is 90 feet and it is run for time. The applicant runs 20 feet, crawls 6 feet through a 2½-foot high simulated tunnel, runs 20 feet, and climbs a 6-foot 6-inch barrier with footholds and handholds. The applicant then runs 20 feet to and around a set of pylons, then back to the barrier, which has footholds and handholds on it. After climbing the barrier a second time, the applicant runs 4 feet to the stop position.

4. *165-Pound Drag:* The applicant drags a 165-pound life-form dummy 30 feet for time. The dummy is gripped in the armpits and dragged backwards.

5. *95-Pound Carry:* The applicant lifts a 95-pound bag, which has handholds, runs with it 30 feet, and places it on a 32-inch platform for time.

6. *½-Mile Shuttle Run:* The applicant runs between two pylons placed 88 feet apart for a total of 15 round trips for time.

Examinees are encouraged to practice ahead of time for the physical performance test.
All physical tests, and especially the ½-mile run, are aided by conditioning ahead of time. Physical training for law enforcement positions requires that new hires be physically fit when they are hired. The physical performance test screens for minimal levels of physical fitness required for State Police Trooper I.

It is very important that applicants adequately prepare themselves to pass the physical performance test. It is recommended that applicants consult a medical doctor before attempting the physical performance skills.

Annual Maintenance Program

Annually, after initial hiring, State Police Troopers may participate in an evaluation of physical fitness consisting of:

1. *Push-Up Test:* 15 push-ups in 60 seconds.
2. *Chin-Up Test:* Five chin-ups in a continuous manner, palms toward body, with full arm extension between each one.
3. *One Mile Continuous Run Test:* Run one mile in less than 9 minutes.
4. *Bent-Knee Sit-Up Test:* 30 bent-knee sit-ups in 90 seconds.
5. *Seated Stretch Test:* Sit on the floor with legs together and knees straight and stretch forward as far as possible. Fingertips must extend to ankles within 6 inches of the heel.

STATE POLICE TROOPER TRAINEE

The State Police are now recruiting able men and women from all walks of life for the position of State Police Trooper Trainee. The selection process begins with a written examination and continues over the following months with several interviews and investigations. At the end of this multiphase process, a select group of candidates will qualify to begin the physically demanding training program. This select group will reflect the commitment of the State Police to affirmative action-equal employment opportunity goals.

Qualifications

Candidates for entry-level Trooper Trainee appointments must:

1. Be at least 18 years old by the date of appointment;
2. Be U.S. citizens by the date of appointment;
3. Be in general good health and have sufficient strength, stamina, and agility as required by the duties of the position;
4. Have good education and/or work record and excellent moral character;
5. Have normal hearing and normal color vision and depth perception, with no marked muscle imbalance. Distant and near visual acuity without vision correction devices shall not be less than 20/50 in either eye with binocular visual acuity of not less than 20/30. Distant and near vision must be correctable to 20/20.

In addition, prior to graduation from the Academy Training Program, successful candidates will be required to obtain and retain a current, valid state motor vehicle operator's license and must establish residence in the state.

The Written Exam

When your completed application is received you will be scheduled for the examination. The exact time and place will be sent to you about 10 days before that date. The exam will include questions to assess your ability to observe and remember details, to analyze facts and make decisions, to reason logically, and to understand and communicate written and oral instructions and questions about your interests. *There will be no makeup exam.* You must pass each phase to be eligible to go on in the selection process. However, because of the large number of applicants, passing one phase may not automatically qualify you for the next.

Physical Assessment

This phase is intended to give an overall measurement of a candidate's physical fitness and preparation for State Police Academy training. Blood pressure and vision will be measured, and candidates must fall within required levels to continue in the process, which includes:

1. A 1.5-mile run measuring cardiovascular efficiency.
2. Push-ups measuring shoulder muscular endurance.
3. Sit-ups measuring abdominal and hip flex or muscle strength.
4. An agility run measuring quickness, speed, and balance.
5. A vertical jump measuring leg muscle strength and explosiveness.
6. A sit and reach test measuring thigh and back muscle extensiveness.
7. A grip test measuring wrist and finger muscle strength.
8. A measure of body fat composition.

Oral Interview

A panel of State Police officers will interview each candidate to measure his/her judgment, motivation for police work, ability to deal effectively with the public, and oral communication ability. A writing sample will also be required and evaluated for written communication ability.

Polygraph & Background Investigations

Candidates successful up to this point in the process will undergo a polygraph examination and thorough background investigation. A psychological evaluation may also be performed. Only those candidates with good education and/or work records and excellent moral character will be chosen.

Medical Exam

Candidates reaching this point in the process will be given a thorough medical evaluation to include eyes, ears, blood, and heart, as well as other tests. All candidates must meet the minimum acceptable standards in each area. Successful completion of all phases of the selection process means that you are eligible to be considered for final appointment as a Trooper Trainee.

State Police Training Program

If you are selected as a State Police Trooper Trainee you will enter the physically and mentally demanding training program at the State Police Academy. The program lasts up to six months and includes classroom instruction and physical conditioning. It requires you to live at the Academy Monday through Friday. After graduation from the program, Trooper Trainees are assigned to one of the State Police Troops throughout the State for a probationary period and on-the-job training.

Basic Qualification and Requirements for Employment as a Highway Patrol Trooper

1. *Age:* Minimum—21 years as of date of application.
2. *Height:* Maximum—6'5" (without shoes).
3. *Weight:* Maximum—240 pounds. (Weight must be commensurate with height and body frame.)
4. *Physical Condition:* Must be in excellent physical condition with no obvious condition that will impair performance of Patrol duties.
5. *Education:* As a minimum, an applicant must have graduated from an accredited high school or hold an approved General Education Development Certificate; college or university level education desired.
6. *Citizenship:* Must be a citizen of the U.S. and must have resided in the state for 12 months immediately preceding date of application. Military service in the state qualifies.
7. *Criminal History:* Must not have pled guilty, entered a plea of no contest, or have been convicted of any crime other than a minor misdemeanor; must not, during the three years preceding the date of his/her application, have been convicted of a traffic offense that required suspension or revocation of driving privileges; must not have accumulated more than eight points against his/her driving record during the preceding three years.
8. *Former Employment:* Must, if a former Patrol member, complete all Patrol pre-employment requirements, including recompletion of Patrol Basic School.
9. *Acceptance of Conditions and Benefits:* Must be willing to live and work in any section of the Sate and to be transferred at the discretion of the Patrol Commander.

10. *Vision Requirements:* Must have 20/20 vision in each eye; uncorrected vision of no more than 20/50 in each eye is acceptable if corrected with lens; must not be color blind or affected by night blindness; must pass depth perception test.

11. *Agility Test:* Must be able to perform an agility test according to standards approved by the Patrol Medical Services Director.

12. *Written Test:* Must pass a specific aptitude test battery and a reading comprehension/writing skills examination. Applicants must also take an examination that measures attitudes desired for law enforcement officers.

13. *Background Investigation:* Must satisfactorily pass a thorough background investigation, including a check of state and Federal Bureau of Investigation records.

14. *Applicant Review Board:* Applicants must be interviewed by the Patrol's Applicant Review Board.

15. *Physical Examination:* Must meet physical standards set by the Patrol Medical Services Director.

16. *Acceptance by Patrol Commander:* Must be accepted by the Patrol Commander to attend the Patrol Basic School.

17. *Completion of Training:* Must successfully complete the Patrol Basic School.

The Kind of Work
You Will Be Doing

This chapter provides essential information about the field in which you will be working. It gives you facts and figures concerning your chosen specialty and points up how desirable and interesting your job can be. When you know more about your job, you'll be more inclined to struggle and study for it.

NATURE OF THE WORK

The laws and regulations that govern the use of our nation's roadways are designed to ensure the safety of all citizens. State Troopers patrol our highways and enforce these laws.

State Troopers issue traffic tickets to motorists who violate the law. At the scene of an accident, they direct traffic, give first aid, call for emergency equipment, including ambulances, and write reports to be used in determining the cause of the accident.

In addition, State Troopers provide services to motorists on the highways. For example, they radio for road service for drivers in mechanical trouble, direct tourists to their destination, or give information about lodging, restaurants, and tourist attractions

State Troopers also provide traffic assistance and control during road repairs, fires, and other emergencies, as well as for special occurrences such as parades and sports events. They sometimes check the weight of commercial vehicles, conduct driver examinations, and give information on highway safety to the public.

In addition to highway responsibilities, State Troopers may investigate crimes, particularly in areas that do not have a police force. They sometimes help city or county police catch lawbreakers and control civil disturbances. State Highway Patrols, however, normally are restricted to vehicle and traffic matters.

Some Troopers work with special State Police units such as the mounted police, canine corps, and marine patrols. Others instruct trainees in State Police Schools, pilot police aircraft, or specialize in fingerprint classification or chemical and microscopic analysis of criminal evidence.

State Troopers also write reports and maintain police records. Some Troopers, including division or bureau chiefs responsible for training or investigation and those who command police operations in an assigned area, have administrative duties.

Training, Other Qualifications, and Advancement

State Civil Service regulations govern the appointment of State Troopers. All candidates must be citizens of the U.S. Other entry requirements vary, but most states require that applicants have a high school education or an equivalent combination of education and experience and be at least 21 years old.

Troopers must pass a competitive examination and meet physical and personal qualifications. Physical requirements include standards of height, weight, and eyesight. Tests of strength and agility often are required. Because honesty and a sense of responsibility are important in police work, an applicant's character and background are investigated.

Although State Troopers work independently, they must perform their duties in line with department rules. They should want to serve the public and be willing to work outdoors in all types of weather.

In all states, recruits enter a formal training program for several months. They receive classroom instruction in state laws and jurisdictions, and they study procedures for accident investigation, patrol, and traffic control. Recruits learn to use guns, defend themselves from attack, handle an automobile at high speeds, and give first aid. After gaining experience, some Troopers take advanced training in police science, administration, law enforcement, or criminology. Classes are held at junior colleges, colleges and universities, or at special police institutions, such as the National Academy of the Federal Bureau of Investigation.

High school and college courses in English, government, psychology, sociology, American history, and physics help in preparing for a police career. Physical education and sports are useful for developing stamina and agility. Completion of a driver education course and training received in military police school also are assets.

State Trooper recruits serve a probationary period ranging from six months to three years. After a specified length of time, Troopers become eligible for promotion. Most states have merit promotion systems that require Troopers to pass a competitive examination to qualify for the next higher rank. Although the organization of police forces varies by state, the typical avenue of advancement is from private to corporal, to sergeant, to first sergeant, to lieutenant, and then to captain. State Troopers who show administrative ability may be promoted to higher-level jobs such as commissioner or director.

In some states, high school graduates may enter State Police work as cadets. These paid civilian employees of the police organization attend classes to learn various aspects of police work and are assigned nonenforcement duties. Cadets who qualify may be appointed to the State Police force at age 21.

Employment Outlook

State Trooper employment is expected to grow much faster than the average for other occupations. Although most jobs will result from this growth, some openings will be created as Troopers retire, die, or leave the occupation for other reasons. As job openings are filled from the ranks of available applicants, the increased interest of women in police work will result in greater employment of women for patrol duties.

Although some Troopers will be needed in criminal investigation and other non-highway functions, the greatest demand will be for Troopers to work in highway patrol. Motorcycles, campers, and other recreational vehicles will continue to add to the nation's traffic flow and require additional officers to ensure the safety of highway users.

Because law enforcement work is becoming more complex, specialists will be needed in crime laboratories and electronic data processing centers to develop administrative and criminal information systems. However, in many departments, these jobs will be filled by civilian employees rather than uniformed officers.

Earnings and Working Conditions

Although starting salaries are normally higher in the West and lower in the South, State Troopers on the average earn about 1.5 times as much as nonsupervisory workers in private industry, except farming.

State Troopers generally receive regular increases, based on experience and performance, until a specified maximum is reached.

State Police agencies usually provide Troopers with uniforms, firearms, and other necessary equipment, or give special allowances for their purchase.

In many states, the scheduled workweek for State Troopers is 40 hours. Although the workweek is longer in some states, hours over 40 are being reduced. Since police protection must be provided around the clock, some officers are on duty over weekends, on holidays, and at night. State Troopers also are subject to emergency calls at any time.

State Troopers usually are covered by liberal pension plans. Paid vacations, sick leave, and medical and life insurance plans frequently are provided.

The work of State Troopers is sometimes dangerous. They always run the risk of an automobile accident while pursuing speeding motorists or fleeing criminals. Troopers also face the risk of injury while apprehending criminals or controlling disorders.

Sources of Additional Information

Information about specific entrance requirements may be obtained from State Civil Service commissions or State Police headquarters, usually located in each state capital.

Job Element Self-Appraisal Form

Every state has different application forms and different application procedures. The Self-Appraisal Form below is part of the application packet of one state. You may or may not find yourself filling out something similar. Now that you have read sample announcements and job descriptions from a variety of states, try filling out this self-appraisal form to see how you "fit."

PLEASE FILL OUT THIS SECTION:

NAME (PRINT) _____

LAST   FIRST   MIDDLE

ADDRESS _____

THIS FORM IS TO BE COMPLETED AND RETURNED WITH YOUR APPLICATION

The Job Element Self-Appraisal Form consists of questions about many of the personal qualities and behaviors that are important in performing the job of a State Trooper. The items have been identified by a thorough study of current job requirements. The information may help you in determining whether you are interested in the job and have some of the needed qualifications.

Directions

You are asked to respond to every question on this form in a direct and honest manner. While your answers to this form will not be scored, you should be aware that many of your answers may be checked in later phases of the examination process. For example, requirements in terms of agility and strength will be checked on the physical performance test.

You may not have had the opportunity to do all the job demands listed on this form. On such questions, you will have to make your best judgment as to whether you would be able to meet the demands. If you think that you probably will be able to perform the job demand, give the appropriate answer. On the other hand, if you think you probably won't be able to do so, answer accordingly. If you are unsure, try performing the job demand before answering the question.

Answer "Yes" or "No" to each of the following questions.

1. Do you have the ability to drive:

   (a) on expressways and limited access highways, such as interstate highways, thruways, or turnpikes?_____

   (b) in city areas?_____

   (c) in suburban areas?_____

2. Are you able to:

   (a) drive at night for extended periods of time?_____

   (b) drive a car for long periods of time under adverse weather conditions?_____

   (c) quickly transfer your foot from the gas pedal to the brake pedal of a car in an emergency?_____

3. While driving a car, can you move your head from side to side without moving your body?_____

4. If you were driving a full-sized sedan without aids or adaptive devices:

   (a) are you tall enough to see over the steering wheel without assuming a body position that would make safe operation of the car difficult?_____

   (b) could you reach all the hand controls, switches, and levers on the dashboard without assuming a body position that would make safe operation of the car difficult?_____

5. Are your legs long enough to reach the gas and brake pedals in a full-sized sedan without the aid of any devices?_____

6. Under normal conditions, do you experience motion sickness while riding in:

   (a) cars?_____

   (b) boats?_____

   (c) planes?_____

7. If you were driving a police car on the way to an emergency, could you maneuver your way through moving traffic using the flashing red lights and siren?_____

8. Are you tall enough to see over the roof of a full-sized sedan (car height approximately five feet)?_____

9. Are your arms long enough to hold an Ithaca Model 37 pump-action shotgun level at shoulder height?_____

10. Can you meet these physical requirements:

    (a) climb over a fence four feet high?_____

    (b) hurdle over an obstacle three feet high?_____

    (c) scale a wall four feet high?_____

    (d) climb to the top of a ladder twenty feet high?_____

    (e) enter a window from the top of a ladder?_____

    (f) climb, unaided, into a window five feet above the ground?_____

(g) climb lengthwise over a full-sized sedan?_____

(h) pass through an opening three feet by three feet?_____

(i) pull a 120-lb. object off the road?_____

(j) lift a 90-lb. weight from ground to waist level and place it in the rear of a station wagon?_____

(k) change a car tire including removal and tightening of lug nuts from a car wheel?_____

(l) remove and replace the spare tire from the trunk of a car?_____

(m) maintain your balance, for example, riding a bicycle?_____

(n) work without regular meal times?_____

(o) use a pry bar to force open a car door?_____

11. (a) Are you missing any fingers, toes, arms, or legs?_____

If you answer "yes," then complete section b of this question.

(b) If so, do you feel that you could still perform the job of a Trooper?_____

12. Can you accurately copy names, addresses, and a long series of numbers and letters as required in filling out a traffic ticket?_____

13. Can you add, subtract, multiply, and divide accurately?_____

14. Are you able to copy information accurately from a driver's license and vehicle registration?_____

15. Do you have the mental and physical abilities needed to make an arrest?_____

16. If a police situation required it, could you use a nightstick to poke or hit someone?_____

17. Could you use a gun to kill an injured or vicious animal at close range?_____

18. If you were a Trooper, could you direct traffic?_____

19. In an emergency situation, could you take the responsibility of directing motorists to drive in the wrong traffic lanes or in a direction that they had not intended to drive?_____

20. Can you learn how to use a two-way radio?_____

21. Are you now or have you been in the military service?

If you answer "yes," then complete section b of this question.

(b) Are you willing to sign a waiver to permit examination of your military records and/or discharge papers?_____

22. Are you able to:

(a) run ½ mile (1,320 feet)?_____

(b) work outdoors in inclement weather for extended periods of time?_____

23. Do you:

    (a) have sufficient strength in each hand to control a .357 magnum handgun (a powerful weapon with considerable recoil)?_____

    (b) have sufficient strength to control a shotgun during rapid fire?_____

24. Have you had any compensation claims for injury connected with your employment, including military service, within the past 10 years?_____

    (If "yes," explain.)

25. Have you ever been discharged, forced, or requested to resign from a job?_____

    (If "yes," explain.)

26. Are you now or have you ever been employed in or compensated for any unlawful activity?_____

    (If "yes," explain.)

27. Do you have:

    (a) frequent and uncontrollable need for sleep?_____

    (b) any speech defects that would interfere with your ability to communicate orally?_____

    (c) any mental or emotional problems that would prevent you from functioning under physical or emotional pressure?_____

    (d) any addiction to unlawful drugs?_____

    (e) any alcohol addiction?_____

    (f) any major physical disabilities?_____

    (g) excessive concern about your health?_____

28. Are you afraid of the dark?_____

29. Are you generally in good health?_____

30. Are you able to maintain your emotional stability without the use of drugs?_____

31. Do you have good peripheral (side) vision?_____

32. Can you focus your eyes quickly on objects at various distances away from you?_____

33. Are you able to distinguish different colors such as in the clothing of suspects or the exterior of automobiles?_____

34. Can you read a state license plate in the daylight at a distance of 40 feet?_____

35. Can you move both eyes in the same direction at the same time?_____

36. Can you observe merging traffic while driving?_____

37. When blinded by oncoming headlights at night, are you able to recover from the glare quickly enough to maintain control of your vehicle?_____

38. (a) Do you wear prescribed glasses?_____

    If you answer "yes," then complete sections b through e of this question.

    If your glasses were broken or removed, could you:
    (b) drive a car?_____
    (c) physically defend yourself in hand-to-hand combat?_____
    (d) effectively use a handgun at 15 yards?_____
    (e) chase a fleeing person across a field?_____

39. Could you hear and understand a normal radio transmission while on patrol?_____

40. Police officers often have to conduct investigations or make arrests involving members of the opposite sex. Would you be afraid to conduct such investigations or make arrests involving members of the opposite sex?_____

41. Are you willing to:
    (a) physically defend yourself?_____
    (b) inflict physical injury on someone, under proper circumstances, when acting in defense of another person?_____

42. Are you aware of the need for safety when handling firearms?_____

43. Are you afraid to handle or shoot firearms?_____

44. Could you withstand boredom such as driving for a long period at night with no other activity, or watching a specific location for 8 hours without relief?_____

45. Are you honest?_____

46. Can you resist a bribe?_____

47. Can you resist the temptation to accept gratuities, for example, special discounts or free meals?_____

48. Can you distinguish between right and wrong?_____

49. Could you remember your work schedule if the hours were changed from week to week?_____

50. Would you be willing to give up your right to strike in a labor-management dispute as a condition of State Police employment?_____

51. A State Trooper must learn law, legal procedures, interpersonal skills, and investigative procedures. Would you be willing to learn:

    (a) how to develop information about the criminal elements in a patrol area_____

    (b) how to make a crime scene search_____

    (c) how to respond to armed robberies_____

    (d) the criteria by which evidence is admitted in a trial_____

    (e) how to plan an investigation_____

    (f) how to interview a person, obtain the desired information, and reduce it to writing_____

    (g) how to recognize and preserve evidence_____

    (h) how to use the Criminal Procedure Law, Penal Law, and Vehicle and Traffic Law_____

    (i) about the Criminal Justice System_____

    (j) how to determine reasonable grounds for an arrest_____

    (k) how to develop criminal informants_____

    (l) how to become a leader and assume responsibility_____

    (m) how much force to use in a given situation_____

    (n) how to identify the symptoms of drug abuse_____

    (o) how to react correctly to a dangerous situation_____

    (p) how to work on your own without supervision_____

    (q) how to maintain your composure on the witness stand_____

    (r) how to recognize and deal with an agitator in a crowd_____

    (s) how to cross-examine a witness at a trial when acting as a prosecutor for your own arrests_____

    (t) how to shoot a revolver and shotgun accurately_____

    (u) proper circumstances under which you can take a human life_____

    (v) emergency removal of a child from a dangerous family situation_____

    (w) distinctions between grades of crime_____

    (x) stop and frisk procedures_____

    (y) regulations regarding reciprocity between states (for example, vehicles, weights, and measures)_____

The Written Examination

Step one in the screening process is nearly always the written examination. Police departments want to avoid any possible accusation of favoritism or prejudice in hiring, so they invariably use written examinations to screen out unqualified candidates. The written examination is in almost all cases a multiple-choice examination. Multiple choice assures objectivity. If the questions are well designed, each question has only one right answer. Such exams are easy to score and are generally considered to be fair. The unique feature of entry-level examinations is that they do not presuppose any knowledge. The applicant taking a state police officer entry exam is not expected to know police rules, regulations, or procedures. On the other hand, the candidate is expected to reason and even think like a police officer. Questions that evaluate the candidate's thinking and reasoning processes will include all the necessary information with which to reason. This means that police officer exams tend to include many lists of rules and procedures. They often include long excerpts from manuals and rulebooks. The test-taker must read and understand the rules that are the basis for each judgment or reasoning question and then must think through the best answer.

READING-BASED QUESTIONS

By now you should have gathered that much of the measure of police intelligence is based upon how well you read and what you do with that which you read. Reading-based questions include questions of fact to be extracted directly from reading passages, questions of inference from reading passages, questions that require a choice of actions based upon rules and a fact situation, and questions of judgment of the behavior of others, again based upon both rules and a fact situation. They may also probe your ability to interpret and judge from what you read by presenting a series of definitions and descriptions of situations and then asking you to classify the situations based on the fact situations.

Since reading-based questions of one form or another constitute the bulk of all police exams, we have devoted a full chapter in this book to preparing you for these questions.

PRACTICAL JUDGMENT QUESTIONS

Closely related to reading-based questions are questions of practical police judgment. These are questions that present you with a fact situation and require you to make a spot decision for appropriate action in that situation. The judgment questions do not presuppose knowledge of the proper police action. Your answer should be based upon good judgment and common sense.

However, some familiarity with "police thinking" should stand you in good stead with these questions. The good judgment that you demonstrate in police practical judgment questions should predict the same good judgment in actual police situations.

OBSERVATION AND MEMORY QUESTIONS

The intelligent police officer reads well, is able to choose a course of action on the basis of knowledge from reading, and can make good judgments in both emergency and non-emergency situations. He or she must also be a keen observer with a good memory. Observation with instant forgetting is totally useless. Observation and memory questions, which appear on many, though by no means all, police officer exams, serve to identify those recruits who are wide awake and know what to watch for. In a way, they also are a test of judgment, for the test-taker must be able to decide what to focus on. Obviously, no one can notice and remember every detail of a scene or event. The intelligent observer can choose what is most important and commit it to memory. The test situation is not, of course, the same as real life. If your exam does not include this type of question, it is because your police department considers observation and memory questions on a written test to be too artificial to be truly predictive. Since this type of question does appear frequently, we have included a chapter for instruction and practice. The information will prove useful whether or not you must answer observation and memory questions on your exam; you will certainly need to sharpen these skills in order to perform your state police duties.

GRAMMAR AND EFFECTIVE EXPRESSION QUESTIONS

Another important line of questioning on police entrance exams has to do with grammar and effective expression. The reason for these questions is obvious. A police officer must communicate in both speech and in writing; his or her message must come across clearly and accurately. All important information must be included, and it must be stated in logical order. There must be no opportunity for misinterpretation or misunderstanding. Police recruits should present their best language skills along with their other qualifications. Grammar and effective expression are, of course, also related to reading. The person who has done extensive reading should be aware of ways to best express information in a clear and orderly fashion. We will not attempt to teach grammar at this late stage. Your logical thinking and your eye for what "looks right" will have to see you through. However, we can forewarn you of various forms that grammar and effective expression questions may take and how to approach them.

Your exam may offer you four sentences and ask you to choose the sentence that is wrong with respect to grammar or English usage. This type of question can prove quite difficult. Often two or even three sentences appear to be wrong. Draw upon your school training. Try the sentences aloud (very softly). You may have to weed out the sentences that you are sure are correct, then guess from among the remaining ones.

Another approach is to offer you four sentences, often all attempting to give the same information, and to ask you which one is best. This is a little easier. Concentrate on literal reading of each sentence. Be sure that the one you choose says what you think it means.

Other exams may ask your advice in rephrasing an awkward sentence or in repositioning a sentence or paragraph for more reasonable presentation.

A common effective expression question gives a series of sentences in random order. You must choose the logical progression of steps—what happened first, next, and so on.

A final form of this question is one that presents a list of facts, then asks you to include all these facts in a statement of one or two sentences. You must take care to include all the facts and to express them in an unambiguous way. Read each choice literally to catch word orders that may make the meaning incorrect or even ridiculous. Check the list of facts often to ensure that all facts are presented clearly and appropriately in the statement.

Related to questions of effective expression are questions of what information is important to include in a statement or report. This type of question relies on judgment as well as on knowing the best way of expressing information. Put yourself in the position of the person receiving and having to act on the information. What would be most useful? What do you need to know? In what order would you find the information most helpful?

READING MAPS

Except in cases of extreme emergency, police officers are required to obey all traffic laws. The police officer who goes to the scene of an accident by entering a one-way street in the wrong direction is likely to create another accident. On the other hand, time may be of the essence. A victim may have injuries that require immediate attention. An officer may have to choose the most efficient legal way to get there. Map questions on police exams involve a combination of reading, logical thinking, and common sense. The police candidate can learn how to use maps effectively while undergoing training; however, the applicant who comes with a well-developed skill will be able to spend more time getting specialized police training. Concentrate on map questions on your exam. Read carefully. Put yourself in the driver's seat, and follow all instructions. Do not hesitate to turn the test booklet as needed to maintain your sense of direction.

FILLING OUT FORMS

Police officers must fill out forms and must read and follow them. A few state police exams include questions based upon a form, instructions for filling out the form, and a fact situation. There is no trick to these questions. Read carefully. Be especially alert to instructions that read "fill in blank 3 only if such and such" or "leave number 7 blank unless this and that both apply." Exclusionary and inclusive words present the keys in answering many form questions.

MISCELLANEOUS QUESTIONS

There is a variety of miscellaneous questions that appear on isolated state police qualification exams. Some or all of them may occur on yours. If they are included, they tend not to comprise a significant part of the exam. These questions include arithmetic, synonyms, verbal analogies, spelling, and various types of coding questions. Read directions carefully, then do your best with these.

Model Examination I includes a variety of different chart and table interpretation and coding questions that have appeared on recent examinations. These questions should serve as your introduction to a line of questioning that is increasing in popularity among examiners.

The Medical Examination

The state police officer's route must be covered at all times. This means that the assigned officer must show up. Otherwise, the scheduling officer must find a substitute and must rearrange the work tours of many other officers. The candidate with a history of frequent illness or one with a chronic ailment that may periodically crop up and interfere with attendance is not an acceptable candidate. Likewise, the applicant with an underlying physical condition that presents no problems in everyday life but that might be aggravated under the stressful activity of a police officer must be rejected.

Every candidate under consideration must undergo a thorough medical examination. This examination always occurs after the applicant has passed the written exam and often before the test of physical fitness or physical performance. The reason many police examining boards conduct the medical examination before the physical test is so that candidates whose health might be jeopardized by the strenuous activity of the physical test are screened out ahead of time. The police department does not want its applicants collapsing on the floor of the physical testing arena. In the interest of cost-efficiency, however, you may be asked to take the physical performance test before your medical examination. Since applicants who cannot qualify on the physical performance test need not undergo the more expensive medical examination, the department saves money. If you are to take the physical performance test before taking your medical examination, you will probably be asked to bring a certificate of fitness to participate in the physical exam, which has been signed by your own doctor. Then, after you have qualified on the physical performance test, the police physician will conduct the departmental examination. Both the physical performance test and the medical exam are administered to one applicant at a time, but the medical exam needs a physician while the physical performance exam can be administered by a police department employee with a stopwatch. Disqualification on the basis of either the physical performance test or the medical exam stops the screening process and eliminates the candidate from further consideration.

The medical exam will resemble an army physical more than a visit to your personal physician. You will start by filling out a lengthy questionnaire relating to your medical history. This questionnaire will be used by the physician to single out special health areas for consideration. It may also be used by the personnel interviewer when you approach the final step of the screening process.

Do not lie on the medical questionnaire. Your medical history is a matter of record at school, in your service, dossier, and in the hospital or clinic files. If you lie you will be found out. If the medical condition does not disqualify you, the fact of your untruthfulness will. On the other hand, there is no need to tell more than is asked. You do not need to expand upon your aches and pains. You needn't make an illness or injury more dramatic than it was. Stick to the facts and do not raise any questions. If you have any current concerns, the police department's examining officer is not the person to ask.

Your medical examination almost certainly will include height and weight measurement, chest x-ray, eye test, hearing test, blood tests, urinalysis, cardiogram, blood pressure, and actual visual and physical examination by the doctor. If you have any doubts as to how you will fare with any of these examinations, you might want to consult your personal physician ahead of time. You may be able to correct a borderline situation before you appear for the exam.

Most police departments provide candidates with height-weight standards and with lists of medical requirements before their scheduled medical examinations. If you receive these, look them over carefully. If they present any problems to you, see your doctor. Your worry may be misplaced, or it may be real. Possibly you will have to change your career goals. Or, likely, you can correct the situation, pass the medical exam, and go on to serve on the police force.

Read over the medical specifications very carefully before you visit your personal physician. Some state police departments require nearly perfect uncorrected vision. Others permit glasses and/or contact lenses. Some departments welcome applicants who have had their vision surgically corrected. Others specify that applicants who have undergone Radial Keratotomy, Epikeratoplasty, or Ortho Keratology are not acceptable. If your own status cannot satisfy there requirements, you may have to move to another state or consider a city, town, or county force that has different requirements.

Not all state police departments have the same standards for medical conditions. Some will accept conditions that are absolutely disqualifying in others. The height-weight charts and the list of medical requirements on the following pages are illustrative. They are typical of those of many police departments. They should serve you as a general guide at this time. If your own medical position is way out of line, you may need to reconsider or embark on a major health reform campaign right away. Once you get your own department's official set of guidelines, follow those standards rather than the ones printed here.

Height and Weight for Females

Acceptable Weight in Pounds According to Frame

Height (in bare feet)		Small Frame	Medium Frame	Large Frame
Feet	Inches			
4	10	92-98	96-107	104-119
4	11	94-101	98-110	106-122
5	0	96-104	101-113	109-125
5	1	99-107	104-116	112-128
5	2	102-110	107-119	115-131
5	3	105-113	110-122	118-134
5	4	108-116	113-126	121-138
5	5	111-119	116-130	125-142
5	6	114-123	120-135	129-146
5	7	118-127	124-139	133-150
5	8	122-131	128-143	137-154
5	9	126-135	132-147	141-158
5	10	130-140	136-151	145-163

Height (in bare feet) Feet	Inches	Small Frame	Medium Frame	Large Frame
5	11	134-144	140-155	149-168
6	0	138-148	144-159	153-173
6	1	142-152	148-163	157-177

NOTE: Although the above table commences at a specified height, no minimum height requirement has been prescribed. This table of height and weight will be adhered to in all instances except where the Civil Service examining physician certifies that weight in excess of that shown in the table (up to a maximum of twenty pounds) is lean body mass and not fat. Decision as to frame size of candidate shall be made by the examining physician.

The following tests will be part of the medical examination:

- Vision
- Hearing
- Serology
- Urinalysis
- Chest X-Ray
- Blood Pressure
- Electrocardiogram

Height and Weight for Males

Acceptable Weight in Pounds According to Frame

Height (in bare feet) Feet	Inches	Small Frame	Medium Frame	Large Frame
5	3	115-123	121-133	129-144
5	4	118-126	124-136	132-148
5	5	121-129	127-139	135-152
5	6	124-133	130-143	138-156
5	7	128-137	134-147	142-161
5	8	132-141	138-152	147-166
5	9	136-145	142-156	151-170
5	10	140-150	146-160	155-174
5	11	144-154	150-165	159-179
6	0	148-158	154-170	164-184
6	1	152-162	158-175	168-189
6	2	156-167	162-180	175-194
6	3	160-171	167-185	178-199
6	4	164-175	172-190	182-204
6	5	168-179	176-194	186-209
6	6	172-183	180-198	190-214

NOTE: Although the above table commences at a specified height, no minimum height requirement has been prescribed. This table of height and weight will be adhered to in all instances except where the Civil Service examining physician certifies that weight in excess of that shown in the table (up to a maximum of twenty pounds) is lean body mass and not fat. Decision as to frame size of candidates shall be made by the examining physician.

The following tests will be part of the medical examination:

- Vision
- Hearing
- Serology
- Urinalysis
- Chest X-Ray
- Blood Pressure
- Electrocardiogram

Candidates are required to meet the physical and medical requirements stated below and in the announcement at the time of the medical examination, at the time of appointment, and at appropriate intervals thereafter.

1. **Weight.** Candidates should have weight commensurate to frame. Weight should not interfere with candidate's ability to perform the duties of the position of Police Officer.

2. **Vision.** Candidates must have binocular visual acuity not less than 20/20 with or without correction; if correction is required, binocular visual acuity not less than 20/40 without correction. Binocular peripheral vision should not be less than 150 degrees.

3. **Color Vision.** Be able to distinguish individual basic colors against a favorable background.

4. **Hearing.** Candidates must be able to pass an audiometric test of hearing acuity in each ear. A binaural hearing loss of greater than 15% in the frequency ranges of 500, 1000, 2000 Hz would be considered disqualifying. Hearing appliances should correct the deficiency so the binaural hearing loss in the combined frequency level of 500, 1000, 2000 Hz is not greater than 15%.

5. **Heart.** Candidates must be free of functionally limited heart disease. Must have functional cardiac classification of no greater than Class I. This determination is to be made clinically or by cardiac stress test.

6. **Lungs.** The respiratory system must be free of chronic disabling conditions that would interfere with the candidate's performance of required duties.

7. **Diabetes.** Candidates who are diabetic must not require insulin injections or oral hypoglycemic agents for control.

8. **Neurological Health.** Candidates must be free of neurological disorders that may affect job performance. Candidates with epilepsy or seizure disorders must provide evidence of one-year seizure-free history without drug control.

9. **Musculoskeletal Health.** Candidates must be free of musculosketetal defects, deformities, or disorders that may affect job performance. Functional use of the arms, hands, legs, feet, and back must be demonstrable at the examination. Candidates will be asked to demonstrate physical fitness through tests of strength, agility, flexibility, and endurance.

10. **Hernia.** Candidates must be free of abdominal and inguinal herniae that would interfere with job performance.

11. **Blood/Vascular Health.** Candidates must be free of blood or vascular disorders that interfere with the performance of duties. Candidates with uncontrolled high blood pressure will be disqualified remediable.

12. **Mental Health.** Candidates must be free of mental illness, serious emotional disturbances or nervous disorders, alcoholism, and drug dependence or abuse.

13. **General Medical Statement.** Candidates must be free of any medical and/or nervous condition that would jeopardize safety and health of others. Candidates with communicable diseases will be disqualified remediable.

FORMULATION OF MEDICAL REQUIREMENTS FROM ANOTHER STATE POLICE DEPARTMENT

The duties of these positions involve physical exertion under rigorous environmental conditions; irregular and protracted hours of work; patrol duties on foot, motor vehicle, and aircraft; and participation in physical training. Applicants must be in sound physical condition and of good muscular development.

Vision

• Binocular vision is required and must test 20/40 (Snellen) without corrective lenses,

• Uncorrected vision must test at least 20/70 in each eye,

• Vision in each eye must be corrected to 20/20,

• Near vision, corrected or uncorrected, must be sufficient to read Jaeger Type 2 at 14 inches, and

• Ability to distinguish basic colors by pseudoisochromatic plate test (missing no more than four plates) is required, as is normal peripheral vision.

Hearing

• Without using a hearing aid, the applicant must be able to hear the whispered voice at 15 feet with each ear; or

• Using an audiometer for measurement, there should be no loss of 30 or more decibels in each ear at the 500, 1000, and 2000 levels.

Speech

• Diseases or conditions resulting in indistinct speech are disqualifying.

Respiratory System

• Any chronic disease or condition affecting the respiratory system that would impair the full performance of duties of the position is disqualifying; e.g., conditions that result in reduced pulmonary function, shortness or breath, or painful respiration.

Cardiovascular System

The following conditions are disqualifying:
- Organic heart disease (compensated or not),
- Hypertension with repeated readings that exceed 150 systolic and 90 diastolic without medication, and
- Symptomatic peripheral vascular disease and severe varicose veins.

Gastrointestinal System

- Chronic symptomatic diseases or conditions of the gastrointestinal tract are disqualifying.
- Conditions requiring special diets or medications are disqualifying.

Endocrine System

- Any history of a systemic metabolic disease, such as diabetes or gout, is disqualifying.

Genitourinary Disorders

- Chronic symptomatic diseases or conditions of the genitourinary tract are disqualifying.

Hernias

- Inguinal and femoral hernias with or without the use of a truss are disqualifying. Other hernias are disqualifying if they interfere with performance of the duties of the position.

Nervous System

- Applicants must possess emotional and mental stability with no history of a basic personality disorder.
- Applicants with a history of epilepsy or convulsive disorder must have been seizure-free for the past two years without medication.
- Any neurological disorder with resulting decreased neurological or muscular function is disqualifying.

Miscellaneous

Though not mentioned specifically above, any other disease or condition that interferes with the full performance of duties is also grounds for medical rejection. Before entrance on duty, all applicants must undergo a pre-employment medical examination and be medically suitable to perform the full duties of the position efficiently and without hazard to themselves and others. Failure to meet any one of the required medical qualifications will be disqualifying for appointment. These standards are considered minimum standards and will not be waived in any case. Applicants found to have a correctable condition may be restored to any existing list of eligibles for further consideration for appointment when the disqualifying condition has been satisfactorily corrected or eliminated.

Physical Performance Tests

The physical performance requirements for all police officers are very similar. All police officers must be able to jump in an instant, must be able to move very quickly, must be strong, must have the stamina to maintain speed and strength for a long time, and must be able to continue physically stressful activity at a high level while withstanding discomfort and pain. The ideal police officer is "Superman." The actual police officer does well to approach those qualities.

While police departments have similar physical performance requirements, they tend to measure fitness in many different ways. Three different police officer physical fitness tests follow. Read them through and note the variations. Try each out to the extent that you can without the actual testing course. See how you do. You may need to get yourself into a regular body-building routine some time before you are called for examination. Strength and fitness cannot be developed overnight. You will need to work yourself up to par over a long period. Set up a program and get started right away. You will not be called for a physical fitness test until after you have passed the written examination and not until there is some possibility that your place on the list will soon be reached. The hiring process moves along slowly, but it does move. You have time, but not that much time. Start now.

A TYPICAL QUALIFYING PHYSICAL FITNESS TEST FOR POLICE OFFICER

Instructions for Candidates

These subtests are electronically timed by your stepping on the Start Mat and the Finish Mat.

Stair Climb / Restrain: (One Trial) (Maximum Time Allowed: Two Minutes)

In this subtest, you will be expected to run up 3 flights of stairs, down 1 flight, push and pull a box 5 times, and run 5 feet to the finish line.

- On the signal GO, step on the Start Mat, run up the stairs on your right, continue up to the landing on the third floor.
- Both feet must be placed on the landing.
- Run quickly down one flight of stairs and into the lobby.

- Grab the box and pull it towards you until the front of the box reaches the tape on the floor.
- Now push it back to its starting position.
- Repeat 4 more times as the examiner announces the count.
- After the last trip, turn RIGHT and step on the Finish Mat.

Dummy Drag: (Two Trials)
(Maximum Time Allowed: One Minute)

In this subtest, you will be expected to drag a dummy 30 feet.

- Step on the Start Mat.
- Grab the dummy under the shoulders.
- Holding the dummy in this position, move backwards around the traffic cone set 15 feet away and return.
- Place the dummy EXACTLY as you found it in the starting position.
- Step on the Finish Mat.

Wall Climb / Obstacle Run: (Two Trials)
(Maximum Time Allowed: One Minute)

In this subtest, you will be expected to go over the five-foot wall and continue through the obstacle run.

- Step on the Start Mat.
- Run to the wall and go over. You are NOT allowed to use the support bars.
- Follow the tape on the floor around the cones.
- If you miss a cone or go around it the wrong way, you must go back and go around the cone CORRECTLY.
- If you knock a cone over, you must STOP and set it up before you continue.
- Step on the Finish Mat.

ANOTHER PHYSICAL FITNESS TEST

Medical evidence to allow participation in the physical fitness test may be required, and the Department of Personnel reserves the right to exclude from the physical test any eligibles who, upon examination of such evidence, are apparently medically unfit. Eligibles will take the physical fitness test at their own risk of injury, although efforts will be made to safeguard them.

Candidates must complete the *entire* course consisting of seven events in not more than *65 seconds*.

Candidates who do not successfully complete events 3, 5, and 6 will fail the test.

Description of Events

1. Run up approximately 40 steps.
2. Run approximately 40 yards, following a designated path including at least four 90 degree turns, to a sandbag.

3. Push the sandbag, weighing approximately 100 pounds, forward a distance of approximately five yards and then back to its original position. (Failure to meet all of the conditions for this event will result in failure of the test as a whole.)

4. Run approximately 10 yards to a dummy, weighing approximately 110 pounds, which is hanging with its lowest point approximately 3 feet above the floor.

5. Raise the dummy so as to lift the attached ring off the metal pipe. Allow the dummy to slide onto the floor or place it on the floor. *You must not drop it or throw it down.* (Failure to meet all of the conditions for this event will result in failure of the test as a whole.)

6. Step up approximately 18 inches and walk across a 12-foot beam by placing one foot in front of the other until you reach the other end. (You must be in control at all times, and falling off the beam will result in failure of the test as a whole.)

7. Run approximately 10 yards to the finish line.

Candidates who fail the test on their first trial will be allowed a second trial on the same date after a rest period.

Candidates who do not successfully complete all the events in their proper sequence will fail the test.

ONE MORE PHYSICAL FITNESS TEST, VERY DIFFERENT IN STYLE

The candidates who qualify on the medical examination will be required to pass the qualifying physical fitness test. A total score of twenty is required for passing this test; the scores attained on the five individual tests are added together to obtain your final score.

Test I: Trunk Flexion Test (Three Chances)

Candidates will assume a sitting position on the floor with the legs extended at right angles to a line drawn on the floor. The heels should touch the near edge of the line and be five inches apart. The candidate should slowly reach with both hands as far forward as possible on a yardstick that is placed between the legs with the fifteen-inch mark resting on the near edge of the heel line. The score is the most distant point (in inches) reached on the yardstick with fingertips.

Rating	Trunk Flexion (Inches)	Points
Excellent	22 and over	6
Good	20-21	5
Average	14-19	4
Fair	12-13	3
Poor	10-11	2
Very Poor	9 and under	1

Test II: Hand Grip Strength Test (Three Chances)

The candidate places the dynamometer (hand grip tester) at the side and, without touching the body with any part of the arm, hand, or the dynamometer, should grip the dynamometer as hard as possible in one quick movement. The best of the three tries will be recorded.

Rating	Hand Grip in Kg.	Points
Excellent	65 and above	6
Good	57-64	5
Average	45-56	4
Fair	37-44	3
Poor	30-36	2
Very Poor	29 and under	1

Test III: Standing Broad Jump (Three Chances)

Candidates will be permitted three chances in consecutive order, and the longest distance will be credited. Candidates will be required to jump from a standing position, both feet together. Distance of jump will be recorded from starting point to back of heels. It is each candidate's responsibility to have a non-skid surface on the soles of his or her sneakers.

Rating	Distance	Points
Excellent	7'10" or better	6
Good	7'0" to 7'9"	5
Average	6'1" to 6'11"	4
Fair	5'6" to 6'0"	3
Poor	5'0" to 5'5"	2
Very Poor	Less than 5'	1

Test IV: One Minute Sit-Up Test

The candidate will start by lying on the back with the knees bent so that the heels are about eighteen inches away from the buttocks. An examiner will hold the ankles to give support. The candidate will then perform as many correct sit-ups (elbows alternately touching the opposite knee) as possible within a one-minute period. The candidate should return to the starting position (back to floor) between sit-ups.

Rating	Sit-Ups in 1 Minute	Points
Excellent	35	6
Good	30-34	5
Average	20-29	4
Fair	15-19	3
Poor	10-14	2
Very Poor	9 and under	1

Test V: Three Minute Step Test

The candidate will step for three minutes on a one-inch bench at a rate of twenty-four steps per minute. The time will be maintained by a metronome. Immediately after the three minutes of stepping, the subject will sit down and relax without talking. A sixty-second heart rate count is taken starting five seconds after the completion of stepping.

Rating	Pulse	Points
Excellent	75-84	6
Good	85-94	5
Average	95-119	4
Fair	120-129	3
Poor	130-139	2
Very Poor	Over 140	1

Sliding Scale Standards

The Americans with Disabilities Act requires that age not be a consideration in hiring except where youth, or maturity, is a bona fide qualification for performance of the job. The federal government has established 37 as the highest age at which persons can and may effectively enter certain federal law enforcement positions. In order to establish an age-based hiring limit, each jurisdiction must justify the age it has chosen. At the time, not all guidelines are clear. Each jurisdiction makes its own interpretation of the requirements of the Americans with Disabilities Act, and its interpretation remains in effect until challenged and overturned by a court of law. Some states have chosen to take the Act at face value and have done away with upper age limits altogether.

When states, or jurisdictions within those states, discard upper age limits, they open themselves to new complications. According to the U.S. Justice Department, physical fitness standards which are the same for everyone violate the Americans with Disabilities Act. In response to this determination, many states have relaxed the physical fitness requirements for state police officers. The following is a recently announced Physical Fitness Screening Test that takes into consideration both age and sex.

Physical Fitness Screening Test

Candidate will go from Stations I through IV in order. Each station is pass/fail. Candidate must pass each station in order to proceed to the next station. Candidate will be allowed up to three minutes rest between stations. Once a station is started, it must be completed according to protocol. See the chart below:

Station I: **Sit-up**—Candidate lies flat on the back, knees bent, heels flat on the floor, fingers interlaced behind the head. Monitor holds the feet down firmly. In the up position, candidate should touch elbows to knees and return with shoulder blades touching floor. To pass this component, candidate must complete the requisite number of correct sit-ups in one minute.

Station II: **Flex**—Candidate removes shoes and places feet squarely against box with feet no wider than eight inches apart. Toes are pointed directly toward ceiling, knees remain extended throughout test. With hands placed one on top of the other, candidate leans forward without lunging or bobbing and reaches as far down the yard stick as possible. The hands must stay together and the stretch must be held for one second. Three attempts are allowed with the best of three recorded to the nearest $1/4$ inch to determine whether the candidate passed/failed.

Station III: **Bench**—Monitor loads weights to $1/2$ of candidate required weight. Candidate is permitted to "press" this weight once. Monitor increases weight to

²/₃ of candidate required weight. Candidate is permitted to "press" this weight once. The required test weight is then loaded. The candidate has up to four (4) attempts to "press" required (maximum) weight. In order to pass, <u>buttocks must remain on the bench</u>. Candidate will be allowed up to two minutes rest between each "press." (Universal Bench Press Equipment)

Station IV: **1.5 Mile Run**—Candidate must be successful on Stations I, II & III in order to participate in Station IV. It will be administered on a track. Candidate will be informed of his/her lap time during the test.

Scoring Chart

AGE/SEX MALE	SIT-UP	FLEX	TEST BENCH	1.5 MI RUN
20-29	38	16.5	99	12.51
30-39	35	15.5	88	13.36
40-49	29	14.3	80	14.29
50-59	24	13.3	71	15.26
60+	19	12.5	66	16.43
FEMALE				
20-29	32	19.3	59	15.26
30-39	25	18.3	53	15.57
40-49	20	17.3	50	16.58
50-59	14	16.8	44	17.54
60+	6	15.5	43	18.44

The Background Check

The police officer is in a position of public trust. He or she must be deserving of that trust. The police department must feel very certain that the police officer will not use his or her position for personal gain, will not use it to harass individuals or groups that he or she dislikes, will not be easily corrupted, and will not take advantage of privileged knowledge. It is for this reason that the background check is such an important part of the police selection process. The background check is a time-consuming process. Therefore, the police personnel office will not initiate the background check until an applicant appears to be qualified in nearly every way; that is, the background check occurs after the written test, physical performance test, and full medical examination.

The standard predictor of future behavior is past behavior. The police department must find out how you have behaved in the past. It will do this by first having you fill out a questionnaire. As with the medical questionnaire, there is no point in lying or cheating. You will be found out and will be disqualified. State the facts clearly. Explain fully and factually.

If you have a totally clean record and face no problems in your personal or family life, then you need have no concern about the background check. Fill in the blanks. List references, and inform those people whose names you have given, so that they are not upset when they are contacted by the police.

Most people have something in their backgrounds that can spark more inquiry. The problem may be financial: If you are strapped for money, the police department may fear that you might be corruptible. The problem may be marital: The police department may worry that you will be distracted. The problem may be one of frequent job changes: The police department questions your stability and the value of investing in your training. The problem may be one of poor credit: Are you responsible and reliable? Or the problem may be one of a brush with the law, minor or major. Most minor infractions can be explained at an interview; reassure the interviewer that these were youthful indiscretions unlikely to recur. Arrests for felonies, and, worse still, convictions present greater obstacles. It may be wise to consult an attorney who specializes in expunging criminal records to see what can be done to clear your name. Some offenses are absolutely disqualifying. You may as well know ahead of time and take all possible steps to make yourself employable by the police department.

A felony record needs the service of an attorney. So might multiple misdemeanor convictions. You can help yourself in many other situations. If you have a poor credit rating, pay up and have your rating upgraded. If you are behind on alimony payments, catch up. If you have an

45

unanswered summons, go to court and answer it. Pay your parking tickets. Even if these past problems turn up in the background check, your positive attitude in clearing them up will be in your favor.

Be sure that you are able to document any claims you make with reference to diplomas, degrees, and honors. You may have to produce these at an interview. Likewise, be certain that you understand the nature and gravity of the problems in your background. Be prepared to admit that you misbehaved and to reassure the examiners that you have matured into a responsible citizen.

The Psychological Evaluation

THE PURPOSE OF THE PSYCHOLOGICAL EVALUATION

Some states subject all police officer candidates to a psychological evaluation before appointment; others, because of the expense involved, limit psychological evaluations to those cases where there are signs that one might be necessary. However, in all cases the sole purpose of a psychological evaluation is to determine the candidate's mental fitness for performing the specific duties of a police officer. The evaluation is *not* concerned with other aspects of mental well-being. In fact, because of this exclusive focus on police work, a candidate might be judged psychologically unfit to be a police officer even if he or she is perfectly suited for other types of employment.

What makes police work so different from other occupations? Soon after orientation and the usual training at the police academy, the police officer begins functioning more or less independently. Although the officer functions under supervision, that supervision is present only periodically and although the officer should be guided by the department's rules of procedure, many times the officer will be thrust into situations where immediate action is required to save lives or protect property. For example, the officer who encounters a pregnant woman about to give birth must take decisive action at once. In such situations, there is no time to consult the rules of procedure. The officer must do whatever is necessary right away.

Another crucial difference is that the police officer carries a gun as part of the job. Prudent use of this weapon requires not only conformance to the rules of procedure but also a good sense of police judgment. The officer who must decide in an emergency whether to use that gun must have a very high degree of psychological stability.

Psychological evaluations of police officer candidates are usually conducted by a psychologist or psychiatrist who is trained to detect signs of deficiencies that could interfere with the proper performance of police work. The job is twofold: to look for signs of potential trouble and to evaluate the sincerity of the candidate. For example, consider the possible responses when the psychologist asks, "Why do you want to become a police officer?" A proper response would be "I want a career in public service, and I feel that effective law enforcement will make for a better society for my children and eventually for my grandchildren." There is nothing wrong with this response. The only thing to be judged is the sincerity of the candidate. Now look at the following response to the same question: "I have always liked uniforms. They bring respect and admiration, and they permit you to perform your duties without interference." Something is wrong here. Or consider this response: "I hate criminals. They take advantage of the weak and elderly. They are cowards, and I want to do everything I can to eliminate them." This intense hatred may indicate the need for further investigation of this candidate's psychological stability.

TYPICAL EVALUATION QUESTIONS

The questions that you will be asked will, for the most part, be quite predictable. The majority of them will be based on your responses to application forms and other papers that you have been required to file. The psychologist will ask you to amplify or to explain the personal data that you listed on those papers. Sometimes you will be asked to describe your feelings about events that happened to you. Also, as a way of encouraging you to talk, you may be asked more open-ended questions about your personal likes, dislikes, or emotions.

You may also be asked your opinion about what you might do in a hypothetical police work situation, but such questions are unlikely to form the bulk of the evaluation. In this case, the psychologist is not testing your knowledge of police procedures but only your ability to make reasoned judgments and to avoid rash behavior. Because most of the questions you will be asked are predictable, it is relatively easy to prepare answers for them. Begin your preparation by looking over the application forms that you filled out and any other papers that you were required to file. You should be able to pick out the points that a psychologist will want you to clarify or explain.

Typical questions you might encounter include the following:

- Why did you choose your area of concentration in school?
- What particularly interests you about that subject?
- Why did you transfer from school x to school y?
- How did you get the job with_____?
- Which of the duties described in your second job did you like best? Which least? Why?
- What did you do during the nine months between your second and third jobs?
- Explain the circumstances of your leaving a particular job.
- Please clarify: armed forces service, arrest record, hospitalization record, etc., as applicable.

Other questions are much like those asked at a routine job interview. They can be anticipated and prepared for as well.

- Why do you want to leave the kind of work you are doing now?
- Why do you want to be a state trooper?
- How does your family feel about your becoming a state police officer?
- What do you do in your leisure time?
- Do you have any hobbies? What are they? What do you particularly like about_____?
- What is your favorite sport? Would you rather play or watch?
- How do you react to criticism? If you think the criticism is reasonable? If you consider the criticism unwarranted?
- What is your pet peeve?
- What are your greatest strengths? Weaknesses?
- What could make you lose your temper?
- Of what accomplishment in your life are you most proud?
- What act do you regret?
- If you could start over, what would you do differently?

- What traits do you value in a co-worker? In a friend?
- What makes you think you would make a good state police officer?

Still other questions may be more specific to police work. You should have prepared answers to:

- How much sleep do you need?
- Are you afraid of heights?
- What is your attitude toward working irregular hours?
- Do you prefer working alone or on a team?
- Are you afraid of dying?
- What would you do with the rest of your life if your legs were crippled in an injury?
- How do you deal with panic? Your own? That of others?
- What is your attitude toward smoking? Drinking? *Playboy* magazine? Gambling?
- What is your favorite TV program? How do you feel about watching news? Sports? Classical drama? Rock music? Opera? Game shows?

Now make a list of your own. The variety of evaluation questions is endless but most can be answered with ease. Preparation makes the whole process much more pleasant and less frightening.

There is one question that strikes terror into the heart of nearly every candidate for police officer or any other job. This question is likely to be the first and, unless you are prepared for it, may well throw you off guard. The question is "Tell me about yourself." For this question you should have a prepared script (in your head, not in your hand). Think well ahead of time about what you want to tell. What could the psychologist be interested in? This question is not seeking information about your birth weight nor about your food preferences. The psychologist wants you to tell about yourself with relation to your interest in and qualifications for police work. Think of how to describe yourself with this goal in mind. What information puts you into a good light with reference to the work for which you are applying? Organize your presentation. Then analyze what you plan to say. What is a psychologist likely to pick up on? To what questions will your speech lead? You must prepare to answer these questions to which you have opened yourself.

Toward the end of the evaluation, the psychologist will most likely ask if you have any questions. You undoubtedly will have had some before hand and should have come prepared to ask them. If all of your questions have been answered in the course of the evaluation, you may tell this to the psychologist. If not, or if the evaluation has raised new questions in your mind, by all means ask them. The evaluation should serve for your benefit; it is not just to serve the purposes of the Police Department.

The invitation of your questions tends to be the signal that the evaluation is nearly over. The psychologist is satisfied that he or she has gathered enough information. The time allotted to you is up. Be alert for the cues. Do not spoil the good impression you have made by trying to prolong the evaluation.

SHOULD YOU REVEAL PERSONAL OPINIONS AND FEELINGS?

The psychologist does not expect candidates to be devoid of personal feelings. After all, everyone has likes and dislikes. However, the mature, psychologically stable person is able to keep those feelings from interfering with the performance of job duties. The police office will encounter a very wide variety of people on the job. Some the officer may find personally likable; others may be unlikeable, even downright unpleasant. However, whatever the officer's true feelings about the persons encountered, he or she must serve those individuals in an effective manner or serious repercussions—even loss of life—may result. This type of behavior takes mental maturity and stability, qualities every officer must possess. It is these qualities that the psychologist is looking for at the evaluation, not an absence of personal feelings. The successful candidate does not have to like everyone he or she meets. What is important is the ability to control personal feelings in order to function effectively.

Sometimes during an evaluation a candidate will express "extreme" views on certain subjects. Unlike typical opinions or feelings, these may indeed be cause for disqualification. An obvious example is a display of unreasonable dislike for people from a particular ethnic or religious background. To the psychologist, this is a sure sign of trouble. The candidate who says, "People from ethnic group X are always the ones who commit the violent crimes," will never be appointed a state police officer.

SHOULD YOU VOLUNTEER INFORMATION?

One very important point to remember at the evaluation is to limit your responses to what is asked. An evaluation session of this type is one of the very few opportunities most people have to reveal their true inner selves to others. The psychologist knows this and will often encourage the person being evaluated to talk freely and openly about personal matters and opinions. An unthinking candidate may use this opportunity to bring up matters that ordinarily he or she would never discuss. The talkative candidate might even know that he or she is getting in too deep but may be unable to refrain from continuing. The psychologist will encourage this type of individual to talk at length in order to reveal personal matters that will indicate the level of the candidate's psychological stability.

One device that psychologists use to make candidates keep talking is to assume a facial expression that indicates further explanation is expected. It is very important not to respond to this suggestion! If you do, you are likely to say things that can only be harmful to you. Try to be satisfied with your original response and have the maturity to stand by it no matter what expression you see on the psychologist's face. Display a sense of self-assurance that convinces the psychologist that you are satisfied with your answers.

HOW TO EXPLAIN PROBLEM INCIDENTS IN YOUR PAST

One concern of many police officer candidates is how to handle questions about problem incidents in their past. More than a few candidates have at some time—usually in their youth—gotten into trouble in some incident involving property damage or even personal injury to others. Such incidents almost always come to light during the candidate's background check, often through school, court, or military records. If you have such an incident in your past and are questioned about it by the psychologist, the wisest course is to accept full responsibility for it and to attribute it to your youthful immaturity at the time. Claiming that the record is false or giving excuses for your bad behavior is not likely to be regarded favorably. The psychologist is much more apt to respond positively if you accept responsibility and—just as important—you attribute any such incident to an immature outlook that you have now outgrown. One mistake of this type will not necessarily disqualify you if you can convince the psychologist that you have become a fully responsible adult and will never do anything of the kind again.

"PENCIL-AND-PAPER" EVALUATIONS

As part of the psychological evaluation, some jurisdictions use standardized personality tests that you answer by marking a sheet of paper. These tests may contain a hundred or more questions. Your responses help the psychologist determine your specific personality traits. Your answer to any one question by itself usually means very little, but your answers to a group of questions, taken together, will have significance to the psychologist. Your wisest course when taking one of these written personality tests is to give honest, truthful answers. Any attempt to make yourself appear different from the way you really are is not likely to be successful.

KEEP A POSITIVE ATTITUDE

One final word of advice: it is important to approach all psychological evaluations with a positive attitude. Think of the evaluation not as an ordeal that you must endure but rather as an opportunity to prove that you are qualified to become a police officer. In truth, the psychologist will be looking for traits that qualify you, not ones that disqualify you. And if disqualifying evidence exists, it is the psychologist's responsibility to consider every factor before making a negative recommendation. So go into the evaluation with confidence and be prepared to "sell" yourself to the psychologist. You will be given every chance to prove your worth.

EVALUATION CHECKLIST

Here are some valuable points to remember as you prepare for the psychological evaluation.

1. Get a good night's sleep the night before the evaluation.
2. Do not take any medication beforehand to calm yourself. You may be tested for drugs before the evaluation.
3. Dress neatly and conservatively.
4. Be polite to the psychologist or psychiatrist.
5. Respond to all questions honestly and forthrightly.
6. Use as few words as possible to communicate your thoughts. When you have finished answering a question, do not let the psychologist's behavior lead you to think that you have not said enough.
7. Admit responsibility for any youthful indiscretions and attribute them to your immaturity at the time of the incident.
8. Do not permit any deep-seated prejudices to assert themselves. If you can control them during the evaluation, you will be able to control them while performing the duties of a police officer.
9. Most important, be yourself. You're bound to do better than if you pretend to be someone you're not.

APPEALS

A police officer candidate who is marked "not qualified" on the psychological evaluation will be afforded an opportunity to appeal. In most jurisdictions, a notice of disqualification will include information on appeal procedures and on any time limitations.

Because the official disqualification is made by a psychologist or psychiatrist, the best way for the candidate to appeal is to engage another psychologist or psychiatrist to testify on the candidate's behalf. To start preparing the appeal, the candidate should obtain the official notice of the examination, the medical standards on which the evaluation was based, and a document telling the precise reason for the disqualification. If these items are not furnished by the examining agency, the candidate should petition for them at once. If necessary, the candidate should be prepared to resort to the procedures specified in the Freedom of Information Act in order to find out the exact reasons for rejection. This information is crucial to preparing a proper appeal. Any psychological testimony on the candidate's behalf must respond to the reasons given for disqualification. It is not enough for a psychologist to simply assert that the candidate is generally mentally stable. The psychologist must show that the candidate is in fact psychologically competent to perform the specific duties of a state police officer.

If you are disqualified as a result of the psychological evaluation, you should certainly consider filing an appeal. Often this kind of show of determination has influenced a hiring jurisdiction to take a chance on a "borderline" candidate. You will find many psychologists and psychiatrists who specialize in helping rejected police officer candidates.

PART TWO

Model Examinations for Practice

Answer Sheet for Model Examination 1

1. Ⓐ Ⓑ Ⓒ Ⓓ   21. Ⓐ Ⓑ Ⓒ Ⓓ   41. Ⓐ Ⓑ Ⓒ Ⓓ   61. Ⓐ Ⓑ Ⓒ Ⓓ   81. Ⓐ Ⓑ Ⓒ Ⓓ

2. Ⓐ Ⓑ Ⓒ Ⓓ   22. Ⓐ Ⓑ Ⓒ Ⓓ   42. Ⓐ Ⓑ Ⓒ Ⓓ   62. Ⓐ Ⓑ Ⓒ Ⓓ   82. Ⓐ Ⓑ Ⓒ Ⓓ

3. Ⓐ Ⓑ Ⓒ Ⓓ   23. Ⓐ Ⓑ Ⓒ Ⓓ   43. Ⓐ Ⓑ Ⓒ Ⓓ   63. Ⓐ Ⓑ Ⓒ Ⓓ   83. Ⓐ Ⓑ Ⓒ Ⓓ

4. Ⓐ Ⓑ Ⓒ Ⓓ   24. Ⓐ Ⓑ Ⓒ Ⓓ   44. Ⓐ Ⓑ Ⓒ Ⓓ   64. Ⓐ Ⓑ Ⓒ Ⓓ   84. Ⓐ Ⓑ Ⓒ Ⓓ

5. Ⓐ Ⓑ Ⓒ Ⓓ   25. Ⓐ Ⓑ Ⓒ Ⓓ   45. Ⓐ Ⓑ Ⓒ Ⓓ   65. Ⓐ Ⓑ Ⓒ Ⓓ   85. Ⓐ Ⓑ Ⓒ Ⓓ

6. Ⓐ Ⓑ Ⓒ Ⓓ   26. Ⓐ Ⓑ Ⓒ Ⓓ   46. Ⓐ Ⓑ Ⓒ Ⓓ   66. Ⓐ Ⓑ Ⓒ Ⓓ   86. Ⓐ Ⓑ Ⓒ Ⓓ

7. Ⓐ Ⓑ Ⓒ Ⓓ   27. Ⓐ Ⓑ Ⓒ Ⓓ   47. Ⓐ Ⓑ Ⓒ Ⓓ   67. Ⓐ Ⓑ Ⓒ Ⓓ   87. Ⓐ Ⓑ Ⓒ Ⓓ

8. Ⓐ Ⓑ Ⓒ Ⓓ   28. Ⓐ Ⓑ Ⓒ Ⓓ   48. Ⓐ Ⓑ Ⓒ Ⓓ   68. Ⓐ Ⓑ Ⓒ Ⓓ   88. Ⓐ Ⓑ Ⓒ Ⓓ

9. Ⓐ Ⓑ Ⓒ Ⓓ   29. Ⓐ Ⓑ Ⓒ Ⓓ   49. Ⓐ Ⓑ Ⓒ Ⓓ   69. Ⓐ Ⓑ Ⓒ Ⓓ   89. Ⓐ Ⓑ Ⓒ Ⓓ

10. Ⓐ Ⓑ Ⓒ Ⓓ   30. Ⓐ Ⓑ Ⓒ Ⓓ   50. Ⓐ Ⓑ Ⓒ Ⓓ   70. Ⓐ Ⓑ Ⓒ Ⓓ   90. Ⓐ Ⓑ Ⓒ Ⓓ

11. Ⓐ Ⓑ Ⓒ Ⓓ   31. Ⓐ Ⓑ Ⓒ Ⓓ   51. Ⓐ Ⓑ Ⓒ Ⓓ   71. Ⓐ Ⓑ Ⓒ Ⓓ   91. Ⓐ Ⓑ Ⓒ Ⓓ

12. Ⓐ Ⓑ Ⓒ Ⓓ   32. Ⓐ Ⓑ Ⓒ Ⓓ   52. Ⓐ Ⓑ Ⓒ Ⓓ   72. Ⓐ Ⓑ Ⓒ Ⓓ   92. Ⓐ Ⓑ Ⓒ Ⓓ

13. Ⓐ Ⓑ Ⓒ Ⓓ   33. Ⓐ Ⓑ Ⓒ Ⓓ   53. Ⓐ Ⓑ Ⓒ Ⓓ   73. Ⓐ Ⓑ Ⓒ Ⓓ   93. Ⓐ Ⓑ Ⓒ Ⓓ

14. Ⓐ Ⓑ Ⓒ Ⓓ   34. Ⓐ Ⓑ Ⓒ Ⓓ   54. Ⓐ Ⓑ Ⓒ Ⓓ   74. Ⓐ Ⓑ Ⓒ Ⓓ   94. Ⓐ Ⓑ Ⓒ Ⓓ

15. Ⓐ Ⓑ Ⓒ Ⓓ   35. Ⓐ Ⓑ Ⓒ Ⓓ   55. Ⓐ Ⓑ Ⓒ Ⓓ   75. Ⓐ Ⓑ Ⓒ Ⓓ   95. Ⓐ Ⓑ Ⓒ Ⓓ

16. Ⓐ Ⓑ Ⓒ Ⓓ   36. Ⓐ Ⓑ Ⓒ Ⓓ   56. Ⓐ Ⓑ Ⓒ Ⓓ   76. Ⓐ Ⓑ Ⓒ Ⓓ   96. Ⓐ Ⓑ Ⓒ Ⓓ

17. Ⓐ Ⓑ Ⓒ Ⓓ   37. Ⓐ Ⓑ Ⓒ Ⓓ   57. Ⓐ Ⓑ Ⓒ Ⓓ   77. Ⓐ Ⓑ Ⓒ Ⓓ   97. Ⓐ Ⓑ Ⓒ Ⓓ

18. Ⓐ Ⓑ Ⓒ Ⓓ   38. Ⓐ Ⓑ Ⓒ Ⓓ   58. Ⓐ Ⓑ Ⓒ Ⓓ   78. Ⓐ Ⓑ Ⓒ Ⓓ   98. Ⓐ Ⓑ Ⓒ Ⓓ

19. Ⓐ Ⓑ Ⓒ Ⓓ   39. Ⓐ Ⓑ Ⓒ Ⓓ   59. Ⓐ Ⓑ Ⓒ Ⓓ   79. Ⓐ Ⓑ Ⓒ Ⓓ   99. Ⓐ Ⓑ Ⓒ Ⓓ

20. Ⓐ Ⓑ Ⓒ Ⓓ   40. Ⓐ Ⓑ Ⓒ Ⓓ   60. Ⓐ Ⓑ Ⓒ Ⓓ   80. Ⓐ Ⓑ Ⓒ Ⓓ   100. Ⓐ Ⓑ Ⓒ Ⓓ

Model Examination 1

Time: 4 Hours—100 Questions

Directions: Each questions numbered 1 through 100 has four possible answers lettered A, B, C, and D. Select the correct answer and darken its letter on your answer sheet.

1. You are driving east on Sunrise Highway. You make a U-turn to pursue a suspect, then make a left turn. In what direction are you now heading?

    (A) north

    (B) south

    (C) east

    (D) west

2. You are driving south. You make a right turn to get to an accident scene and pass a military convoy traveling the opposite way. In what direction is the convoy headed?

    (A) north

    (B) south

    (C) east

    (D) west

3. You are traveling north on State Highway 12. At the junction of State 12 and County Road 113, you turn and proceed west on County 113. At the next stop sign, you stop and yield the right of way to a car crossing County 113 and entering the intersection from your right. The car is traveling

    (A) north

    (B) south

    (C) east

    (D) west

4. You are pursuing a car that was just involved in a hit-and-run accident and is now speeding north on High Street. In an attempt to lose you, the car turns left, then left, then left again. As the fleeing car goes through a red light, it is hit in the right side by a car legally entering the intersection. The car that hits the fugitive car is traveling

(A) north

(B) south

(C) east

(D) west.

5. As you are patrolling the southbound highway, you see smoke billowing from an area to your right. In order to investigate the source of the smoke, you should turn into the next exit to the

(A) north

(B) south

(C) east

(D) west

6. You are traveling in a southwesterly direction on the parkway, and traffic is merging into your lane from the left. The merging traffic is traveling

(A) north

(B) south

(C) east

(D) west

7. If you travel west one block on Grand Street, turn left onto North Street for one block, then turn right onto River Road for just one block, right again for one block on Church Street, and then take a left, you will be headed

(A) west on Grand Street

(B) north on North Street

(C) east on Grand Street

(D) west on River Road

Answer questions 8 through 17 by choosing the most grammatical and precise sentence.

8. (A) If he would have answered the detective honestly, he would not have been arrested.

(B) If he had answered the detective honestly, he would not have been arrested.

(C) He would not of been arrested if he had answered the detective honestly.

(D) If he'd answered the detective honestly, he wouldn't of been arrested.

9. (A) There are some people which don't know how to be happy.

(B) Some people can't be happy in no way.

(C) There are some people who don't know how to be happy.

(D) There are some people whom simply can't find happiness.

10. (A) Picking the cartridge up off the floor, the officer placed it on the counter.

    (B) The officer placed the cartridge on the counter after picking it up off the floor.

    (C) Picking the cartridge off of the floor, it was the officer who placed it on the counter.

    (D) The officer placed the cartridge on the counter and picked it up from the floor.

11. (A) If you talk right, people will know you are in possession of a good education.

    (B) If you speak good, people will know that your education is good.

    (C) By talking real good, you show how good your education is.

    (D) If you speak correctly, people will know that you are well educated.

12. (A) The suspect said he had done nothing wrong.

    (B) The suspect said he hadn't done nothing wrong.

    (C) The suspect says he ain't done anything wrong.

    (D) The suspect says he done nothing wrong.

13. (A) In order to watch his favorite team play, 40 miles it was that he drove.

    (B) He drove 40 miles in order to watch his favorite team play.

    (C) He drove, in order to watch his favorite team play, 40 miles.

    (D) His favorite team was playing, and he drove 40 miles in order to watch them play.

14. (A) Sergeant Miller, every morning at breakfast, the paper she likes to read.

    (B) At breakfast every morning it is the paper that Sergeant Miller likes to read.

    (C) At breakfast, reading the paper is what Sergeant Miller likes to do every morning.

    (D) Sergeant Miller likes to read the paper every morning at breakfast.

15. (A) If Trooper Howard had joined our barracks sooner, she might of made Sergeant by now.

    (B) If Trooper Howard would have joined our barracks sooner, she could of become a Sergeant already.

    (C) If Trooper Howard had joined our barracks sooner, she might be a Sergeant today.

    (D) If Trooper Howard joined our barracks sooner, she would be a Sergeant now.

16. (A) Entering the room, a strange mark on the floor attracted the officer's attention.

    (B) The officer entered the room and attracted the attention of a strange mark on the floor.

    (C) The officer's attention was attracted by a strange mark on the floor entering the room.

    (D) As the officer entered the room, his attention was attracted by a strange mark on the floor.

17. (A) The door opens, and in walk Captain Gomez and Officer Hua.

    (B) The door opens, and in walked Captain Gomez and Officer Hua.

    (C) The door opened, and in walk Captain Gomez and Officer Hua.

    (D) The door opened, and in walks Captain Gomez and Officer Hua.

18. The speed limit on the bridge is 35 mph, but Henry Smith crosses doing 42 mph. By what percent is he exceeding the speed limit?

    (A) 7%

    (B) 17%

    (C) 20%

    (D) 22%

19. The supply sergeant is filling out requisition forms and requests your ammunition needs for the next four months. Last month you used 270 rounds, including those needed for target practice. Assuming that you will be using about the same amount per month, how much ammunition should you request?

    (A) 880 rounds

    (B) 980 rounds

    (C) 1080 rounds

    (D) 1180 rounds

20. At 6:15 A.M. on a fog-bound morning, seven passenger cars, two vans, three tractor-trailers, and a bus pile up in a chain-reaction collision on the thruway. At 6:19 A.M. the first patrol car arrives on the scene and immediately radios for assistance. By 6:33 A.M. three ambulances, two fire engines, five tow trucks, and eight additional patrol cars have arrived. Between 6:33 A.M. and 7:15 A.M. three of the tow trucks hook up to damaged cars and remove them from the scene. How many vehicles remain at the accident site at 7:15 A.M.?

    (A) 32

    (B) 26

    (C) 25

    (D) 20

21. State Patrol Barracks C, home base to 20 patrol cars, is responsible for patrolling 235 miles of thruway and the surrounding vicinity. One Thursday morning, three cars were out of service for maintenance and repairs and four cars were assigned to off-highway duties. If all remaining cars were assigned equal territories, approximately how many miles of thruway did each car patrol?

    (A) 12

    (B) 17

    (C) 18

    (D) 19.5

22. The average gasoline usage of a patrol car in highway service is 28 miles per gallon. Officer Prince took out a car with a full tank of gas and an odometer reading of 4,682 and returned it with an odometer reading of 5,067. Approximately how many gallons of gasoline did Officer Prince use?

    (A) 28

    (B) 13.65

    (C) 12.85

    (D) 13.75

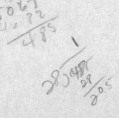

23. State troopers are permitted to place two in-state personal telephone calls per day at no charge. Excess phone calls are charged to the trooper at the rate of $0.50 each for the first two calls and $0.75 for each additional call. Out-of-state calls are billed at telephone company rates. Officer Zappa has been conducting family business by telephone during his break period. One day Officer Zappa made a long-distance call for which the charge was $2.35. His total telephone bill for that day was $5.60. How many telephone calls did Officer Zappa make that day?

    (A) 8

    (B) 7

    (C) 9

    (D) 6

24. Two troopers left the barracks at 3:00 P.M. Officer Tolski drove north maintaining an average speed of 42 mph. Officer Hara drove south at a steady speed of 38 mph. How many miles apart were the troopers at 4:30 P.M.?

    (A) 6

    (B) 80

    (C) 120

    (D) 150

25. A trooper left Barracks A at 9:15 A.M. and arrived at Barracks C at 2:45 P.M. How long did the trip take this trooper

    (A) 6 hours 30 minutes

    (B) 5 hours 30 minutes

    (C) 5 hours 15 minutes

    (D) 4 hours 45 minutes

26. A large group of demonstrators has gathered at a construction site to protest alleged discriminatory practices in hiring. The captain has dispatched 24 officers to avert a potential riot. No sooner have the officers arrived at the site when a call comes over the radio requesting that five officers report to a serious accident seven miles to the north. Shortly afterwards three officers are requested to control traffic at an intersection at which the traffic signal has malfunctioned. At the construction site, a worker is suddenly injured by a swinging boom, and two officers take the injured worker to the hospital in their patrol car. Then the captain arrives to survey the situation. What is the total number of law enforcers on hand to avert a riot?

    (A) 14

    (B) 15

    (C) 21

    (D) 22

27. Cars in police service receive very hard use and must be serviced every 3,000 miles or sooner. Officer Lindner's vehicle was last serviced at 8,782 miles. Officer Lindner drives an average of 140 miles a day, and his odometer currently reads 10,461. Within how many more working days must Officer Lindner bring in the car for servicing?

    (A) 14

    (B) 8

    (C) 10

    (D) 9

28. Officer Cohen's personal car was using 12 gallons of gasoline to travel 240 miles. Officer Cohen took the car to the mechanic for a tune-up and carburetor adjustment. After this service, Officer Cohen discovered that the car used only 80 percent as much gasoline as before. How many miles can Officer Cohen now drive with 12 gallons of gasoline?

    (A) 320

    (B) 280

    (C) 300

    (D) 342

29. The schedule of speeding penalties is as follows:

10% to 14% over the speed limit	$ 25
15% to 19% over the speed limit	$ 35
20% to 24% over the speed limit	$ 50
25% to 29% over the speed limit	$ 70
30% to 34% over the speed limit	$100
35% to 39% over the speed limit	$125
40% to 44% over the speed limit	$150
more than 44% over the speed limit	$200

    In a 40 mph zone, Officer David gave one ticket each to drivers clocked at 45 mph, 48 mph, and 53 mph and two tickets to drivers clocked at 60 mph and 58 mph respectively. Later that day while working in a 55 mph zone, Officer David gave two tickets to drivers traveling at 64 mph, one ticket to a driver clocked at 71.5 mph, and one ticket to a speeder doing 85 mph. If all ticketed drivers plead or are proven guilty, what is the total of fines to be collected from Officer David's tickets?

    (A) $945

    (B) $845

    (C) $910

    (D) $810

Questions 30 through 35 are based on the personnel chart below.

Personnel Chart

Name	Sex	SS Number	Date of Birth	Date Hired	Position	Supervisor
Hail, C.B.	M	123-45-6789	5/7/57	1/2/90	cook	Hood, R.B.
Hale, T.J.	F	083-68-1218	6/12/60	4/1/88	trooper	Dale, A.A.
Hales, N.A.	F	221-91-0031	4/28/53	5/10/74	property clerk	Tuck, F.R.
Hall, F.X.	M	118-22-5410	1/9/48	6/6/76	custodian	Hood, R.B.
Hals, F.T.	F	630-98-1234	12/21/64	11/23/85	sergeant	Allen, G.
Hill, R.L.	F	562-76-7977	9/30/30	10/4/86	security	Tuck, F.R.
Hill, P.C.	M	987-40-3939	10/14/41	9/2/72	mechanic	John, L.T.
Hilly, J.G.	M	406-18-6238	7/2/73	4/8/94	trooper	Dale, A.A.

30. Which person is supervised by F.R. Tuck?
    (A) P.C. Hill
    (B) F.X. Hall
    (C) N.A. Hales
    (D) T.J. Hale

31. The job held by the oldest person is
    (A) mechanic
    (B) security
    (C) cook
    (D) trooper

32. The oldest trooper was born on
    (A) 9/30/30
    (B) 12/21/64
    (C) 7/2/73
    (D) 6/12/60

33. The person who has been employed here for the longest time is
    (A) P. C. Hill
    (B) C. B. Hail
    (C) R. L. Hill
    (D) F. X. Hall

34. F. T. Hals's social security number is

(A) 630-89-1234

(B) 118-22-5410

(C) 118-22-5401

(D) 630-98-1234

35. The person whose social security number is 987-40-3939 is a

(A) cook

(B) trooper

(C) security guard

(D) mechanic

Questions 36 through 41 are based on the work schedule below.

Work Schedule

	Sun	Mon	Tues	Wed	Thurs	Fri	Sat
Group 1	South Quadrant	training	West Quadrant	off	South Quadrant	off	East Quadrant
Group 2	East Quadrant	off	training	North Quadrant	West Quadrant	West Quadrant	off
Group 3	North Quadrant	West Quadrant	off	West Quadrant	off	training	North Quadrant

Group 1	*Group 2*	*Group 3*
Supervisor: Jose Primo	*Supervisor: Steve Chen*	*Supervisor: Jane Shulz*
Mary Clark	Robert Park	Clifford Rose
James McDonald	Linda LaRue	Gino Abate
Thoru Moro	Barbara Benson	Ben Trotsky
Akeel Morris	Marvin Cohen	Charles O'Day

Training at: 146 Butler Road
Training supervisor: Gregor Ozmanian

July

Sun	Mon	Tues	Wed	Thurs	Fri	Sat
				1	2	3
4	5	6	7	8	9	10
11	12	13	14	15	16	17
18	19	20	21	22	23	24
25	26	27	28	29	30	31

36. Where is Gino Abate working on July 21?

    (A) North Quadrant

    (B) 146 Butler Road

    (C) West Quadrant

    (D) Not working

37. A person who will be working in only two quadrants during the month of July is

    (A) Linda LaRue

    (B) Jane Shulz

    (C) Thoru Moro

    (D) Gregor Ozmanian

38. On what date will Akeel Morris report for training?

    (A) July 2

    (B) July 4

    (C) July 19

    (D) July 22

39. The supervisor of the group that will work in the south quadrant on July 15 is

    (A) Jose Primo

    (B) Jane Shulz

    (C) Mary Clark

    (D) Gregor Ozmanian

40. A person who will be off on July 25 is

    (A) Steven Chen

    (B) Charles O'Day

    (C) Gregor Ozmanian

    (D) Robert Park

41. Which group will work in the west quadrant on July 11?

    (A) Group 1

    (B) Group 2

    (C) Group 3

    (D) Cannot be determined

Questions 42 through 46 are based on the daily arrest report below:

Daily Arrest Report

Area	Arresting Officer	Burglary	Murder	Arson	Assault	Total
Arch	Sgt. Tomas	X			X	2
Cove	Sgt. Blau		X		X	2
Dale	Sgt. Paik	X			X	2
Hill	Sgt. Leary			X		1
Wall	Sgt. Rossi	X		X		2
	Total	3	1	2	3	9

Those arrested today are: D. Tramp, A. Wilson, E. Brown, M. Allen, L. King, J. Harris, B. Davis, S. Grant, G. Evans.

- M. Allen lives in Dale.
- E. Brown was arrested in her home vicinity.
- S. Grant was arrested by Sgt. Tomas.
- D. Tramp was arrested for murder.
- J. Harris and E. Brown are roommates.
- Sgt. Leary arrested only male suspects.
- No person arrested by Sgt. Paik lives in the area in which the arrest took place.
- Sgt. Rossi did not arrest any residents of Arch.
- L. King is a juvenile.
- A. Wilson was carrying a fur jacket and silver candlesticks in a pillowcase when arrested.
- E. Brown lives in Arch.
- G. Evans is on probation stemming from prior conviction for assaulting his wife.

42. The person who could NOT have been arrested by Sgt. Leary is

    (A) G. Evans
    (B) L. King
    (C) J. Harris
    (D) Cannot be determined from information given

43. Which of these suspects could Sgt. Paik have arrested?

(A) M. Allen

(B) B. Davis

(C) D. Tramp

(D) E. Brown

44. The person who might have been arrested by Sgt. Rossi on suspicion of arson is

(A) J. Harris

(B) A. Wilson

(C) L. King

(D) S. Grant

45. D. Tramp was arrested by

(A) Sgt. Blau

(B) Sgt. Paik

(C) Sgt. Tomas

(D) cannot be determined from information given

46. Sgt. Leary arrested M. Allen on a charge of

(A) burglary

(B) arson

(C) murder

(D) cannot be determined from information given

In the diagrams for questions 47 and 48, symbols are used to represent vehicles, pedestrians, animals, and their movements.

- Vehicles are shown by the symbol: front ◁▭ rear
- Pedestrians are represented by a circle: ○
- Animals are represented by a square: □
- Solid lines show the path and direction of a vehicle, person, or animal *before* an accident happened: ——→
- Dotted lines show the path and direction of a vehicle, person, or animal *after* an accident happened: – – – →

47. Car 1 was driving north on State Road #112 when a deer crossing the road from the left of the car ran into the roadway directly in front of the car. Car 1 glanced off the rear end of the deer and swerved to the left. Car 2 proceeding south on State Road #112 swerved to its right to avoid a head-on collision with Car 1, and stopped in the underbrush off the shoulder. Which of the four diagrams below best represents the accident described?

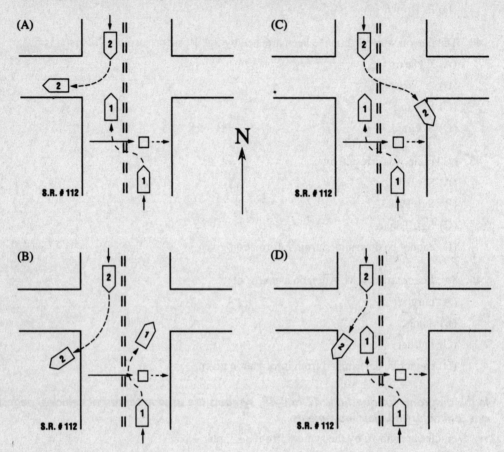

48. Officer Wood was standing beside a radar-equipped patrol car on the west shoulder of southbound I-95 and observed the following: Car 1 was proceeding south on I-95 in accordance with the posted speed limit. Car 2 approaching I-95 from the east on Hilton Crossway and signaling for a left turn came to a full stop at the intersection. Car 3, directly behind car 2, was signaling for a right turn and not paying attention. Car 3 hit car 2 from behind. Car 2 swerved into the northbound roadway so as to avoid a collision in the southbound direction. Which of the four diagrams below best represents the accident observed by Officer Wood?

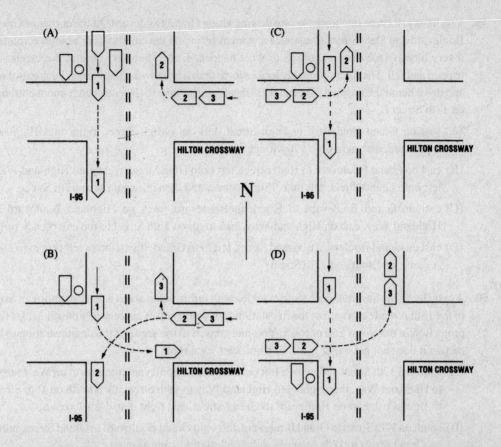

Use the map below to answer questions 49 and 50. The flow of traffic is indicated by the arrows. If there is only one arrow shown, then traffic flows only in the direction indicated by the arrow. If there are two arrows shown, then traffic flows in both directions. You must follow the flow of traffic.

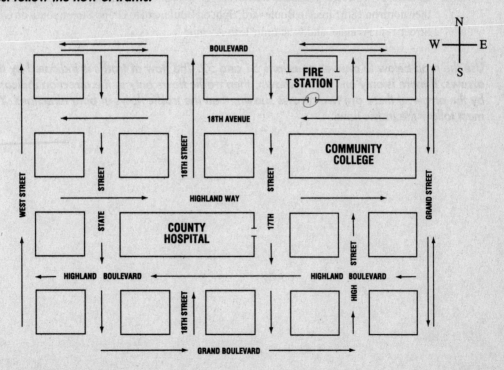

49. You have just come into town and are driving along Grand Boulevard. At the corner of Grand Boulevard and State Street, you notice a woman sitting on the curb holding a handkerchief to a very bloody face. You inquire as to what happened, and she tells you that she carelessly tripped and fell. The injury probably looks worse than it is, but you place her in your patrol car and drive her to the hospital. The quickest legal route to take to the emergency room entrance on 17th Street is

(A) east on Grand Boulevard to High Street, left onto High Street, right onto Highland Boulevard, and right onto 17th Street

(B) east on Grand Boulevard to High Street, left onto High Street, right onto Highland Way, left onto Grand Street, left onto 18th Avenue, and then left again onto 17th Street

(C) east on Grand Boulevard to Highland Boulevard, west on Highland Boulevard to Highland Way, east on Highland Way, and south on 17th Street to the emergency room

(D) east on Grand Boulevard to Grand Street, left onto Grand Street, then a left turn onto 18th Avenue, and south on 17th Street

50. As you leave the hospital, your radio crackles with information about a demonstration in front of the 18th Avenue entrance of the fire station. A noisy group of citizens is protesting poor fire protection in the North End of town. You must report to the scene of the demonstration to be certain it does not get out of hand. The quickest legal route is

(A) south on 17th Street and make a left onto Highland Boulevard, then north on West Street to Highland Way, then right onto Highland Way to 18th Street, then north on 18th Street to Boulevard, east on Boulevard to Grand Street, and right onto 18th Avenue

(B) south on 17th Street to Grand Boulevard, left onto Grand Boulevard to Grand Street, north on Grand Street to 18th Avenue, and then left onto 18th Avenue

(C) exit the hospital and go left on 17th Street to Highland Way, follow Highland Way east to Grand Street, then turn north onto Grand Street for one block, and left onto 18th Avenue

(D) south on 17th Street to Highland Boulevard, go west on Highland Boulevard to 18th Street, then north on 18th Street to Boulevard, right on Boulevard to Grand Street, south on Grand Street 18th Avenue, and west onto 18th Avenue

Use the map below to answer questions 51 and 52. The flow of traffic is indicated by the arrows. If there is only one arrow shown, then traffic flows only in the direction indicated by the arrow. If there are two arrows shown, then the traffic flows in both directions. You must follow the traffic flow.

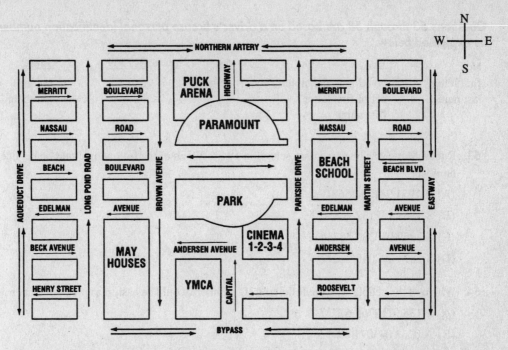

51. You have been asked to give a highway-safety talk to the students at Beach School. Entering town on Capital Highway, the best way for you to get to the school is to

(A) turn west on Andersen Avenue and go to Long Pond Road, then turn right onto Long Pond Road to Beach Boulevard, and turn right to go through the park to the Beach School

(B) go east on Roosevelt to Parkside Drive, then turn left onto Parkside Drive and continue to Beach School

(C) turn left onto Andersen Avenue, then turn left to go south on Brown Avenue, then right for one block on Bypass, right again onto Long Pond Road to Beach Boulevard, and right onto Beach Boulevard for the ride through the park to Beach School

(D) turn west on Andersen Avenue to Brown Avenue, south on Brown Avenue to Bypass, east on Bypass to Eastway, north on Eastway to Beach Boulevard, and left onto Beach Boulevard to Beach School

52. You are helping to direct traffic at the hockey game at Puck Arena when word comes over your radio of a patron with a gun at the movie house. You must get to Cinema 1-2-3-4 as quickly as possible without endangering lives by traveling against traffic. Your best route is to

(A) go east on Merritt Boulevard to Martin Street, south on Martin Street to Edelman, and turn right onto Edelman Avenue to the movie house

(B) go south on Brown Avenue to Andersen Avenue, then turn left onto Andersen Avenue to Cinema 1-2-3-4

(C) take Capital Highway through the park to Cinema 1-2-3-4

(D) take Brown Avenue south to the Bypass, turn left onto Bypass for one block, and left onto Capital to the movie house

Questions 53 through 58 are based on a driver's license personal identification numbers as explained below.

G	14	69	042969	74862
first letter last name	position in the alphabet of first letter first name	height	date of birth	random numbers

53. Robert Stone was in elementary school in 1943. Which of the following could be his license number?

(A) R 1971 981334 56818

(B) S 1868 122132 90756

(C) S 2059 030336 58734

(D) S 1874 092043 71212

54. Which of the people with the following ID numbers would be easiest to pick out in a crowd?

(A) T 1386 110765 67727

(B) A 0263 043071 09791

(C) Z 2469 090941 12345

(D) F 2058 101828 62262

55. Which of the following could NOT be a real ID number?

(A) C 0648 020955 31652

(B) E 1160 120929 68517

(C) H 0366 023049 68712

(D) O 1568 070915 63480

56. Which of the following is most likely to have special restrictions on his or her driver's license?

(A) I 1040 103050 77134

(B) K 1460 061972 84356

(C) D 0863 010377 95604

(D) M 1370 082246 74569

57. Which of the following is least likely to be a driver's license ID number?

(A) A 2172 052411 54367

(B) P 1568 041943 84685

(C) K 1048 092888 65823

(D) T 2366 123179 65125

58. Which one of the following is Donato Panetta's driver's license number?

(A) D 1690 032456 88610

(B) P 0369 062763 54769

(C) P 0426 082695 44126

(D) P 0459 102030 65241

Questions 59 through 64 are based on roadside mile markers as explained below.

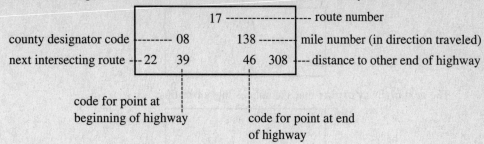

```
                                    17 ------------------------ route number
county designator code --------- 08           138 -------- mile number (in direction traveled)
next intersecting route --- 22  39            46  308 ---- distance to other end of highway


            code for point at
            beginning of highway        code for point at end
                                        of highway
```

59. A driver traveling east on Route 13 passes a marker that looks like this:

```
                    13
              11          25
          44  02          61  144
```

He makes a right turn onto Route 44 and proceeds to drive six more miles. The next marker he passes could look like

(A)
```
                13
          11          28
      44  02          61  141
```

(B)
```
                44
          11          16
      13  12          76  210
```

(C)
```
                44
          11          112
      06  63          08  92
```

(D)
```
                44
          11          86
      44  10          19  103
```

60. A highway traveler passes a road marker that looks like this:

		101		
	09		26	
66	56		33	306

The next highway marker that she notices looks like this:

		101		
	19		32	
66	56		33	300

This marker indicates that

(A) the traveler has turned onto another highway

(B) the route number has changed

(C) the traveler has gone ten miles since the last marker she noticed

(D) the traveler has crossed a county line

61. A trooper patrolling an assigned sector passes a route marker that looks like:

		112		
	04		172	
18	21		36	260

Thirty minutes later, the marker the trooper passes looks like this:

		112		
	04		172	
48	36		21	160

Indications are that the trooper

(A) has made a U-turn

(B) has exceeded the speed limit in the line of duty

(C) is now on a cloverleaf

(D) has changed highways

62. A motorist passes a roadside marker that looks like this:

		76		
	24		19	
89	110		41	92

As the motorist continues his trip, he makes a number of turns. Which of the following roadside markers might this motorist now pass?

(A)

		76		
	32		22	
08	25		41	96

(B)

		113		
	24		53	
66	81		05	123

(C)

		08		
	32		56	
38	41		110	379

(D)

		89		
	24		88	
89	05		94	100

63. A state highway officer passes a marker that looks like this:

		46		
	12		33	
80	54		101	260

One hour later, the same officer passes a marker that looks like this:

		46		
	15		83	
36	54		101	210

We can be certain that the officer

(A) traveled at least 60 miles

(B) crossed at least three county lines

(C) made a number of U-turns

(D) crossed more than one intersection

64. A highway patrol car passed a marker that looked like this:

```
                29
         03           74
   41    84           09    122
```

Some time later this same car passed a marker that looked like this:

```
                29
         15           42
   88    09           84    154
```

This car definitely did NOT

(A) cross a county line

(B) travel at least 32 miles

(C) make a single right turn

(D) make a U-turn

Questions 65 through 70 are based on vehicle identification numbers as explained below.

year	engine size	plant made	style	day assembled	shift	individual identifying #s
A-1988	A-3.7l	1-Dearborn, MI	A-2dr sedan	1-Mon	L-1st	
B-1989	B-3.15l	2-Gary, IN	B-4dr sedan	2-Tues	M-2nd	
C-1990	C-3.9l	3-Detroit #1	C-3dr hatchback	3-Wed	N-3rd	
D-1991	D-3.9l diesel	4-Detroit #2	D-station wagon	4-Thurs		
E-1992	E-3.39l	5-Toledo, OH	E-convertible	5-Fri		
F-1993	F-3.45l	6-Flint, MI	F-5dr van	6-Sat		
G-1994		7-Ontario				
H-prototype						

- Pacers and Canters come in 2dr or 4dr sedans.
- Vans are made only at the Ontario, Gary, and Detroit #1 plants.
- Diesel engines are assembled only in the Detroit plants.
- Convertibles do not have diesel engines.
- Vans are made only with 3.7l and 3.9l engines.
- Vans use gasoline or diesel fuel.
- Only sedans are assembled on the 3rd shift.
- There is no third shift on Saturday.
- Ontario does not manufacture 3.45l engines.
- Station wagons are not assembled on Saturday.
- No convertibles were made in 1988 and 1989.
- Prototypes are all made with diesel engines.
- Prototypes do not follow the above guidelines.

65. The vehicle with ID#DC5C4MN2X438 is a

   (A) 1991 sedan with a 3.9*l* engine assembled in Toledo during the third shift on a Thursday

   (B) 1991 Pacer hatchback with a 3.9*l* engine assembled in Detroit during the second shift on a Friday

   (C) 1991 hatchback with a 3.9*l* engine assembled in Toledo during the second shift on a Thursday

   (D) 1991 hatchback prototype with a 3.9*l* diesel engine assembled in Toledo during the second shift on a Thursday

66. A 1994 station wagon with a 3.45*l* engine could be identified by which one of the following serial numbers?

   (A) GF6D3L1H5T07

   (B) GF1D6MP9684B

   (C) HF7D21U674RS

   (D) GF4D2N2M9064

67. The vehicle with ID#BF1A63F732RZ is a

   (A) 1989 2dr convertible with a 3.45*l* engine made in Dearborn on a Friday third shift

   (B) 1989 2dr Canter with a 3.45*l* engine made in Dearborn on a Friday third shift

   (C) 1990 2dr Pacer with a 3.39*l* engine made in Dearborn on a Saturday third shift

   (D) prototype 1989 Pacer with a 3.9*l* diesel engine made in Dearborn on a Friday second shift

68. Which of the following serial numbers identifies a prototype 1994 convertible?

   (A) GH3F2L9Y14R7

   (B) HE4F6N2P8VB5

   (C) HD6E4MI17X22

   (D) HD3E1M60G916

69. The vehicle identified by serial number EC4B5NKJ0273 could be

   (A) a diesel-powered Pacer

   (B) a prototype Canter

   (C) a 2dr convertible

   (D) a 4dr Pacer

70. Which of the following serial numbers identifies a van?

   (A) FA7E2L5P7UY6

   (B) CD2E1M7RE123

   (C) DC5E4N0O748B

   (D) GA2E6N5HJ864

Questions 71 through 73 are based on the following rules for use of the community room at Barracks B.

Now that our new training facility has been completed and we are no longer pressed for space, Barracks B is offering use of the old common room for use by the people of the region we serve. This use, of course, will be governed by certain rules and conditions.

Availability: The common room is reserved for the exclusive personal use of troopers assigned to Barracks B on Monday and Wednesday between 6:00 P.M. and 8:00 P.M., on Saturday between 10:00 A.M. and 3:30 P.M. unless specifically relinquished by the troopers in residence, and on Sunday from 4:00 P.M. on. The common room is available for use by recognized community groups on Monday and Tuesday from 9:00 A.M. to 2:00 P.M., on Friday from 10:00 A.M. to 11:30 A.M. and from 1:00 P.M. to 4:00 P.M. Weekend use of the common room by members of the community is limited to Saturday from 6:00 P.M. to 11:00 P.M. and Sunday from 10:00 A.M. to 2:00 P.M. At all other times the common room is to be left vacant or occupied by scheduled activities within the barracks.

Procedure for use of the facility by members of Barracks B: A trooper who wishes to reserve the common room for a private purpose may do so by applying to the superintendent in writing at least 20 days before the date requested. The application must describe the nature of the activity, the number of people expected, and any special facilities that will be needed (chairs, food service, extra lighting, booths, etc.). A $25 charge for cleanup will be deducted from the trooper's paycheck on the next payday following the event. If a group of troopers wishes to reserve the common room for a special group event, this $25 charge must be paid in advance of the event from money contributed by members to the group.

Procedure for application by members of the public: The recognized leader of a community group must submit a signed application in writing at least 20 days before the date requested. The application must state the general nature of the function, the number of persons expected to attend, and the special facilities required. A community group must post a refundable bond in the sum of $100 at the time permission for use is granted. Routine cost of cleanup is $25 payable by money order on the date of the event. Should cleanup costs exceed this sum, the excess will be deducted before the bond money is returned. An individual citizen may reserve the common room for a personal function subject to the same rules except that a cancellation fee of $50 will apply as well.

Priority: Within the day and time restrictions outlined above, the application with the earliest date of filing will receive priority. In case of applications for the same date that are filed on the same date, priority is as follows: (1) members of Barracks B; (2) youth groups; (3) senior citizen groups; (4) civic groups; (5) social groups.

Other rules:

1. Under no circumstances may the common room be used between the hours of 11:00 P.M. and 8:00 A.M.

2. The maximum legal occupancy of the common room is 138 people.

3. No group or individual may reserve the common room for use on a regular basis, nor may any such group or individual reserve the common room for more than two functions in any month.

4. Any group disrupting the regular activities of the barracks will be denied future use of the facilities.

71. Who might be using the common room on Thursday afternoon at 4:00?

 (A) A quilting group consisting of 18 elderly women

 (B) A Girl Scout troop having its regular weekly meeting

 (C) An off-duty trooper in a penny-ante poker game

 (D) A local physician teaching an advanced CPR class to ten troopers

72. Which request for use of the common room is most likely to be granted?

 (A) On March 15 Officer Carroll requests use of the common room on Sunday, April 1, from 11:00 A.M. to 2:00 P.M. for a Christening Party with 80 guests.

 (B) On March 3 the Boy Scouts request use of the common room on Saturday, March 31, from 6:00 P.M. to 10:00 P.M. and on Sunday, April 1, from 10:00 A.M. to 2:00 P.M. for a bazaar with an estimated total attendance of 300 people coming and going over the two-day span of time.

 (C) On March 3 a senior citizen group requests use of the common room on Sunday, April 1, from 10:00 am to 2:00 P.M. for a tax clinic to be attended by about 40 people in all.

 (D) On March 3 the Eton Squares, a local dance club, requests use of the common room for a square dance on Saturday, March 31, from 6:00 P.M. to 11:00 P.M. with expected attendance of about 75 people.

73. Officer Barone will be married on June 14. His fellow officers decide to throw a bachelor party in Barone's honor in the common room on Sunday, June 9. On May 1, a group of Barone's trooper friends, led by Officer Yamato, approach the superintendent to apply for use of the common room Sunday, June 9, from 7:00 P.M. to 11:00 P.M.. Their application states that approximately 15 troopers and 15 friends from the community will attend and that the group will supply food, drink, and music, but will need tables, chairs, and a microphone. The superintendent grants this request and tells Officer Yamato that

 (A) he will have $25 deducted from the first paycheck following June 14

 (B) he must post $100 bond and give the superintendent $25 within the next few weeks

 (C) he should collect a total of $25 from the participating troopers and pay this sum over to the superintendent before June 9

 (D) there will be no charge if the troopers clean up after themselves, but if the event is canceled there will be a $50 fee

Questions 74 through 76 are based on the following rules for the use of a college gym.

Since budgetary constraints have halted construction of the gym and pool at our new state police barracks, the superintendent of the barracks has made special arrangements with Elmtop Community College for our use of college athletic facilities at specified times and subject to certain restrictions.

Locker room: The locker room and showers are available to our troopers at any time that the swimming pool is available for our use. For any other use of the college facilities—gym, weight room, outdoor track—troopers are asked not to overtax college facilities but rather to use shower and changing facilities at the barracks and to travel between campus and barracks in exercise clothing.

Swimming pool: The swimming pool is reserved for our exclusive use from 6:00 AM to 7:30 AM on Monday, Tuesday, and Saturday and from 8:30 P.M. to 10:00 P.M. on Friday. In addition, upon presentation of trooper identification, troopers may be admitted at no charge to the general public swim session from 7:30 A.M. to 9:00 A.M. on Tuesday and Thursday, from 8:00 P.M. to 9:30 P.M. on Monday and Wednesday, and from 9:00 A.M. to 11:00 A.M. on Saturdays. Sundays from 4:00 P.M. to 6:00 P.M. there is a "women only" swim period to which women troopers are welcome. Likewise, the "men only" swim period on Sundays from 1:00 P.M. to 3:00 P.M. is open to men troopers.

Weight room: The weight room is "ours" between the hours of 5:30 A.M. and 7:30 A.M. every morning except Wednesday and Friday.

Gym: We have use of the gym for individual purposes or for organized group activities (see barracks bulletin board for schedule of organized games) every morning at the same times that we have use of the weight room and on Saturday between 1:00 P.M. and 3:00 P.M.

Track: The track is available for use by the general public at any time that it is not specifically reserved for use by a college group. College use changes each semester; a schedule is posted on the bulletin board in each college locker room. As a general rule, the track is available every day before 9:00 A.M. and after 8:00 P.M. Lighting at the track makes this an attractive exercise option at these uncrowded hours.

74. Women troopers may use the facilities from

    (A) 6:00 A.M. to 9:00 A.M. on Tuesday and from 4:00 P.M. to 6:00 P.M. on Sunday

    (B) 8:30 P.M. to 10:00 P.M. on Friday and from 1:00 P.M. to 6:00 P.M. on Sunday

    (C) 7:30 A.M. to 9:00 A.M. on Tuesday and from 5:30 A.M. to 7:00 A.M. on Thursday

    (D) 6:00 A.M. to 7:30 A.M. on Monday, from 3:00 P.M. to 5:30 P.M. on Saturday, and on Thursday after 8:00 P.M.

75. What athletic activity is occurring at the college on Wednesday evening?

    (A) Troopers' weight lifting

    (B) Women's swim

    (C) Free swim for the general public

    (D) Trooper's volleyball tournament in the gym

76. On Thursday at 6:00 A.M., a trooper could be engaging in any of these activities EXCEPT

    (A) working out with weights

    (B) shooting foul shots

    (C) trying to break the 3-minute mile

    (D) swimming laps

Answer questions 77 through 79 on the basis of the information in the following paragraph.

All automotive accidents, no matter how slight, are to be reported to the Safety Division by the employee involved on Accident Report Form S-23 in duplicate. When the accident is of such a nature that it requires the filling out of the State Motor Vehicle Report Form MV-104, this form is also prepared by the employee in duplicate and sent to the Safety Division for comparison with the Form S-23. The Safety Division forwards both copies of Form MV-104 to the Corporation Counsel, who sends one copy to the State Bureau of Motor Vehicles. When the information on the Form S-23 indicates that the employee may be at fault, an investigation is made by the Safety Division. If this investigation shows that the employee was at fault, the employee's dispatcher is asked to file a complaint on Form D-11. The foreman of mechanics prepares a damage report on Form D-8 and an estimate of the cost of repairs on Form D-9. The dispatcher's complaint, the damage report, the repair estimate, and the employee's previous accident record are sent to the Safety Division where they are studied together with the accident report. The Safety Division then recommends whether or not disciplinary action should be taken against the employee.

77. According to the paragraph, the forwarding of Form MV-104 to the State Bureau of Motor Vehicles is done by the

    (A) Corporation Counsel

    (B) dispatcher

    (C) employee involved in the accident

    (D) Safety Division

78. According to the paragraph, the Safety Division investigates an automotive accident if the

    (A) accident is serious enough to be reported to the State Bureau of Motor Vehicles

    (B) dispatcher files a complaint

    (C) employee appears to have been at fault

    (D) employee's previous accident record is poor

79. Of the forms mentioned in the paragraph, the dispatcher is responsible for preparing the

    (A) accident report form

    (B) complaint form

    (C) damage report

    (D) estimate of cost of repairs

Answer questions 80 through 82 on the basis of the information in the following passage.

Society's historical approach to criminals can be conveniently summarized as a succession of three Rs: revenge, restraint, and reformation. Revenge was the primary response prior to the first revolution in penology in the 18th and 19th centuries. During that revolution, revenge was replaced by an emphasis upon restraint. When the second revolution occurred in the late 19th and 20th centuries, reformation became an important objective. Attention was focused upon the mental and emotional makeup of the offender, and efforts were made to alter these primary sources of difficulty.

We have now entered yet another revolution in which a fourth concept has been added to the list of Rs: reintegration. This has come about because students of corrections feel that a singular focus upon reforming the offender is inadequate. Successful rehabilitation is a two-sided coin that includes reformation on one side and reintegration on the other.

It can be argued that this third revolution is premature. Society itself is still very ambivalent about the offender. It has never really replaced all vestiges of revenge or restraint but has merely supplemented them. Thus, although it is unwilling to kill or lock up all offenders permanently, it is also unwilling to give full support to the search for alternatives.

80. According to the passage, revolutions against accepted treatment of criminals have resulted in all of the following approaches to handling criminals EXCEPT

    (A) revenge
    (B) restraint
    (C) reformation
    (D) reintegration

81. According to the passage, the second revolution directed particular attention to

    (A) preparing the offender for his or her return to society
    (B) making the pain of punishment exceed the pleasure of crime
    (C) exploring the inner feelings of the offender
    (D) restraining the offender from continuing a life of crime

82. The author of the passage suggests that the latest revolution will

    (A) fail and the cycle will begin again with revenge or restraint
    (B) be the last revolution
    (C) not work unless society's correctional goals can be defined
    (D) succumb to political and economic pressures

Answer questions 83 through 85 on the basis of the information in the following paragraph.

The practice of occasionally adulterating marijuana complicates analysis of the effects of marijuana use in noncontrolled settings. Behavioral changes that are attributed to marijuana may actually derive from the adulterants or from the interaction of tetrahydrocannabinols and adulterants. Similarly, in today's society marijuana is often used simultaneously or sequentially with other psychoactive drugs. When drug interactions occur, the simultaneous presence of two or more drugs in the body can exert effects that are more than those that would result from the simple addition of the effects of each drug used separately. Thus, the total behavioral response may be greater than the sum of its parts. For example, if a given dose of marijuana induced two units of perceptual distortion, and a certain dose of LSD given alone induced two units of perceptual distortion, the simultaneous administration of these doses of marijuana and LSD may induce not four but five units of perceptual distortion.

83. According to the paragraph, the concurrent presence of two drugs in the body can

    (A) compound the effects of both drugs
    (B) reduce perceptual distortion
    (C) simulate psychotic symptoms
    (D) be highly toxic

84. On the basis of the paragraph, it is most reasonable to assume that tetrahydrocannabinols are

    (A) habit-forming substances
    (B) components of marijuana
    (C) similar to quinine or milk-sugar
    (D) used as adulterants

85. Based on the paragraph, it is most reasonable to state that marijuana is

    (A) most affected by adulterants when used as a psychoactive drug

    (B) erroneously considered to be less harmful than other drugs

    (C) frequently used in conjunction with other mind-affecting drugs

    (D) occasionally used as an adjunct to LSD in order to reduce bad reactions

For questions 85 through 88, arrange the five sentences into a logical sequence to create your own coherent story.

86. 1. A man crawled across the sand.
    2. A man saw a pool of water in the distance.
    3. A man ran out of gas crossing the desert.
    4. A helicopter pilot spotted a body sprawled in the sand.
    5. A family sent out an alarm for a missing person.

    (A) 3-4-1-2-5

    (B) 5-3-2-1-4

    (C) 3-2-1-5-4

    (D) 4-5-3-2-1

87. 1. Acreage is destroyed.
    2. An airplane sprays the fields.
    3. A crop is planted.
    4. A person is assigned a task.
    5. Seedlings sprout.

    (A) 4-5-2-1-3

    (B) 3-4-5-1-2

    (C) 2-4-3-5-1

    (D) 3-5-4-2-1

88. 1. A person came to investigate.
    2. Witnesses were questioned.
    3. A large crate was missing.
    4. A dog barked.
    5. A green van was sought.

    (A) 5-1-3-2-4

    (B) 4-1-3-2-5

    (C) 4-3-2-5-1

    (D) 3-1-2-5-4

For questions 89 through 96, complete the sentence.

89. The body that was found in the woods smelled so bad that the trooper knew_____.

    (A) it must have been lying there for many days.

    (B) it must have laid there many days.

    (C) it must of lain there for many days.

    (D) it must have layed there for many days.

90. Our training supervisor has more patience_____.

    (A) than any officer on the force.

    (B) then any other training officer in the whole entire place.

    (C) than any training supervisor I ever had on any job.

    (D) than any other officer here.

91. Perhaps we could keep details of our getting lost as a secret_____.

    (A) among you and me.

    (B) between you and I.

    (C) between you and me.

    (D) among the two of us.

92. By May 1, each trooper is expected to hand in_____.

    (A) a schedule of when they want to take vacation.

    (B) his preferred vacation schedule.

    (C) their vacation plans.

    (D) a detailed plan of when they would like to have a vacation.

93. An assignment sometimes handed out as a reward is that of delivering bus-safety lectures to _____ groups.

    (A) childrens

    (B) children's

    (C) childrens'

    (D) childrens's

94. The officer was willing to _____ all of the new working conditions _____ the shift rotation schedule.

    (A) except . . . accept

    (B) accept . . . accept

    (C) accept . . . except

    (D) except . . . except

95. It is _____ bad that _____ of the patrol cars will be out of service when they are needed so badly to control holiday weekend traffic.

(A) too . . . to

(B) to . . . two

(C) too . . . too

(D) too . . . two

96. _____ should listen to the weather forecast so that _____ may anticipate a heavy snowstorm.

(A) People . . . one

(B) One . . . they

(C) One . . . he

(D) We . . . one

For questions 97 through 100, choose the best statement of the underlined portion.

97. The suspect fleeing the scene of the crime with a bloody knife in his hand was seized and arrested. While the suspect was in custody, his clothing was searched and one-half ounce of heroin was found in his pockets. <u>The suspect complained that the police did not have a search warrant though the Court will say that a person in custody has no right to expect a privileged privacy of his things.</u>

(A) The suspect complained that the police did not have a search warrant, but the Court ruled that a person in custody has a diminished expectation of privacy.

(B) The suspect complained that he had no right of privacy in custody because the police did not have a Court search warrant.

(C) The Court said that a suspect who complains about his privacy has no right to expect a search warrant in custody.

(D) Correct as written.

98. Frank questioned the witness about the car that she had seen speeding from the scene. The witness said that the car looked like one of those things you see in war pictures, but it was red. <u>Frank says to the sergeant that the suspect was probably driving a red Jeep.</u>

(A) The suspect was probably escaping in a red Jeep is what the sergeant hears from Frank.

(B) The sergeant is being told by Frank that the witness is thinking that she probably saw a red Jeep driving away.

(C) Frank then told the sergeant that a red Jeep was observed leaving the scene.

(D) Correct as written.

99. Officers Reiner and Orsini were investigating a report of a man with a gun at the mile 3580 scenic overlook. They approached a man who seemed to fit the description they were given and asked for identification. <u>Officer Orsini then frisked the man and felt an object in the man's pocket that might have been suspicious.</u>

   (A) Officer Orsini frisks the man and feels an object that makes him very suspicious.

   (B) When Officer Orsini frisked the man, he felt an object that raised his suspicions.

   (C) Then Officer Orsini took to frisking the man and feeling a suspicious feeling object.

   (D) Correct as written.

100. The suspect crashed through a roadblock and was placed under arrest for reckless driving. In the police car, she quickly swallowed contents of a plastic pouch that she pulled from her pocket. <u>The troopers then drove her directly to a hospital to have her stomach pumped so that they could learn what she had swallowed.</u>

   (A) So the troopers had to take her to the hospital and pump out her stomach so that they could get back for her that what she swallowed.

   (B) The troopers took her to a hospital and arrested her when they pumped out of her stomach what she swallowed.

   (C) So then the troopers have to take her to the hospital and have her stomach pumped so they can arrest her.

   (D) Correct as written.

ANSWER KEY

1. B	21. C	41. D	61. A	81. C
2. C	22. D	42. D	62. B	82. C
3. B	23. A	43. B	63. D	83. A
4. A	24. C	44. C	64. C	84. B
5. D	25. B	45. A	65. C	85. C
6. D	26. B	46. B	66. A	86. C
7. A	27. D	47. D	67. B	87. D
8. B	28. C	48. A	68. D	88. B
9. C	29. A	49. D	69. D	89. A
10. B	30. C	50. B	70. A	90. D
11. D	31. B	51. C	71. D	91. C
12. A	32. D	52. D	72. B	92. B
13. B	33. A	53. B	73. C	93. B
14. D	34. D	54. A	74. A	94. C
15. C	35. D	55. C	75. C	95. D
16. D	36. C	56. A	76. D	96. C
17. A	37. B	57. C	77. A	97. A
18. C	38. C	58. D	78. C	98. C
19. C	39. A	59. C	79. B	99. B
20. B	40. C	60. D	80. A	100. D

EXPLANATORY ANSWERS

1. **(B)** If you are driving east and make a U-turn, you will be heading west. A left turn when driving west heads you south.

2. **(C)** If you are driving south and make a right turn, you will be heading west. The convoy going in the other direction is going east.

3. **(B)** If you are traveling west, a car approaching from your right is traveling south.

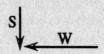

4. **(A)** The car is traveling north. With the first left turn, it is traveling west; with the second left, south; with the third left, east. If the car is headed east, then its right side faces to the south, and the car that hits it is traveling north.

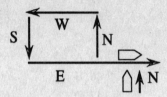

5. **(D)** If you are traveling south, west is on your right.

6. **(D)** If you are traveling in a southwesterly direction, the merge on your left is a merge from the east and is going west.

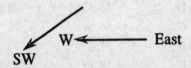

7. **(A)** If you are traveling west on Grand Street and turn left, you will be going south on North Street. Your right turn will have you going west on River Road. The next right will direct you north on Church Street. The next left will have you once more proceeding west on Grand Street.

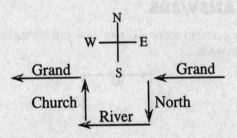

8. **(B)** The proper subjunctive form (the form used for a wish or for a condition contrary to fact) is *if he had,* not *if he would have.* Therefore, (A) is incorrect. The participle *been* requires an auxiliary verb. *Of* is not an auxiliary verb; *had* is. Both (C) and (D) should read "would not *have* been."

9. **(C)** *Which* applies only to things, so (A) is incorrect. (B) contains a double negative. (D) is incorrect because the subject of *don't know how to be happy* should be *who.*

10. **(B)** In (D), the sequence is reversed. (A) and (C) leave the sequence of action unclear.

11. **(D)** *Talk* and *speak* are verbs so must be modified by adverbs, not by adjectives. In addition, all three incorrect choices involve pretentious construction or errors of tense.

12. **(A)** Choice (B) involves a double negative. In (C), *ain't* is an unacceptable word. (D) requires an auxiliary verb; it could also be stated using a simple past tense, as in, "he did nothing wrong."

13. **(B)** Simple is best. Both (A) and (C) are awkward, unwieldy constructions. (D) introduces disagreement of noun and pronoun. "Team" is a singular noun even though it includes a number of individuals; the correct pronoun is "it."

14. **(D)** All other choices are awkward.

15. **(C)** The incorrect answers all involve problems with the auxiliary verb.

16. **(D)** Who entered the room? Whose attention was attracted? Only choice **(D)** makes it clear.

17. **(A)** The opening of the door and the entry of the captain and officer happen at the same time. All other choices mix present and past tenses.

18. **(C)** $42 - 35 = 7$; he is exceeding the speed limit by 7 mph; $7 \div 35 = .20$; 7 is 20% of 35.

19. **(C)** $270 \times 4 = 1080$

20. **(B)** 7 cars + 2 vans + 3 trucks + 1 bus = 13 vehicles involved in the accident; 1 patrol car + 3 ambulances + 2 fire engines + 5 tow trucks + 8 patrol cars = 19 rescue vehicles; $13 + 19 = 32$ vehicles at the scene. 3 tow trucks remove 3 damaged vehicles = 6 vehicles leave. $32 - 6 = 26$ vehicles remain.

21. **(C)** 3 out of service + 4 with other duties = 7 not patrolling. $20 - 7 = 13$ available to patrol. $235 \div 13 = 18$ miles patrolled by each.

22. **(D)** $5,067 - 4,682 = 385$ miles driven. $385 \div 28 = 13.75$ gal.

23. **(A)** $2.35 + $1.00 = $3.35 for one long distance plus two in-state calls. $5.60 - $3.35 = $2.25 $\div$ .75 = three more in-state calls. $1 + 2 + 3 = 6 + 2$ free calls = 8 calls in all.

24. **(C)** 42 mph $\times$ 1.5 hrs. = 63 miles to the north; 38 mph $\times$ 1.5 hrs. = 57 miles to the south; $63 + 57 = 120$ miles apart.

25. **(B)** 9:15 A.M. to noon = $12:00 - 9:15 = 11:60 - 9:15 = 2$ hrs. 45 min. Noon to 2:45 P.M. = 2 hrs. 45 min; 2 hrs. 45 min. + 2 hrs. 45 min. = 4 hrs. 90 min. = 5 hrs. 30 min.

26. **(B)** 24 – 5 to the accident – 3 to direct traffic – 2 to the hospital = 14 + 1 captain = 15 officers on hand.

27. **(D)** $8,782 + 3,000 = 11,782$ by which reading car must be serviced. $11,782 - 10,461 = 1,321$ miles Lindner may drive. $1,321 \div 140 = 9.44$ average working days to reach servicing mileage. Car may drive no more than 3,000 miles between servicing, so must be brought in within 9 days.

28. **(C)** 240 miles $\div$ 12 gal. = 20 mpg original mileage. 80% of 12 gal. = $12 \times .80 = 9.6$ gal. 240 miles $\div$ 9.6 = 25 mpg; 12 gal. $\times$ 25 mpg = 300 miles per 12 gal.

29. **(A)** Calculate percentage over the speed limit by subtracting the speed limit from the speed driven and dividing the difference by the speed limit. Thus, 45 mph in a 40 mph zone is: $45 - 40 = 5$; $5 \div 40 = 12.5\%$. Similarly, 48 mph is 20% over the 40 mph limit, 53 mph is 33.5% over, and both 58 mph and 60 mph are more than 44% over the 40 mph limit. 64 mph is 16.36% over the 55 mph limit (and there were two such tickets), 71.5 mph is 30% over the 55 mph limit, and 85 mph is 54.5% over the 55 mph limit. Totaling up all the speeders and their fines:

    1 car exceeding by 12.5% = $25

    2 cars exceeding by 16.36% = $70 ($35 each)

    1 car exceeding by 20% = $50

    1 car exceeding by 30% = $100

    1 car exceeding by 33.5% = $100

    3 cars more than 44% over = $600 ($200 each)

    Total fines = $945

30. **(C)** N.A. Hales is supervised by F.R. Tuck.

31. **(B)** The oldest employee, R.L. Hill, was born 9/30/30. R.L. Hill is security.

32. **(D)** The oldest trooper, T.J. Hale, was born 6/12/60.

33. **(A)** The person longest employed is the mechanic, P.C. Hill, who was hired 9/2/72.

34. **(D)** F.T. Hals's social security number is 630-98-1234.

35. **(D)** The mechanic's social security number is 987-40-3939.

36. **(C)** July 21 is a Wednesday, and Gino Abate is in group 3. On Wednesday group 3 is in the west quadrant.

37. **(B)** During July group 3 will work in only the north and west quadrants. Jane Shulz is supervisor of group 3.

38. **(C)** Akeel Morris is in group 1 and group 1 reports for training on Monday. July 19 is a Monday.

39. **(A)** July 15 is a Thursday. Group 1 works in the south quadrant on Thursday. The supervisor of group 1 is Jose Primo.

40. **(C)** July 25 is a Sunday. Since Gregor Ozmanian is the training supervisor and no groups are scheduled for training on Sunday, Ozmanian will have the day off.

41. **(D)** July 11 is a Sunday. This particular work schedule does not specify what group is working in the west quadrant on Sunday in July.

42. **(D)** The only restrictive information given with regard to Sgt. Leary is that Leary arrested only male suspects. G. Evans beats his wife, so he is definitely male and might have been arrested by Leary. L. King is a juvenile, gender unspecified. J. Harris is roommate of E. Brown, who is female, but J. Harris may well be a man. Sgt. Leary could have arrested any of these; we can't tell.

43. **(B)** Eliminate: Sgt. Paik arrested no resident of the district of arrest; M. Allen lives in Dale where Paik worked. D. Tramp was arrested for murder. E. Brown was arrested in her home vicinity, which is Arch. There is no reason why Sgt. Paik might not have arrested B. Davis.

44. **(C)** Eliminate: Sgt. Rossi did not arrest any residents of Arch; as roommate of E. Brown who lives in Arch, J. Harris lives in Arch. A. Wilson was carrying a pillowcase containing a fur jacket and silver candlesticks when arrested, most likely for burglary rather than arson. S. Grant was arrested by Sgt. Tomas. There is no reason why Sgt. Rossi might not have arrested L. King on suspicion of arson.

45. **(A)** D. Tramp was arrested for murder. The only arrest for murder on this date was made by Sgt. Blau.

46. **(B)** Sgt. Leary made only one arrest on this date, and the arrest was for arson. It is stated that Sgt. Leary arrested M. Allen, so the charge against Allen must have been arson.

47. **(D)** Mentally hop into the cars and follow the narrative.

48. **(A)** Put yourself into Officer Wood's place and follow the story carefully.

49. **(D)** Choice (A) cannot be correct because 17th Street is one-way southbound. (B) is perfectly legal but includes some extra corner-turns, which make it not the "best" route. (C) is impossible from the outset because Grand Boulevard never intersects Highland Boulevard. Do not waste time looking at the rest of a proposed route once you have found the point at which it become impossible.

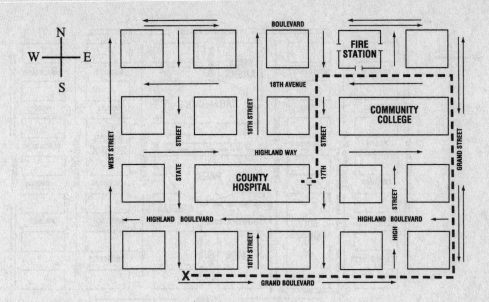

50. **(B)** Choice (A) is entirely legal, but it is unnecessarily long and roundabout. (C) starts out going north on a one-way southbound street. (D) is physically impossible because the hospital intervenes, making it impossible to go from Highland Boulevard to Boulevard on 18th Street.

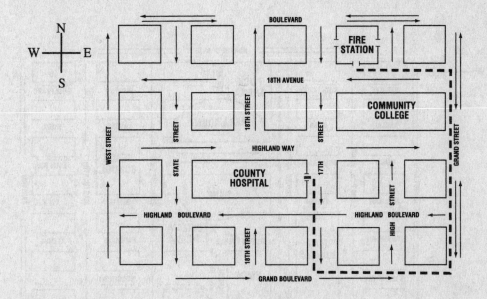

51. **(C)** Choice (A) is impossible because Andersen Avenue does not go through to Long Pond Road. Choice (B) involves going the wrong way on one-way Roosevelt. (D) is not illegal, but is a much longer route than that recommended in **(C)**.

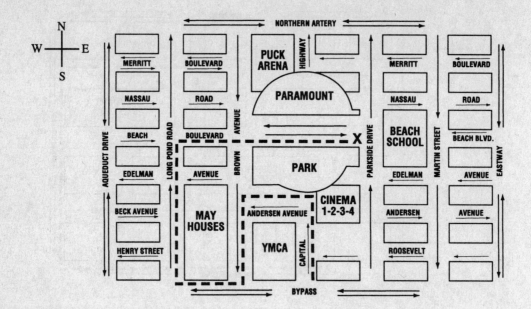

52. **(D)** Choice (A) is incorrect because Merritt Boulevard is a two-way street only on the west side of Puck Arena; from Puck Arena one cannot go east on Merritt Boulevard. Andersen Avenue between Brown Avenue and Cinema 1-2-3-4 is a west-bound street making choice (B) incorrect. As for choice (C), Capital Highway does not go through the park.

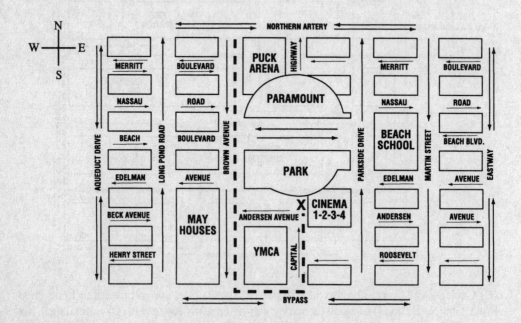

53. **(B)** Choices (A) and (B) both miscode Robert Stone's name. Choice (D) offers 1943 as a birth year; a person born that year could not have been in elementary school.

54. **(A)** Eighty-six inches is 7 ft. 2 in. This tall person should stand out in a crowd.

55. **(C)** No one can have a birthdate of February 30.

56. **(A)** Forty inches is 3 ft. 4 in. A person of this height must have a specially equipped automobile.

57. **(C)** A person born is 1988 is too young to have a driver's license; a person born in 1888 is too old.

58. **(D)** Choice (A) reverses first and last names; the height of 7 ft. 6 in. is unusual but not impossible. In (B), the letter "D" is miscoded. In (C) the year '95 must refer to 1995 because the person is only 2 ft. 2 in. tall; a person born in 1895 could still have a driver's license, but a person born in 1995 is too young.

59. **(C)** The driver has turned onto Route 44, so the top center number must be 44; eliminate choice (A). The driver does not make a U-turn, so the next intersecting route cannot be the Route 13 from which he has just turned; eliminate (B). Route 44 cannot intersect with itself, so (D) cannot be correct.

60. **(D)** The number that designates the county has changed; the traveler has crossed a county line. The number that indicates distance traveled along the highway has increased by six while the number that indicates distance remaining along this highway has decreased by six; the traveler has driven six miles.

61. **(A)** The trooper has made a U-turn. The trooper is still on Route 112, but the order of the locations between which mileage is calculated has been reversed. Distance is now being calculated from locality 36 to locality 21, whereas on the earlier marker it was calculated from locality 21 to locality 36.

62. **(B)** If he had made a number of turns and returned to Route 76, the beginning and end points of Route 76 would still be the same, so eliminate (A). In (C) the route on which the motorist is traveling runs between the same two cities as the original route, but the distance between them is vastly greater; this cannot be. A highway cannot intersect itself as in (D).

63. **(D)** We can be certain only that the officer traveled 50 miles, so eliminate (A). We know for certain only that the officer crossed at least one county line; county lines do not run in order. The officer may have made any number of U-turns, but we have no way of knowing. The officer is traveling in the same direction on the same highway, but the next intersection has a different number, so the officer must at least have crossed Route 80.

64. **(C)** Answer this question by simple elimination. The car definitely did cross a county line, travel at least 32 miles, and make a U-turn. One right turn could not head the car in the opposite direction on the same highway.

65. **(C)** Just follow along letter for letter and number for number to find the only possible answer meeting all requirements.

66. **(A)** Neither (B) nor (D) is possible because station wagons are not assembled on Saturdays or on third shifts. (C) is impossible because prototypes must have diesel engines.

67. **(B)** The first letter, B, identifies a 1989 model; the fourth letter, A, identifies this 1989 car as a 2dr sedan, either a Pacer or a Canter.

68. **(D)** The year of a prototype is irrelevant, so eliminate (A). All prototypes have diesel engines, so eliminate (B). Diesels are made only in Detroit, so eliminate (C).

69. **(D)** This car is a 4dr sedan, not a prototype, with a 3.9l gasoline engine.

70. **(A)** Eliminate (B) because diesel engines are not made in Gary. Eliminate (C) because vans are not made in Toledo. Eliminate (D) because vans are not assembled on Saturday or on third shifts.

71. **(D)** The Thursday slot at 4:00 P.M. is a time for the common room to be left vacant or to be used by scheduled trooper activities. A CPR class clearly is a scheduled use. Choice (B) is

additionally wrong because use of the common room for regular weekly meetings is not permitted.

72. **(B)** If Officer Carroll had asked at least 20 days in advance, he would have gotten the common room for his christening, but he waited too long. In the order of priorities, youth groups take precedence over senior citizens and social groups. Since the Boy Scouts' application covered both dates requested at the same time by other legitimate groups, the Boy Scouts preempted both the seniors' tax clinic and the square dance.

73. **(C)** A single trooper requesting the use of the common room may have the cleanup fee deducted from a paycheck, but a group should take up a collection and pay in advance of the event. The bond is required only of outside groups; and no one is exempt from the cleanup fee.

74. **(A)** Women troopers may use the locker room any time they may use the pool. Trooper swim is from 6:00 A.M. to 7:30 A.M. on Tuesday, running into free general swim from 7:30 A.M. to 9:00 A.M. Women troopers may also swim at the "women only" session from 4:00 P.M. to 6:00 P.M. on Sunday. 1:00 P.M. to 3:00 P.M. on Sunday is "men only." The general swim on Thursday does not begin until 7:30 A.M. There is no swim for which troopers are eligible after 8:00 P.M. on Thursday.

75. **(C)** Wednesday from 8:00 P.M. to 9:30 P.M. is free swim for the general public. Troopers never have access to weight room or gym in the evening.

76. **(D)** The pool is not open to troopers at 6:00 A.M. on Thursday. The gym, weight room, and track are all available.

77. **(A)** The employee sends two copies of Form MV-104 to the Safety Division which sends both copies to the Corporation Counsel. The Corporation Counsel, in turn, sends one copy to the State Bureau of Motor Vehicles.

78. **(C)** The Safety Division investigates only when the employee appears to have been at fault.

79. **(B)** The dispatcher files the complaint form, Form D-11. The accident report form is filed by the employee, and both damage report and estimate of cost of repairs are filed by the foreman of mechanics.

80. **(A)** Revenge was the approach prior to the first revolution.

81. **(C)** The second revolution focused attention upon the mental and emotional makeup of the offender, that is, the offender's inner feelings.

82. **(C)** If society is still ambivalent about the offender, society's correctional goals are not fully defined. Hence, the third revolution may be premature.

83. **(A)** "The simultaneous presence of two or more drugs in the body can exert effects that are more than would result from the simple addition of the effect of each drug used separately."

84. **(B)** Adulterants interact with tetrahydrocannabinols, so tetrahydrocannabinols must be components of marijuana.

85. **(C)** The whole point of the passage is to discuss the problems created by the practice of using marijuana along with other mind-affecting drugs.

86. **(C)** 3-2-1-5-4

The story must begin with the man's running out of gas as he drove across the desert. Getting out of his car, he was deluded by a mirage; he though he saw water in the distance. He began walking toward the illusory water, eventually becoming so dehydrated that he fell to his knees and crawled. When his family finally missed him, they sent out an alarm and a highway patrol search helicopter was dispatched. By the time the helicopter pilot spotted him, it was too late.

87. **(D)** 3-5-4-2-1

   A crop of a substance that is grown to produce illegal drugs (probably marijuana) is planted. Seedlings sprout. At this point someone recognizes the growing crop and alerts the state police. The captain assigns a pilot the task of eliminating this crop. The pilot flies over the fields spraying them with a substance that is toxic to the plants, thereby destroying the acreage.

88. **(B)** 4-1-3-2-5

   A dog, presumably a watch dog, barked. The dog's barking alerted a man, probably a watchman, to investigate. The watchman discovered that a large crate was missing. Clearly the dog's barking was in response to a burglary. Upon questioning, a witness mentioned seeing a green van at the site, so a green van was sought.

89. **(A)** *Laid* is a form of the verb *to lay*, but what we need here is a form of the verb *to lie*. The requisite auxiliary verb is *have*, not *of*. *Layed* is an altogether incorrect form.

90. **(D)** Since the training supervisor is already on the force, the comparison must be completed by making it clear that the supervisor has more patience that *any other*. Choice (B) answers this problem but is wordy and redundant.

91. **(C)** Since we are only two, the correct term is *between* rather than *among*. Between is a preposition that must be followed by the objective *me*.

92. **(B)** Each trooper is one person; the pronoun must be singular.

93. **(B)** *Children* is a plural noun that forms the possessive by adding "apostrophe *s*."

94. **(C)** *Accept* means "agree to." *Except* means "but."

95. **(D)** *Too* means "extremely." *Two* stands for the number 2. *To* refers to "going toward," which does not apply in this sentence.

96. **(C)** In order to maintain parallelism within the sentence, both blanks must be filled with the same number. In choices (A) and (D), the first word is plural and the second is singular. In (B), the first word is singular and the second is plural. In **(C)**, both *one* and *he* are singular.

97. **(A)** Read carefully. None of the other choices really makes sense.

98. **(C)** The first two sentences of the paragraph are written in the past tense. The third sentence must continue in the past tense.

99. **(B)** In the original, the object itself was feeling suspicious. Obviously, it is the trooper who felt suspicious, not the object. Choice (A) shifts into the present tense. (C) is too colloquial and is poorly written.

100. **(D)** The troopers had already arrested the woman, so you can eliminate (B) and (C) without considering any mistakes other than simple sequence of events. (A) is grammatically incorrect (that what); the stated purpose is also not reasonable in context with the first two sentences.

Answer Sheet for Model Examination 2

1. Ⓐ Ⓑ Ⓒ Ⓓ	21. Ⓐ Ⓑ Ⓒ Ⓓ	41. Ⓐ Ⓑ Ⓒ Ⓓ	61. Ⓐ Ⓑ Ⓒ Ⓓ	81. Ⓐ Ⓑ Ⓒ Ⓓ
2. Ⓐ Ⓑ Ⓒ Ⓓ	22. Ⓐ Ⓑ Ⓒ Ⓓ	42. Ⓐ Ⓑ Ⓒ Ⓓ	62. Ⓐ Ⓑ Ⓒ Ⓓ	82. Ⓐ Ⓑ Ⓒ Ⓓ
3. Ⓐ Ⓑ Ⓒ Ⓓ	23. Ⓐ Ⓑ Ⓒ Ⓓ	43. Ⓐ Ⓑ Ⓒ Ⓓ	63. Ⓐ Ⓑ Ⓒ Ⓓ	83. Ⓐ Ⓑ Ⓒ Ⓓ
4. Ⓐ Ⓑ Ⓒ Ⓓ	24. Ⓐ Ⓑ Ⓒ Ⓓ	44. Ⓐ Ⓑ Ⓒ Ⓓ	64. Ⓐ Ⓑ Ⓒ Ⓓ	84. Ⓐ Ⓑ Ⓒ Ⓓ
5. Ⓐ Ⓑ Ⓒ Ⓓ	25. Ⓐ Ⓑ Ⓒ Ⓓ	45. Ⓐ Ⓑ Ⓒ Ⓓ	65. Ⓐ Ⓑ Ⓒ Ⓓ	85. Ⓐ Ⓑ Ⓒ Ⓓ
6. Ⓐ Ⓑ Ⓒ Ⓓ	26. Ⓐ Ⓑ Ⓒ Ⓓ	46. Ⓐ Ⓑ Ⓒ Ⓓ	66. Ⓐ Ⓑ Ⓒ Ⓓ	86. Ⓐ Ⓑ Ⓒ Ⓓ
7. Ⓐ Ⓑ Ⓒ Ⓓ	27. Ⓐ Ⓑ Ⓒ Ⓓ	47. Ⓐ Ⓑ Ⓒ Ⓓ	67. Ⓐ Ⓑ Ⓒ Ⓓ	87. Ⓐ Ⓑ Ⓒ Ⓓ
8. Ⓐ Ⓑ Ⓒ Ⓓ	28. Ⓐ Ⓑ Ⓒ Ⓓ	48. Ⓐ Ⓑ Ⓒ Ⓓ	68. Ⓐ Ⓑ Ⓒ Ⓓ	88. Ⓐ Ⓑ Ⓒ Ⓓ
9. Ⓐ Ⓑ Ⓒ Ⓓ	29. Ⓐ Ⓑ Ⓒ Ⓓ	49. Ⓐ Ⓑ Ⓒ Ⓓ	69. Ⓐ Ⓑ Ⓒ Ⓓ	89. Ⓐ Ⓑ Ⓒ Ⓓ
10. Ⓐ Ⓑ Ⓒ Ⓓ	30. Ⓐ Ⓑ Ⓒ Ⓓ	50. Ⓐ Ⓑ Ⓒ Ⓓ	70. Ⓐ Ⓑ Ⓒ Ⓓ	90. Ⓐ Ⓑ Ⓒ Ⓓ
11. Ⓐ Ⓑ Ⓒ Ⓓ	31. Ⓐ Ⓑ Ⓒ Ⓓ	51. Ⓐ Ⓑ Ⓒ Ⓓ	71. Ⓐ Ⓑ Ⓒ Ⓓ	91. Ⓐ Ⓑ Ⓒ Ⓓ
12. Ⓐ Ⓑ Ⓒ Ⓓ	32. Ⓐ Ⓑ Ⓒ Ⓓ	52. Ⓐ Ⓑ Ⓒ Ⓓ	72. Ⓐ Ⓑ Ⓒ Ⓓ	92. Ⓐ Ⓑ Ⓒ Ⓓ
13. Ⓐ Ⓑ Ⓒ Ⓓ	33. Ⓐ Ⓑ Ⓒ Ⓓ	53. Ⓐ Ⓑ Ⓒ Ⓓ	73. Ⓐ Ⓑ Ⓒ Ⓓ	93. Ⓐ Ⓑ Ⓒ Ⓓ
14. Ⓐ Ⓑ Ⓒ Ⓓ	34. Ⓐ Ⓑ Ⓒ Ⓓ	54. Ⓐ Ⓑ Ⓒ Ⓓ	74. Ⓐ Ⓑ Ⓒ Ⓓ	94. Ⓐ Ⓑ Ⓒ Ⓓ
15. Ⓐ Ⓑ Ⓒ Ⓓ	35. Ⓐ Ⓑ Ⓒ Ⓓ	55. Ⓐ Ⓑ Ⓒ Ⓓ	75. Ⓐ Ⓑ Ⓒ Ⓓ	95. Ⓐ Ⓑ Ⓒ Ⓓ
16. Ⓐ Ⓑ Ⓒ Ⓓ	36. Ⓐ Ⓑ Ⓒ Ⓓ	56. Ⓐ Ⓑ Ⓒ Ⓓ	76. Ⓐ Ⓑ Ⓒ Ⓓ	96. Ⓐ Ⓑ Ⓒ Ⓓ
17. Ⓐ Ⓑ Ⓒ Ⓓ	37. Ⓐ Ⓑ Ⓒ Ⓓ	57. Ⓐ Ⓑ Ⓒ Ⓓ	77. Ⓐ Ⓑ Ⓒ Ⓓ	97. Ⓐ Ⓑ Ⓒ Ⓓ
18. Ⓐ Ⓑ Ⓒ Ⓓ	38. Ⓐ Ⓑ Ⓒ Ⓓ	58. Ⓐ Ⓑ Ⓒ Ⓓ	78. Ⓐ Ⓑ Ⓒ Ⓓ	98. Ⓐ Ⓑ Ⓒ Ⓓ
19. Ⓐ Ⓑ Ⓒ Ⓓ	39. Ⓐ Ⓑ Ⓒ Ⓓ	59. Ⓐ Ⓑ Ⓒ Ⓓ	79. Ⓐ Ⓑ Ⓒ Ⓓ	99. Ⓐ Ⓑ Ⓒ Ⓓ
20. Ⓐ Ⓑ Ⓒ Ⓓ	40. Ⓐ Ⓑ Ⓒ Ⓓ	60. Ⓐ Ⓑ Ⓒ Ⓓ	80. Ⓐ Ⓑ Ⓒ Ⓓ	100. Ⓐ Ⓑ Ⓒ Ⓓ

Model Examination 2

MEMORY BOOKLET

Directions: You will be given 10 minutes to study the scene that follows and to try to notice and remember as many details as you can. You may not take any notes during this time.

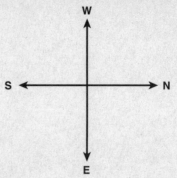

TEST QUESTION BOOKLET

Time: 3 Hours—100 Questions

Directions: Now that the Memory Booklets have been collected, you have 3 hours in which to answer the test questions. Questions 1 to 10 are based on the scene that you just studied. Answer these questions first. Then proceed directly to the remaining 90 questions. Choose the best answer to each question and mark its letter on your answer sheet.

Answer questions 1-10 on the basis of the scene in the memory booklet.

1. The car that is on fire is
   (A) on the southbound shoulder
   (B) upended
   (C) partly off the road
   (D) the private car closest to the ambulance

2. How many people appear to be seriously injured?
   (A) None
   (B) Two
   (C) Four
   (D) Six

3. The people in the right-hand southbound lane who are not state troopers are
   (A) sitting in the roadway
   (B) looking at the accident scene
   (C) standing on the shoulder
   (D) standing in the roadway

4. The fire engine is
   (A) approaching from the north
   (B) putting out the fire
   (C) crossing the divider
   (D) in front of the ambulance

5. The number of state troopers on the scene who have gotten out of their cars is
   (A) 3
   (B) 5
   (C) 6
   (D) 7

6. The passenger car that is not in the roadway is
   (A) on fire
   (B) on the divider
   (C) touching another car
   (D) upside down

7. The vehicles in the left lane, southbound are
   (A) a fire engine and a police car
   (B) two passenger cars
   (C) a fire engine, a police car, and two passenger cars
   (D) a police car and two passenger cars

8. The people on the divider are
   (A) sitting
   (B) standing
   (C) some sitting, some standing
   (D) there are no people on the divider

9. This accident happened
   (A) at night
   (B) at high noon
   (C) in the afternoon
   (D) in the morning

10. Among the southbound cars are
    (A) a tanker truck, a bus, and three motorcycles
    (B) a large double trailer, a tanker truck, and two motorcycles
    (C) a tow truck, a car transport, a large double trailer, and a tanker truck
    (D) two large trailer trucks, a tanker truck, and a motorcycle

Questions 11 and 12 are based on the following scenario.

You are a highway patrol officer traveling north in the right lane on Route 75 at 50 mph. You have driven exactly five miles when a speeding car passes on your left, swerves around you, and speeds right on intersecting County Road 34. You broadcast alerts to the police departments of towns near which Road 34 passes, turn to follow, and accelerate to 90 mph in pursuit of the speeding car. Fifteen minutes later the cloud of dust that you have been following turns to the right, loses control, and smashes into a tree. You are at the scene of the accident in seconds.

11. In what direction was the speeding car traveling when it lost control?
    (A) North
    (B) South
    (C) East
    (D) West

12. About how many miles have you driven in pursuit?

(A) 15

(B) 20

(C) 24

(D) 28

Questions 13 and 14 are based on the following procedure.

When making a highway stop for any reason, highway patrol officers must take the following steps in the prescribed order:

1. Request the operator's driver's license and registration certificate.
2. Compare picture and information on license with the operator at the wheel.
3. Compare information on the registration with vehicle and with operator information.
4. If operator is not owner, ask for explanation.
5. Scan interior of car for suspicious objects or occupants.
6. Ask operator to step out of car; pat for weapons; conduct sobriety test by asking operator to walk straight line.
7. For routine violation by sober driver, issue summons.
8. If outcome of any step is unsatisfactory, request backup assistance to take operator into custody.

13. State Highway Patrol Officer Hellman traveling east notices a westbound car with one headlight burned out. Officer Hellman makes a U-turn, overtakes the offending car, and pulls it over. Hellman asks the operator for license and registration. The operator is a 17-year-old young man and the license he presents is clearly his. The registration is in the name of a woman with a different surname. Officer Hellman asks for an explanation, and the young man says that the car belongs to his mother who is remarried. Officer Hellman should now

(A) issue a summons because the car has only one headlight

(B) ask the driver to step out of the car to test his sobriety

(C) scan the interior of the car for suspicious objects

(D) call for backup so the young man can be taken into custody for driving a car not his own

14. State Trooper Malone follows a car that is weaving back and forth over two lanes and even over the double yellow line. Malone then signals that the car should pull to the side. When the driver rolls down the window, Trooper Malone is struck with the strong odor of marijuana from the smoke-filled car. The three passengers in the car are all smoking. Trooper Malone asks the driver to step out of the car to prove that he is not high on drugs.

This action by Malone is

(A) correct; the driver was operating the car as if he were drunk

(B) incorrect; Malone should have called for assistance to take the driver and marijuana-smoking passengers into custody

(C) correct; the suspicious objects and passengers in the car were obvious

(D) incorrect; he should have first asked to see driver's license and registration

15. Taxes are deducted each pay period from the amount of salaries or wages, including payments for overtime, paid to law enforcement personnel in excess of the withholding exemptions allowed under the Internal Revenue Act. The amount of tax to be withheld from each payment of wages to any employee will be determined from the current official table of pay and withholding exemptions to be found on page 32 of the employee manual.

    The paragraph best supports the statement that salaries of law enforcement personnel

    (A) do not include overtime

    (B) are determined by provisions of the Internal Revenue Act

    (C) are paid from tax revenues

    (D) are subject to tax deductions

16. A state police officer attempting to extract information from a witness should not ask questions that can be answered by a "yes" or "no." An officer is interviewing a witness to a car accident that resulted in serious injury to two people. The officer has reason to believe that the car involved went through an intersection against the light. Of the following, the proper question for the officer to ask the witness would be:

    (A) Did you see the car go through a red light?

    (B) Can you recall if the light turned red before the car went through the intersection?

    (C) What color was the light at the time the car went through the intersection?

    (D) Was the light red when the car went through the intersection?

17. State Trooper Cato has just assisted the victim of a hit-and-run accident. He has seen the victim safely removed by ambulance, has broadcast a description of the vehicle, and has made these notes in his memo book:

    > Location: intersection of Route 3 and Main Street
    > Occurrence: hit-and-run accident
    > Victim: elderly black woman, unconscious
    > Witness: Mary Clark of 323 North State Road
    > Vehicle: red sports car with Nevada license plates
    > Response by: Highland Hospital ambulance #1; driver: Barry Brown; EMT: Bill Briggs

    Trooper Cato must file a report about this incident as part of his daily activity log. Which of the following expresses the information most clearly, accurately, and completely?

    (A) A red sports car from Nevada killed an old black lady in front of Mary Clark of 323 North State Road. Barry Brown and Bill Briggs picked her up in ambulance #1.

    (B) Mary Clark of 323 North State Road reported that an elderly black woman was hit by a red sports car at the intersection of Main Street and Route 3. Ambulance #1 with Barry Brown driving and Bill Briggs, EMT, responded and took the unconscious victim to Highland Hospital.

    (C) An old black woman was hit by Mary Clark in a red sports car from Nevada at 323 North State Road. Highland Hospital ambulance #1 took her away with Barry Brown and Bill Briggs in attendance.

    (D) Mary Clark was hit by an elderly black woman at the intersection of Route 3 and Main Street. The red sports car was from Nevada, and the ambulance was Highland Hospital #1 driven by Barry Brown and Bill Briggs.

18. The service plaza serving both directions on the thruway is on the east shoulder of the northbound lanes. A car traveling southbound may gain entry to this service plaza by making a right turn onto a feeder road that loops around, crosses the highway, and merges with the cars on the feeder entered by cars making a right turn from the northbound lanes. Cars wishing to park in the lot of the service plaza proceed straight ahead from the feeder into the lot. Cars that need gasoline make a left turn before the entrance to the parking lot and then a right turn into the gasoline service lines. When a car that had been traveling southbound arrives at a gasoline pump, in what direction is it facing?

(A) North

(B) South

(C) East

(D) West

19. Detectives assigned to investigate violent crimes with no obvious motive and no apparent witnesses must direct their whole effort toward success in their work. If they wish to succeed in such investigations, their work will be by no means easy, smooth, or peaceful; on the contrary, they will have to devote themselves completely and continuously to a task that requires all their ability.

   The paragraph best supports the statement that an investigator's success depends most upon

(A) persistence in the face of difficulty

(B) training and experience

(C) superior ability

(D) ambition to advance rapidly in rank

20. A state trooper should not ask leading questions, that is, questions which suggest the answer that the officer desires. A state trooper arrives at the scene of an accident that involved a red car and a green car. It would be proper for the officer to ask a witness to the accident:

(A) "You observed the red car hit the green car, didn't you?"

(B) "Did you see the green car hit the red car?"

(C) "The red car caused the accident, didn't it?"

(D) "Just what caused the accident between the red car and the green car?"

21. Toll charges on a certain toll road are roughly calculated on the basis of two cents per mile per axle. A ten-wheeler that enters the toll road at mile 75 and exits at mile 130 will pay a total toll of

(A) $ 1.10

(B) $ 2.20

(C) $ 5.50

(D) $11.00

22. State Police Officer Rescigno is investigating a shoe store break-in at the Eastview Mall. The break-in evidently had occurred during the previous night. She compiles the following information:

> Location: Manny's Shoes and Boots, first floor, west wing, Eastview Mall
> Incident: burglary
> Date of event: night of Tuesday, May 3 to Wednesday, May 4
> Time of event: between 9:40 P.M. and 8:15 A.M.
> Reporter: Manny Monroe, owner, of 350 Main Street, East Hills
> Damage: broken window; empty cash register

Officer Rescigno must write a report of this incident for follow-up. Which of the following expresses the information most clearly, accurately, and completely?

(A) Manny Monroe of 350 Main Street, East Hills, reports that his Manny's Shoes and Boots located at Eastview Mall on the first floor of the west wing was broken into between 9:40 P.M. May 3 and 8:15 A.M. May 4. Contents of the cash register are missing.

(B) Manny Monroe had a burglary between closing on May 3 and opening May 4. He got a broken window and they emptied the cash register and took his money.

(C) Manny's Shoes and Boots on the first floor of the west wing of Eastview Mall had a burglary at night on May 3rd. They broke a window and took the money.

(D) Manny's Shoes and Boots was burgled through a broken window on the first floor of Eastview Mall's west wing during the night May 3–4. The burglars took everything out of the cash register. Mr. Monroe lives at 350 Main Street, East Hills and keeps the store open from 8:15 A.M. to 9:40 P.M.

23. Highway Patrol Officer Patel answers a motorist's request for directions by telling the motorist to: "Proceed south, as you are now headed, for two blocks; turn right at the traffic light and, at the next intersection, turn right again. Immediately after you see a gas station on your right, make a left turn and go one block. The post office is in the strip mall on your left." In what direction will the car be traveling when the motorist reaches his destination?

(A) North

(B) South

(C) East

(D) West

24. State troopers often respond to the scene of traffic accidents involving two vehicles. In situations in which one of the drivers involved in the accident has left the scene before the arrival of a trooper, the responding trooper must use the following procedures in the order given:

    1. Question the driver of the remaining vehicle as to the license plate number of the vehicle that fled.

        a. If the complete license plate number is known, call Vehicle Inquiry Section to determine name and address of owner.

        b. Write down name and address of owner of vehicle that fled.

        c. Give name and address of owner of vehicle that fled to driver remaining at scene of accident.

    2. Obtain from driver remaining at scene all details of accident including description of vehicle that fled.

    3. Call Stolen Vehicle Desk.

    4. Prepare Complaint Form in duplicate.

State Trooper Yoshida has arrived at the scene of a traffic accident involving two cars. One of the drivers fled the scene immediately after the impact, but the driver of the remaining vehicle, Myra Lamonica, did notice that the last three digits of the license plate were 7-9-7, and she gives this information to Trooper Yoshida. Which one of the following actions should Trooper Yoshida take next?

(A) Call Vehicle Inquiry Section to determine name and address of owner.

(B) Call Stolen Vehicle Desk.

(C) Write down name and address of Myra Lamonica.

(D) Ask Lamonica for a description of the other car and for details of the accident.

25. Of the following, the most grammatical and precise sentence is:

(A) Speed limits do not know about road and weather conditions so you should not always be guided by them.

(B) Consider road and weather conditions and modify your driving speed accordingly.

(C) Road and weather conditions can change speed limits.

(D) Driving at the posted speed limit should be slowed down by bad road and weather conditions.

Answer questions 26 and 27 on the basis of the following procedure.

When speaking to a traffic violator, a highway patrol officer should adhere to the following:

1. Use the words "Sir" or "Ma'am" until you get to know the name of the violator; then the use of Mr. Jones or Ms. Smith is proper.

2. Advise the driver of the violation he or she has committed.

3. Do not argue with the motorist.

4. Be impersonal in your conversation; do not mention yourself.

5. Do not be critical of the motorist.

26. Officer Thomas stops a motorist for speeding. The officer approaches the car, and the driver says, "I haven't done anything wrong. Why did you stop me?" An appropriate reply from Officer Thomas would be

    (A) "I stopped you for speeding."

    (B) "Buddy, you were speeding to a fire."

    (C) "Sir, you were exceeding the speed limit."

    (D) "Sir, I know exactly how fast you were going. You were speeding."

27. Officer Provo stops a motorist because of erratic driving on a busy highway. The motorist had come close to hitting several cars. The motorist extends his license to the officer who notes his name as being William Doran. The motorist asks the officer why he was stopped, declaring that he was not driving too fast. Officer Provo calmly says, "Mr. Doran, you are a lousy driver." Officer Provo's statement to the motorist is

    (A) improper; the officer should first ask the motorist how much he has had to drink

    (B) proper; the officer is being truthful

    (C) improper; the officer is criticizing the motorist

    (D) proper; the officer is using the motorist's name respectfully

28. Choose the most logical order of the sentences to create a coherent story.

    1. The officer asked the witness if his brother had been drinking.
    2. The witness angrily replied that his brother was sober.
    3. A highway patrol officer on the scene was interviewing the witness to a serious car accident.
    4. The accident had resulted in the death of the witness's brother, driver of one of the vehicles.

    (A) 3 - 4 - 1 - 2

    (B) 3 - 1 - 2 - 4

    (C) 4 - 3 - 1 - 2

    (D) 1 - 2 - 3 - 4

29. State troopers must be trained in the safe and efficient operation of motor vehicles. Principles and techniques are thoroughly explained in the classroom before students are allowed to participate in the actual performance of practical exercises. Under close supervision and guidance, the students train until they recognize their personal limitations as well as limitations of the vehicle. The training curriculum should include courses in: highway response, defensive driving, skid control, transportation of prisoners, pursuit driving, evasive maneuver driving techniques, and accident investigation.

    The paragraph best supports the statement that

    (A) it is important for police officers to understand the principles of motor vehicle operation

    (B) the training curriculum is specific to the special requirements of police driving

    (C) state troopers have personal limitations so must be closely supervised

    (D) vehicle maintenance is an important part of police driver training

30. A highway patrol officer pulls into a gas station at an easy-off/easy-on location parallel to the highway and discovers a holdup in progress. When he identifies himself as a law officer, the robber takes off at high speed and reenters the highway. The officer gives chase. They proceed west on the highway for three miles. Then they make a right turn off the highway onto a secondary road for another mile and a half, and then a left turn onto a dirt road. Driving at high speed on the dirt road, the holdup man's car develops a flat tire. The man jumps out of the driver's seat and runs directly into the woods. The highway patrol officer follows on foot, but loses sight of his suspect. The officer than turns around and runs back to his car to radio for assistance. In what direction is he running?

    (A) North

    (B) South

    (C) East

    (D) West

31. State Police Officer vanNess on routine highway patrol on the Cross River Bridge notices a car pulled to the side of the bridge with driver's door open, motor running, and no one inside. She quickly radios for help and jumps from her patrol car. She finds a young Hispanic man clinging to the underside of the bridge, grabs him by both hands, and waits for backup. Officer vanNess attempts to question and reason with the man, but the man speaks no English. Before backups arrive, another motorist pulls up and asks if he can be of assistance. The motorist, while not fluent, knows enough Spanish to keep the man engaged until assistance arrives. Officer vanNess jots the following notes in her memo book:

    > Location: mid-span, southbound shoulder, Cross River Bridge
    > Time: 3:40 P.M.
    > Event: threatened suicide
    > Description: 23-year-old Hispanic male, slight build, about 5 ft. 8 in., primary language Spanish, wearing denim cutoffs, gray tank top, and canvas sneakers. Name not revealed. Individual's wife just left him, taking baby.
    > Assisting bystander: James Hogan of 381 Baird Boulevard, North City, CT

    Having transported the individual to the county hospital, Officer vanNess must prepare a report to enter into her activity record and to transmit to psychiatrists who will examine and treat the threatened suicide. Which of the following expresses the information most clearly, accurately, and completely?

    (A) A 23-year-old Hispanic male whose wife left him speaking Spanish tried to jump off the Cross River Bridge at 3:40 P.M. James Hogan talked him out of it wearing denim cutoffs, gray tank top, and canvas sneakers.

    (B) A 23-year-old Spanish-speaking male wearing denim cutoffs, gray tank top, and canvas sneakers is 5 ft. 8 in. and has a slight build. His wife and baby left him and he won't tell us his name. He wanted to jump off the Cross River Bridge but James Hogan told him not to at 381 Baird Boulevard, North City, CT.

    (C) At 3:40 P.M., James Hogan and I convinced an unidentified 23-year-old Hispanic male, about 5 ft. 8 in., slightly built, and wearing denim cutoffs, gray tank top, and canvas sneakers, not to jump from the middle of the Cross River Bridge.

    (D) At 3:40 P.M., an unidentified 23-year-old Hispanic male, about 5 ft. 8 in., slightly built, wearing denim cutoffs, gray tank top, and canvas sneakers, threatened to jump from the south side of the Cross River Bridge. A Spanish-speaking motorist, James Hogan of 381 Baird Boulevard, North City, CT, learned that his wife had just left him and stopped him from jumping.

32. State troopers assigned to patrol in a radio car are instructed to adhere to the following rules concerning the use of the police radios in patrol cars:

1. The use of the radio is to be restricted to performance of duty only.
2. All conversations should be to the point and as short as possible.
3. Names of people are not to be used.
4. All conversations should begin by identifying the vehicle by number.
5. A message received is to be acknowledged by "ten-four."

    State Troopers Abel and Flynn apprehend two men in the act of stealing a stereo tape and disc player from a car in a service area parking lot. They place the men in their car—car 14—and radio in a report of the activity. Which one of the following messages would be in conformance with the procedure specified?

(A) "Officers Abel and Flynn, car one-four, proceeding to barracks number 3 with two prisoners."

(B) "Car one-four, proceeding to barracks number 3 with two prisoners."

(C) "Car one-four, Troopers Abel and Flynn, proceeding to barracks number 3 with two prisoners, ten-four."

(D) "Car one-four proceeding to barracks number 3 with prisoners Bossey and Warren; ten-four."

33. Of the following, the most grammatical and precise sentence is:

(A) In arresting and detention of suspects, a trooper has to give advice about Miranda rights.

(B) Constitutional rights like Miranda warnings are advice given by arresting officers.

(C) A suspect being arrested or detained must be given a Miranda warning, that is, must be advised of his or her constitutional rights.

(D) A trooper must give the suspect their Miranda warning and tell them they have constitutional rights before anyone can be arrested.

34. Choose the most logical order of the sentences to create a coherent story.

1. Everyone entering the elevators for the upper floors of the municipal building must pass through a metal detector.
2. The man was not permitted to take the exam.
3. As the man approached the elevator, the alarm began to sound.
4. A sign in the lobby read, "All applicants for the state trooper exam must check their weapons."

(A) 1 - 3 - 4 - 2

(B) 4 - 3 - 1 - 2

(C) 1 - 4 - 2 - 3

(D) 4 - 1 - 3 - 2

35. An assumption commonly made in regard to the reliability of testimony is that when a number of persons report the same matter, those details upon which there is an agreement may generally be considered substantiated. Experiments have shown, however, that there is a tendency for the same errors to appear in the testimony of different individuals, and that, apart from any collusion, agreement of testimony is no proof of dependability.

   This paragraph suggests that

   (A) if the testimony of a group of people is in substantial agreement, it cannot be ruled out that those witnesses have not all made the same mistake

   (B) if details of the testimony are true, all witnesses will agree to it

   (C) if most witnesses do not independently attest to the same facts, the facts cannot be true

   (D) unless there is collusion, it is impossible for a number of persons to give the same report

36. State Police Officer Waksman cruising in an unmarked car on Main Street in Littleton answers an alert on the car radio and begins to follow two robbery suspects. The suspects go south for two blocks, then turn left for two blocks, then make another left turn for one more block. At this point, the suspects sense that they are being followed. They hurriedly make a left turn, travel two more blocks, and then make a right turn. In what direction are the suspects now headed?

   (A) North

   (B) South

   (C) East

   (D) West

37. A black Ford Escort pulled up at the tollbooth, and the driver pointed a gun at the toll collector and demanded money. The frightened toll collector tossed a sack of tokens at the gunman. The driver was thrown off guard by the weight of the sack hurled at him and sped off without demanding bills. State Trooper Prensky, responding to the booth, learned that the sack had contained 50 rolls of $3.50 tokens. Each roll is made up of 10 tokens. What was the value of the sack of tokens?

   (A) $ 35.00

   (B) $ 175.00

   (C) $ 500.00

   (D) $1750.00

38. State Police Officer Thomases, on patrol in an unincorporated village policed by her barracks, notices an elderly gentleman wandering aimlessly in the elementary schoolyard. The man tells Officer Thomases that he thinks that his name is Bob and that he was a student at this school but was kidnapped by aliens in a flying saucer and just escaped. Officer Thomases puts the man in her car and broadcasts the following alert to her sergeant and to officers in other patrol cars:

   Incident: lost, disoriented adult
   Location: schoolyard of Central Consolidated Elementary School
   Description: white male, about 80, 5 ft. 7 in., weight 150, thin gray hair, blue eyes, wearing gray pants, white shirt, and green windbreaker, "Bob"

   Which of the following expresses the information most clearly, accurately, and completely?

   (A) An old man who might be Bob says that he was left in front of Central Consolidated School by aliens who kidnapped him. He is about 5 ft. 7 in., weighs about 150 lbs., and has thin gray hair and blue eyes. He is wearing gray pants, white shirt, and a windbreaker.

(B) Bob is an old man who was kidnapped by aliens and returned to the schoolyard at Central Consolidated Elementary where he used to go to school. He is confused wearing gray pants, a white shirt, and a green windbreaker. He has gray hair and blue eyes and is average size.

(C) A confused white man, about 80, was found in the schoolyard of Central Consolidated Elementary. The man is about 5 ft. 7 in, weighing about 150 lbs., with thin gray hair and blue eyes. He is wearing gray pants, white shirt, and a windbreaker and is uncertain of his name and address.

(D) A man with thin gray hair and blue eyes wearing gray pants, a white shirt, and a green windbreaker says he is Bob who was left by aliens in the schoolyard at Central Consolidated where he used to go to school before they kidnapped him. He is 5 ft. 7 in. and weighs 150 lbs.

Answer questions 39 and 40 on the basis of the following procedure.

1. When a suspect in custody requests medical attention or is in apparent need of it, the officer should arrange for the suspect to be promptly examined by a doctor.

2. In the event that a suspect in custody is in need of medical treatment, the officer should notify a supervisor immediately so that an ambulance can be summoned. Suspects who are drug addicts and who are in need of treatment for their addiction should be taken to a hospital by a radio car.

3. Under no circumstances should an officer prescribe any medication for a suspect in custody.

4. An officer should not attempt to diagnose a suspect's illness or injury and should not attempt to treat the suspect except in a situation where first aid is required. First aid should be administered promptly.

39. Bill Adams, a suspect well known to police because of his long record, is in custody when he claims that he has a severe headache as a result of being badly beaten. There are no apparent signs of a physical injury, but the suspect is demanding medical attention.

The state police officer in charge of Bill Adams should

(A) consider the suspect's long record before deciding to call a doctor

(B) see that Bill Adams is promptly examined by a doctor

(C) give the suspect two aspirins

(D) ignore the suspect's request for medical attention since there are no apparent physical injuries

40. It is a hot summer day, and Trooper Domonkos has in his custody a suspect who is a drug addict. The suspect opens his shirt to reveal a large unhealed wound which is obviously infected. Trooper Domonkos suggests to the suspect that he call a doctor in to examine him, but the suspect refuses, saying the wound is of no consequence. In this instance, Trooper Domonkos should

(A) request that his supervisor call an ambulance

(B) closely examine the wound in order to evaluate its severity

(C) adhere to the suspect's wishes and do nothing about the matter

(D) take the suspect at once to a hospital in a radio car

Questions 41 through 46 are based on the personnel chart below.

PERSONNEL CHART

Name	Sex	SS Number	D.O.B.	Date Hired	Position	Supervisor
Cain, G.C.	M	112-22-8765	4/8/48	5/12/73	sergeant	Barton, H.
Cane, P.T.	M	221-63-5432	9/21/56	10/10/80	custodian	Frank, L.T.
Canes, L.D.	F	868-91-0870	12/9/70	6/22/96	dispatcher	Holmes, R.G.
Coan, R., Jr.	M	555-06-9892	5/16/39	12/5/79	mechanic	Frank, L.T.
Coen, B.B.	F	342-78-1234	1/25/63	8/18/81	cook	Smith, A.N.
Cone, A.F.	F	630-12-7654	1/21/68	3/30/91	trooper	Cain, G.C.
Cone, F.J.	F	366-42-4759	11/3/72	5/7/95	trooper	Cain, G.C.
Cope, E.M.	M	633-41-8076	3/6/63	9/13/87	paramedic	Holmes, R.G.

41. Which person is supervised by A.N. Smith?

(A) G.C. Cain

(B) A.F. Cone

(C) B.B. Coen

(D) R. Coan, Jr.

42. The job held by the oldest person is

(A) sergeant

(B) dispatcher

(C) mechanic

(D) custodian

43. The person whose social security number is 633-41-8076 is a

(A) dispatcher

(B) paramedic

(C) custodian

(D) trooper

44. The social security number of the person who has been employed here for the longest time is

(A) 221-63-5432

(B) 555-06-8982

(C) 212-22-8765

(D) 112-22-8765

45. The oldest trooper was born on

(A) 1/21/68

(B) 1/25/63

(C) 5/ 7/95

(D) 11/ 3/72

46. A.F. Cone's social security number is

(A) 630-12-7554

(B) 630-12-7564

(C) 630-12-7654

(D) 630-12-7645

Answer questions 47 and 48 on the basis of the following Employee Leave Regulations.

As a full-time permanent state employee under the Career and Salary Plan, Trooper Fogarty earns an "annual leave allowance." This consists of a certain number of days off a year with pay and may be used for vacation, for personal business, or for observing religious holidays. During his first 8 years of state service, he will earn an "annual leave allowance" of 20 days a year (an average of 1-2/3 days off a month). After he has finished 8 full years of state employment, he will begin earning an additional 5 days off a year. His "annual leave allowance" will then be 25 days a year and will remain at this level for 7 full years. He will begin earning an additional 2 days off a year after he has completed a total of 15 years of state employment.

A "sick leave allowance" of 1 day a month is also given to Trooper Fogarty, but it can be used only in case of actual illness. When Fogarty returns to work after using "sick leave allowance," he must have a doctor's note if the absence is for a total of more than 3 days, but he may also be required to show a doctor's note for absences of 1, 2, or 3 days.

47. According to the preceding passage, Trooper Fogarty's "annual leave allowance" consists of a certain number of days off a year that he

(A) does not get paid for

(B) should use if he is sick

(C) may use for personal business

(D) may not use for observing religious holidays

48. According to the preceding passage, when he uses "sick leave allowance," Trooper Fogarty may be required to show a doctor's note

(A) even if his absence is for only 1 day

(B) only if his absence is for more than 2 days

(C) only is his absence is for more than 3 days

(D) only if his absence is for 3 days or more

49. Choose the most logical order of the sentences to create a coherent story.

1. There was a turnpike crash between two trucks, one of which overturned.

2. One highway patrol officer called for an ambulance for the driver of the overturned truck, who appeared to be seriously injured.

3. Cartons of cigarettes, some burst open, were scattered all over the highway.

4. Another highway patrol officer noticed that the federal tax stamps on the cigarettes were counterfeit.

(A) 1 - 2 - 3 - 4

(B) 1 - 3 - 2 - 4

(C) 3 - 1 - 2 - 4

(D) 3 - 2 - 4 - 1

50. Choose the most grammatical and precise statement.

(A) Without prior authorization, personal telephone calls are prohibited by on-duty state police officers.

(B) State police officers without prior authorization on duty are prohibited from making personal telephone calls.

(C) State police officers are prohibited from making personal telephone calls while on duty without prior authorization.

(D) State police officers without prior authorization are prohibited from making personal telephone calls while on duty.

Questions 51 through 56 are based on the work schedule below.

WORK SCHEDULE

	Sun	Mon	Tues	Wed	Thurs	Fri	Sat
Group 1	South Quadrant	West Quadrant	training	off	West Quadrant	South Quadrant	off
Group 2	East Quadrant	training	off	North Quadrant	South Quadrant	off	West Quadrant
Group 3	North Quadrant	off	South Quadrant	East Quadrant	off	training	North Quadrant

Group 1	Group 2	Group 3
Supervisor: Mark Cross	*Supervisor: Mary Gelb*	*Supervisor: Andy Mao*
Traci Baron	Scott McKeon	Ramon Martinez
Evan Luwisch	Demetria Kougios	Horace Logan
Janice Payson	Bruce Nelson	Kathy Choong
Warren Correa	Marina Drabek	David Cotino

Training at: 9848 State Road

Training supervisor: Herbert Talmini

September

Sun	Mon	Tues	Wed	Thurs	Fri	Sat
		1	2	3	4	5
6	7	8	9	10	11	12
13	14	15	16	17	18	19
20	21	22	23	24	25	26
27	28	29	30			

51. Where is Bruce Nelson working on September 17?

(A) 9848 State Road

(B) South Quadrant

(C) Not working

(D) East Quadrant

52. On what date will Kathy Choong report for training?

(A) September 18

(B) September 3

(C) September 1

(D) September 28

53. A person who will be working in all four quadrants during the month of September is

(A) Mark Cross

(B) Ramon Martinez

(C) Demetria Kougios

(D) Herbert Talmini

54. The supervisor of the group that will work in the east quadrant on September 9 is

(A) Herbert Talmini

(B) Mark Cross

(C) Andy Mao

(D) cannot be determined

55. A person who will be off on September 24 is

    (A) Evan Luwisch

    (B) Marina Drabek

    (C) Mark Cross

    (D) Herbert Talmini

56. Which group will work in the north quadrant on September 18?

    (A) Group 1

    (B) Group 2

    (C) Group 3

    (D) cannot be determined

57. Choose the most grammatical and precise sentence.

    (A) On account of the prediction that there would be heavy snow, it was required of the troopers that they put chains on their cars.

    (B) Due to the fact that it was due to snow heavily, troopers were told to put on chains.

    (C) Because heavy snow was predicted, troopers were directed to use tire chains.

    (D) The forecasters said that it was going to snow hard which led the troopers to put chains on their tires.

58. The civil service commission shall designate a qualified trainer to administer the physical fitness screening test to determine the underlying physiological capacity of a candidate to learn and perform the essential job functions of an entry-level state police officer. Such test shall be administered prior to the making of a conditional offer of employment and shall be administered to the candidate prior to the post-offer medical examination to be conducted by a qualified physician or practitioner unless the civil service commission can demonstrate that it could not reasonably conduct such screening test at the pre-offer stage of employment.

    The paragraph best supports the statement that

    (A) physical fitness screening is the first step in the hiring process for state police officers

    (B) an applicant may be offered employment before physical fitness screening if the civil service commission could not conduct this screening before the offer was made

    (C) the purpose of physical fitness screening is to determine if the candidate will be able to pass the medical examination

    (D) the medical examination is administered by a qualified trainer or practitioner

59. Prior to the administration of the test by the qualified trainer, the civil service commission may ask the candidate to assume legal responsibility and release such commission of liability for injuries resulting from any physical or mental disorders. In addition, the commission may furnish such candidate with a description of the physical fitness screening test and require certification from the candidate's physician that he or she is physically capable of participating in the physical fitness screening test. If the commission requests such certification from one candidate, it must request such certification from all candidates.

The paragraph best supports the statement that

(A) the physical fitness test causes injuries to persons with physical or mental disorders

(B) the civil service commission is not liable for injuries to state police candidates

(C) all candidates must be treated equally with respect to certifying fitness for the fitness test

(D) persons with physical or mental disorders must be furnished with a description of the physical fitness screening test

60. If a candidate is unable to perform an element of the test, the civil service commission may provide for an alternative element to be substituted, which, in the judgment of such commission, will render a demonstrably valid assessment of the individual's physiological capacity for the particular factor to be measured.

The paragraph best supports the statement that

(A) the civil service commission may offer substitute tasks to measure fitness if a candidate has failed to pass on one of the established measures

(B) individuals may offer substitute tasks to prove their fitness if unable to adequately perform on a designated element

(C) candidates are offered second chances to prove their fitness for employment

(D) an alternative may be offered for only one element of the test

Answer questions 61 and 62 on the basis of the drawing below. This drawing shows parts of the magazine of a police revolver and the order in which these parts fit together.

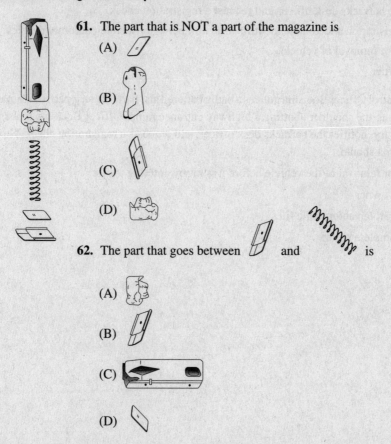

61. The part that is NOT a part of the magazine is

(A)

(B)

(C)

(D)

62. The part that goes between   and   is

(A)

(B)

(C)

(D)

63. State Highway Patrol Officer Zildgian has just issued a summons to a driver and has obtained the following information:

> Time of Occurrence: 6:08 A.M.
> Place of Occurrence: U.S. Highway 202 at milepost 74
> Offense: illegal U-turn
> Driver: Malcolm Brooks, age 29
> Address of Driver: 76 Shady Lane, Martinsburgh

Officer Zildgian is making an entry in his daily activity log regarding the incident. Which of the following conveys the information most clearly, accurately, and completely?

(A) Malcolm Brooks, age 29, made a U-turn at 76 Shady Lane. I arrested him.

(B) At 6:08 A.M. I stopped 29-year-old Malcolm Brooks of 76 Shady Land, Martinsburgh, for making an illegal U-turn on Highway 202 at mile 74 and gave him a summons.

(C) 29-year-old Malcolm Brooks made an illegal U-turn on Highway 202 at 76 Shady Lane. This happened early this morning, and I gave him a summons.

(D) When Malcolm Brooks, age 29, made an illegal U-turn on Highway 202 at milepost 74, I gave him a summons at 76 Shady Lane, Martinsburgh, at 6:08 A.M.

64. Highway patrol officers occasionally discover vehicles which appear to have been abandoned along the roadside. An officer coming upon such a vehicle should do the following:

1. Make a memo book entry describing the vehicle and the location at which the vehicle was found.
2. Notify the barracks desk officer and request a registration check.
3. Check registration and vehicle identification number against stolen automobile files.
4. Arrange for removal of vehicle.
5. Notify owner.

Highway Patrol Officer Boersma notices a badly battered and partially stripped red Camaro unattended along the shoulder abutting a highway entrance ramp. Officer Boersma makes a memo book entry, notifies the barracks desk officer, and requests a registration check. Next, Officer Boersma should

(A) arrange for removal of the vehicle before it is hit by entering traffic

(B) notify the owner

(C) check the stolen automobile files

(D) write a complete report

Answer questions 65 through 67 on the basis of the following map. The flow of traffic is indicated by the arrows. You must follow the flow of traffic.

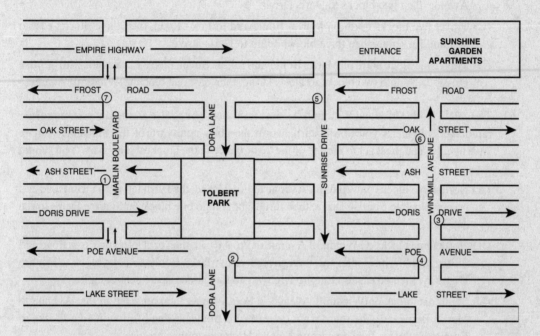

65. If you are located at point (1) and travel north three blocks, then turn east and travel one block, then turn south and travel five blocks, then turn west and travel one block, you will be closest to point

(A) 2

(B) 3

(C) 5

(D) 7

66. You are located at Marlin Boulevard and Ash Street while patrolling in the town depicted on the map portion and receive a call to respond to the corner of Doris Drive and Windmill Avenue. Which of the following is the most direct route for you to take in your patrol car, making sure to obey all traffic regulations?

   (A) Travel two blocks south on Marlin Boulevard to Poe Avenue, then three blocks east to Windmill Avenue, then north one block to Doris Drive.

   (B) Travel three blocks north on Marlin Boulevard to Empire Highway, then one block east to Sunrise Drive, then two blocks south to Dora Lane, then one block east to Windmill Avenue, then two blocks to Doris Drive.

   (C) Travel two blocks north on Marlin Boulevard to Frost Road, then three blocks east to Windmill Avenue, then three blocks south to Doris Drive.

   (D) Travel one block north on Marlin Boulevard to Oak Street, then east two blocks to Sunrise Drive, then south two blocks to Doris Drive, then east one block to Windmill Avenue.

67. The call to Doris Drive and Windmill Avenue turns out to be a false alarm, but your patrol car radio suddenly alerts you to a disturbance in the entry courtyard of the Sunshine Garden Apartments. You must get to the site of the disturbance in the quickest legal way. You should drive:

   (A) North three blocks on Windmill Avenue to Frost Road, then turn left onto Frost Road and go one block to Sunrise Drive, then turn right and go one block on Sunrise Drive to the entrance.

   (B) North three blocks on Windmill Avenue to Frost Road, then turn left onto Frost Road and follow it to Marlin Boulevard, then go right onto Marlin Boulevard one block to Empire Highway, then go east on Empire Highway to the garden apartment complex.

   (C) South one block on Windmill Avenue to Poe Avenue, then go west on Poe Avenue to Marlin Boulevard, then turn right onto Marlin Boulevard and follow it five blocks to Empire Highway, then go east on Empire Highway to the entrance.

   (D) North one block on Windmill Avenue to Ash Street, then west on Ash Street one block to Sunrise Drive, then south on Sunrise Drive two blocks to Poe Avenue, then follow Poe Avenue west to Marlin Boulevard, then turn right onto Marlin Boulevard and go to Empire Highway, and turn right onto Empire Highway and drive to the entry.

68. The characteristics that should be emphasized in a wanted person report are those which most easily set an individual apart from the general public. Which one of the following descriptions would be of greatest help to a state police officer trying to locate a wanted person in a large crowd of people on a cold winter day?

   (A) The person is wearing a blue coat and has short-cropped hair.

   (B) The person has a patch on his right eye and a long thin scar on his left cheek.

   (C) The person talks with a lisp and has two upper front teeth missing.

   (D) The person has a scar on his right knee and has blue eyes.

69. Choose the most logical order of the sentences to create a coherent story.

1. He observed a vehicle accident with several injured persons lying on the roadway.
2. Officer Wolchock immediately requested that two ambulances be dispatched to the scene.
3. Highway Patrol Officer Wolchock on vehicle patrol was traveling on a local freeway.
4. Prompt action was taken to establish traffic control to protect the injured parties from further injury.

(A) 3 - 1 - 4 - 2

(B) 1 - 3 - 4 - 2

(C) 3 - 1 - 2 - 4

(D) 1 - 3 - 2 - 4

70. Choose the most grammatica

(A) Johnny Carabitsis come   lligan that he seen the
   victim fall to the groun   tim and run off.

(B) Johnny Carabitsis exite   Trooper Milligan that he
   observed that the victim   ir of white males running
   away after searching hi

(C) Exiting the store, Johnr   per Milligan that the victim
   fell down and the two   white men ran away.

(D) Johnny Carabitsis can   Milligan that he had seen the
   victim fall down and   victim and had then run off.

In the diagrams for question   represent vehicles, pedestrians, and their move

- Vehicles are shown by the symbol: front
- Pedestrians are represented by a circle: ○
- Animals are represented by a square: □
- Solid lines show the path and direction of a vehicle, person, or animal *before* an accident happened: ⟶
- Broken lines show the path and direction of a vehicle, person, or animal *after* an accident happened: — — — — ⟶

71. Car 1 was driving north on County Road #3; car 2 was driving south on the same road. The two cars were nearly abreast when a squirrel began to cross the roadway from west to east. Car 1 swerved onto the right shoulder to avoid hitting the squirrel. Just past the middle of the roadway, the squirrel changed its mind, turned around, and began to scamper back across the road from east to west. Car 2 slammed on its brakes. Car 3, unable to see the road in front of car 2 and therefore unaware of any reason for car 2 to stop suddenly, rear-ended car 2. Which of the four diagrams below best represents the accident described?

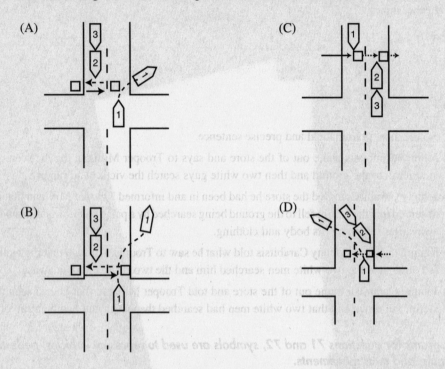

72. The diagram below represents a highway accident. Which of the narratives following the diagram best describes the accident depicted?

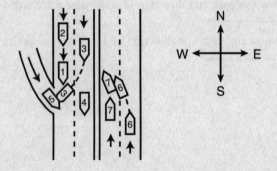

(A) Car 1, car 2, and car 3 were all driving southbound in the right lane of a divided highway when car 5 cut in from the right and smashed into car 3. Traffic in the left lane and northbound traffic were unaffected.

(B) Car 6, traveling in the right lane, northbound, attempted to illegally pass car 7 on the right causing car 7 to jump the divider and forcing car 3 from the left lane to the right lane of southbound traffic. Car 3 then hit car 5 which was entering the highway from an entrance ramp and car 3, in turn, was hit by car 1. Car 2 stopped in time and didn't hit anyone.

(C) Car 1 and car 2 were traveling southbound in the right lane of a divided highway and were passed by car 3 in the left lane. Car 3 then impatiently cut into the right lane in front of car 1, hitting car 5 which was entering the highway from an entrance ramp on the right. Meanwhile car 6, distracted by rubbernecking, veered from the right lane of the northbound roadway into the left lane, hitting car 7 and pushing car 7 up onto the divider.

(D) Car 4, traveling slowly in the left southbound lane of a divided highway, caused car 3 to cut into the right lane and to hit car 1. Car 1 then hit car 5 which was entering the highway from an entrance ramp. Car 7, northbound, attempting a U-turn into the southbound lanes, got hung up on the divider and was hit by car 6 which was entering the left lane of the northbound roadway.

73. Fill in the blank:

The Freedom of Information Act gives private citizens _____ government files.

(A) excess to

(B) access from

(C) excess of

(D) access to

74. Fill in the blanks:

The _____ object of the penal law is to define crime and _____ punishments.

(A) final . . . declare

(B) principal . . . prescribe

(C) principle . . . proclaim

(D) only . . . demand

75. Every person must be informed of the reason for his or her arrest unless that person is arrested in the actual commission of a crime. Sufficient force to effect the arrest may be used, but the courts frown on brutal methods.

According to this statement, a person does not have to be informed of the reason for his or her arrest if

(A) brutal force was not used in effecting it

(B) the courts will later free the defendant

(C) the person arrested knows force will be used if necessary

(D) the reason for the arrest is clearly evident from the circumstances

Answer questions 76 through 84 solely on the basis of the following information. Read the passage thoroughly and review the Report of Arrest form before attempting to answer the questions.

State Police Officer Chris Hazarika passing by an in-town all-night convenience store late at night hears a male voice shouting for help. Officer Hazarika enters the store through the front door where he is met by the franchise owner, Barry Nielsen, who tells the officer that he has just been robbed by a tall, slim, young, white man who can still be seen running in the distance. The officer chases after the youth who climbs into a light blue two-door Toyota bearing the New York license plate X45-2CP. The car fails to start, and Officer Hazarika catches up to it and arrests its occupant in front of 72 Lenox Street. From crime to arrest, barely five minutes of time have elapsed. The officer then takes the prisoner to the state police substation located in the village hall. There it is determined that the prisoner's legal name is Peter Bright, that he lives alone in apartment 5 at 72 Camptown Road in the nearby town of Libertyville, and his telephone number is 841-9708. Bright's nickname is "Fatso," and he is single. He was born in Rochester, NY, on April 15, 1969, and his Social Security number is 987-06-5432. Bright is employed by the Springwater Bottling Company, 276 High Street, Libertyville. An arrest record is completed and is assigned the number 18431.

Nielsen arrives at the state police substation and is able to describe the incident in detail. He states that at approximately 10:30 P.M. on August 14, 1996, a young, slim, white man entered his store. He approximated the weight of the man to be 145 lbs. and his height to be 5 ft. 11 in. The man had brown hair and eyes. Nielsen said he went to wait on the man who suddenly pointed a knife at Nielsen and said, "Give me all your money, or else." Nielsen noticed that the man had a red and blue tattoo of the head of an Indian Chief on his right forearm. Nielsen picked up an empty soda bottle from the counter and threw it at the man, hitting him in the chest. The man turned and ran out of the store, heading south on Lenox Street. Nielsen then headed for the door, yelling for help.

Nielsen was born on June 17, 1957, and he lives with his wife at 694 Judson Drive in Mount Lawrence. His business address is 26 Lenox Street, Mount Lawrence. His home telephone number is 336-6787 and his business phone number is 336-4234.

76. Which one of the following dates should be entered in the box numbered (1)?

(A) April 15, 1969

(B) August 14, 1996

(C) August 15, 1996

(D) April 14, 1969

77. Which one of the following times should be placed in the box numbered (2)?

(A) 10:25 P.M.

(B) 10:30 P.M.

(C) 10:35 P.M.

(D) 10:45 P.M.

78. Which one of the following should be placed in the box numbered (7)?

(A) April 15, 1996, 10:30 P.M.

(B) August 14, 1996, 10:25 P.M.

(C) June 17, 1996, 10:35 P.M.

(D) August 14, 1996, 10:30 P.M.

REPORT OF ARREST

ARREST INFORMATION	(1) Date of arrest	(2) Time of arrest	(3) Place of arrest	(4) Station	(5) Arrest number

DESCRIPTION OF INCIDENT		
(6) Prisoner's weapon (description)		(7) Date and time
(8) Prisoner's auto (color, year, make, model, license plate number, state)		
(9) Type of business	(10) Location of incident (be specific)	

DESCRIPTION OF PRISONER

(11) Last name First name Middle initial			(12) Date of birth			
(13) Sex	(14) Race	(15) Eyes	(16) Hair	(17) Weight	(18) Height	(19) Age
(20) Address City State			(21) Apt. no.	(22) Home phone number		
(23) Citizenship Citizen ☐ Non-Citizen ☐		(24) Place of birth	(25) Marital status			
(26) Social Security number	(27) Where employed (company and address)					
(28) Nickname	(29) Scars, tattoos (describe fully and give location)					

DESCRIPTION OF COMPLAINANT

(30) Last name First name Middle initial		(31) Date of birth
Telephone Numbers (32) Business (33) Home		(34) Address City State

79. Which of the following should be entered in the box numbered (6)?

(A) Knife

(B) Bottle

(C) Gun

(D) Ax

80. Of the following, which one should be entered in the box numbered (8)?

(A) Light blue, 1993 two-door Toyota, X45-2CP, New York

(B) Light blue, two-door Toyota, X45-C2P, New York

(C) Light blue, two-door Nissan, X45-2PC, New York

(D) Light blue, two-door Toyota, X45-2CP, New York

81. Which of the following should be entered in the box numbered (12)?

(A) June 17, 1957

(B) April 15, 1969

(C) June 17, 1969

(D) August 14, 1957

82. Of the following, which should be entered in the box numbered (27)?

(A) Springwater Bottling Company, 267 High Street, Libertyville

(B) Springwater Bottling Company, 26 Lenox Street, Mount Lawrence

(C) Springwater Bottling Company, 276 High Street, Libertyville

(D) Springwater Bottling Company, 276 High Street, Mount Lawrence

83. Of the following, which one should be entered in the box numbered (34)?

(A) 964 Judson Drive, Mount Lawrence

(B) 72 Camptown Road, Libertyville

(C) 694 Judson Drive, Libertyville

(D) 694 Judson Drive, Mount Lawrence

84. Of the following, which one should be entered in the box numbered (32)?

(A) 336-9767

(B) 336-6787

(C) 336-4234

(D) 841-9708

Answer question 85 on the basis of the information below.

Under the Penal Law, a highway patrol officer is a peace officer. A peace officer is charged with keeping the peace whether officially on duty or not and whether in uniform or not. A peace officer must attempt to prevent crime from occurring, must attempt to stop crime in progress, and must attempt to assist crime victims.

85. Highway Patrol Officer Mahoney has completed his day's tour of duty and is on his way home. He has just parked his car in his usual space, three blocks from his home, when he comes upon a woman screaming that her purse has just been snatched. Officer Mahoney begins to chase the perpetrator, who is still visible running up the street. The purse snatcher suddenly turns, shoots, and kills Officer Mahoney. Highway Patrol Officer Mahoney's widow files to collect "death-in-the-line-of-duty" benefits. Mrs. Mahoney's request is

   (A) proper; Officer Mahoney was murdered in cold blood

   (B) improper; Mahoney was off duty when he was killed

   (C) proper; it is the duty of peace officers to assist victims of crimes in progress

   (D) improper; Mahoney deliberately put himself in unnecessary danger

Answer questions 86 through 88 on the basis of the following procedure.

The final step in an accident investigation is the making out of the report. In the case of a traffic accident, the officer should go right from the scene to his or her office to write up the report. However, if a person was injured in the accident and taken to a hospital, the officer should visit the victim there before going to the office to prepare a report. This personal visit to the injured person does not mean that the officer must make a physical examination, but the officer should make an effort to obtain a statement from the injured person or persons. If this is not possible, information should be obtained from the attending physician as to the extent of the injury. In any event, without fail, the name of the physician should be secured and the report should state the name of the physician and the fact that the physician told the officer that, at a certain stated time on a certain stated date, the injuries were of such and such a nature. If the injured person dies before the officer arrives at the hospital, it may be necessary to take the responsible person into custody at once.

86. When a person has been injured in a traffic accident, the one of the following actions which it is necessary for the officer to take in connection with the accident report is to

   (A) prepare the report immediately after the accident and then go to the hospital to speak to the victim

   (B) do his or her utmost to verify the victim's story prior to preparing the official report of the accident

   (C) be sure to include the victim's statement in the report in every case

   (D) try to get the victim's version of the accident prior to preparing the report

87. When one of the persons injured in a motor vehicle accident dies, the above procedure provides that

   (A) if the injured person is already dead when the officer appears at the scene of the accident, the officer must immediately take the responsible person into custody

   (B) if the injured person dies after arrival at the hospital, the officer must either arrest the responsible person or get a statement from him or her

   (C) if the injured person dies in the hospital prior to the officer's arrival there, the officer may have to immediately arrest the responsible person

   (D) the officer may refrain from arresting the responsible person, but only if the responsible person is also seriously injured

88. When someone has been injured in a collision between two automobiles and is given medical treatment shortly thereafter by a physician, the one of the following actions which the officer must take with regard to the physician is to

    (A) obtain the physician's name and diagnosis of the injuries, regardless of the place where treatment was given

    (B) obtain the physician's approval of the portion of the report relating to the injured person and the treatment given prior to and after arrival at the hospital

    (C) obtain physician's name, opinion of the extent of the person's injuries, and signed statement regarding the treatment the physician gave the injured person

    (D) set a certain stated time on a certain stated date for interviewing physician, unless physician is an attending physician in a hospital

89. Choose the most logical order of the sentences to create a coherent story.

    1. Security staff are now checking packages being carried by employees into the state office building.

    2. This checking resulted in discovery and confiscation of a revolver on December 18.

    3. The suspect stated that he carried it to keep it away from his children.

    4. The weapon was turned over to state police officers for further investigation.

    (A) 2 - 3 - 4 - 1

    (B) 1 - 2 - 3 - 4

    (C) 4 - 3 - 1 - 2

    (D) 4 - 3 - 2 - 1

90. Fill in the blanks:

    If the interviewer does not _____ the witness, it is better to proceed _____ permitting the witness to know that _____ statements are being doubted.

    (A) understand . . . quickly . . . his

    (B) like . . . cautiously . . . their

    (C) believe . . . cautiously . . . its

    (D) believe . . . without . . . his

Questions 91 through 96 are based on the following explanation of the coding on a state motor vehicle operator's license.

H12027005087110199905

H	12	02	70	050871	101999	05
first letter, last name	position in alphabet of first letter, first name	gender	height	date of birth	expiration date	county

91. Which of the following is Martha Goldstein's license number?

   (A) M07026212236512239703

   (B) G13026808177511149710

   (C) G13025911089306069801

   (D) M13016309247909249608

92. John Jacobson graduated from junior high school in 1950. Which of the following could be his license number?

   (A) J10017407123605169911

   (B) J10016812313112020004

   (C) J10016109285009289608

   (D) J10027001244404259715

93. Which of the people with the following license numbers would be easiest to pick out in a crowd?

   (A) P26017212122903309801

   (B) B03025302294005059906

   (C) F11027604257005229911

   (D) G22016910197208279709

94. Which of the following could NOT be a real driver's license number?

   (A) A18015711234506260003

   (B) K05027006197312299914

   (C) T20036408287209079806

   (D) W05016601108004269903

95. Which of the following is least likely to be a driver's license number?

   (A) X01028210197710199909

   (B) V26015607265709249805

   (C) L11016108287809079707

   (D) Y19016305159009189813

96. Which of the following is most likely to have special restrictions on his or her driver's license?

   (A) O07026503254311159701

   (B) H20013807265809129907

   (C) P22017004306604329811

   (D) T09026511277210199904

97. Choose the most grammatical and precise statement:

   (A) The traffic light being red, the intersection should not be entered by a driver.

   (B) A driver with a traffic light turning red should not enter the intersection.

   (C) A driver making the observation that the traffic light at the intersection is about to turn red should refrain from entering that intersection until it is red no more.

   (D) If the light at the intersection is red, a driver should not enter the intersection.

98. On the basis of a tip from a reliable informer, State Police Officer Carey has verified the location of a cocaine processing factory. He has made a number of notes in his memo book and must now write a report and request search warrant and backups before actually raiding the establishment. These are Officer Carey's notes:

   Date: Monday, November 4
   Location: 481 West Martini Parkway, Apt. 4-R
   Activity: processing and packaging cocaine for street sale
   Time of activity: 9:00 P.M. to 3:00 A.M.
   Persons involved: at least five unidentified males, one female
   Basis of request: tip from reliable paid informant, John Doe, and personal observation of activity from undercover post

   Which of the following expresses this information most clearly, accurately, and completely?

   (A) On the basis of informant, John Doe, I observed five men and one woman carrying on drug-related activity at 481 West Martini Parkway, Apt. 4-R, between 9:00 P.M. and 3:00 A.M. I would like a search warrant and assistance to follow this information.

   (B) Five men and one woman are packing cocaine at 481 West Martini Parkway, Apt. 4-R from 9 to 3 on November 4. John Doe and I want to raid the premises.

   (C) According to John Doe, five men and one woman pack cocaine from 9:00 P.M. to 3:00 A.M. on November 4 at Apt. 4-R, 481 West Martini Parkway. I saw them.

   (D) Five men, one of them is John Doe, and one woman went into 481 West Martini Parkway, Apt. 4-R on November 4 from 9:00 A.M. to 3:00 P.M. to do drugs. I saw them and want a search warrant to raid the place.

99. Highway Patrol Officer Clements left Barracks #2 and began driving south on I-95. As Officer Clements cruised along at the posted 55 mph speed limit, her car was passed by a red sports car doing 75 mph. Officer Clements turned on her flashing lights and siren and gave chase. The speeding car exited the highway on a southwest ramp. At the end of the ramp, the car turned right onto State Route 201 running parallel to the interstate. When the driver of the car realized that the state police car was still in hot pursuit, he made a quick U-turn on Route 201. Three miles later, the sports car turned right onto County Road 680 and, at the next intersection, collided with a car crossing from its right. In what direction was the unfortunate car traveling when it was hit by the red car?

   (A) North

   (B) South

   (C) East

   (D) West

100. Suppose that 10% of those who commit serious crimes are convicted and that 15% of those convicted are sentenced for more than three years. The percentage of those committing serious crimes who are sentenced for more than three years is

(A) 15%

(B) 1.5%

(C) 0.15%

(D) 0.015%

ANSWER KEY

1. C	21. C	41. C	61. B	81. B
2. B	22. A	42. C	62. D	82. A
3. B	23. D	43. B	63. B	83. D
4. A	24. D	44. D	64. C	84. C
5. C	25. B	45. A	65. A	85. C
6. D	26. C	46. C	66. D	86. D
7. A	27. C	47. C	67. B	87. C
8. D	28. A	48. A	68. B	88. A
9. C	29. B	49. B	69. C	89. B
10. B	30. A	50. D	70. D	90. D
11. B	31. D	51. B	71. A	91. B
12. C	32. B	52. A	72. C	92. A
13. C	33. C	53. C	73. D	93. C
14. D	34. D	54. C	74. B	94. C
15. D	35. A	55. D	75. D	95. D
16. C	36. A	56. D	76. B	96. B
17. B	37. D	57. C	77. C	97. D
18. C	38. C	58. B	78. D	98. A
19. A	39. B	59. C	79. A	99. B
20. D	40. A	60. A	80. D	100. B

EXPLANATORY ANSWERS

1. **(C)** The car that is on fire is right side up, partly in the right-hand lane and partly on the shoulder.

2. **(B)** There are two people lying in the roadway. It is reasonable to assume that these victims are seriously hurt. Those who are sitting and standing are probably not seriously hurt.

3. **(B)** The right-hand southbound lane consists of bumper-to-bumper traffic. The people who are stuck in this traffic are rubbernecking, that is, they are looking at the accident.

4. **(A)** The fire engine is in the left lane, southbound. It is approaching from the north.

5. **(C)** Two troopers are near the people lying in the roadway; two are on the shoulder near the seated victims; one is talking to the group of four standing off on the shoulder; and one is in the roadway near the broadside car.

6. **(D)** The passenger car that is entirely on the shoulder is upside down.

7. **(A)** In the left lane southbound is a fire engine about to cross to the northbound side followed by a police car.

8. **(D)** There are no people on the divider.

9. **(C)** All the shadows are to the east of the vehicles, bushes, and people. If the shadows are to the east, the sun is in the west, and it is afternoon.

10. **(B)** Stuck among the cars in the southbound direction are a large double trailer, a tanker truck, and two motorcycles.

11. **(B)**

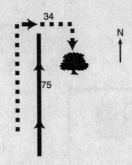

12. **(C)** Driving at 90 mph for 15 minutes, you have driven 22-1/2 miles, closest to 24. The five miles you drove before the car passed you were not miles driven in pursuit. Read questions carefully.

13. **(C)** All steps must be taken in the required order. Officer Hellman must next scan the interior of the car for suspicious occupants or objects. Then Hellman must pat down the operator for weapons and check for sobriety. Only after these steps are taken should the summons be issued for the burned-out headlight violation.

14. **(D)** Remember, the steps must be taken in order. First comes the check of driver's license and registration.

15. **(D)** The paragraph tells us that the payroll department complies with IRS regulations in withholding taxes from salaries and wages. The IRS determines the tax, not the salaries.

16. **(C)** All other choices can be answered by "yes" or "no."

17. **(B)** Choice (A) is an overstatement; the lady was not necessarily killed. (C) gets it all wrong; Mary Clark was the witness, not the driver. (C) also incorrectly places the location of the accident at Mary Clark's residence. (D) has the location right, but confuses the people involved.

18. **(C)** Southbound cars make a loop and join northbound cars to enter the service plaza.

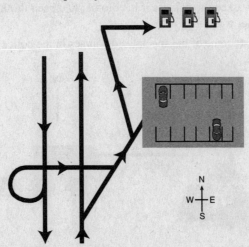

19. **(A)** By saying that investigators must devote themselves completely though the work may not be easy, smooth, or peaceful, the paragraph is saying that they must be persistent in the face of difficulty.

20. **(D)** All other choices are leading questions.

21. **(C)** The truck travels 130 − 75 = 55 miles.

A ten-wheeler has five axles. At 2 cents per mile per axle, the truck must pay 5 × .02 or 10 cents per mile. 55 × $ .10 = $5.50.

22. **(A)** Choice (D) does include all of the necessary information, but (A) is more clearly written.

23. **(D)**

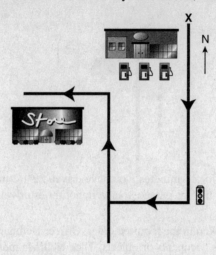

24. **(D)** The complete license number of the vehicle that fled is not known, so the name and address of its owner cannot be immediately determined. Trooper Yoshida must get as much information as possible from the remaining driver.

25. **(B)** All four sentences do get their messages across, but the sentence that addresses the driver and tells the driver what to do is clearly best. The other choices do not have appropriate subjects.

26. **(C)** Refer to rules 1 and 2 of the procedure.

27. **(C)** Officer Provo is indeed addressing the driver properly, but Provo is otherwise out of order because he is criticizing the driver's ability (Rule 5) and not advising him of his violation (Rule 2). There is no mention in the question that the driver may have been drinking.

28. **(A)** A highway patrol officer on the scene was interviewing the witness to a serious car accident. The accident had resulted in the death of the witness's brother, driver of one of the vehicles. The officer asked the witness if his brother had been drinking The witness angrily replied that his brother was sober.

29. **(B)** The paragraph lists some of the specialized courses in the police driving curriculum.

30. **(A)**

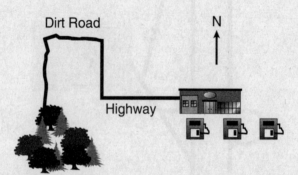

31. **(D)** Choices (A) and (B) are garbled and incorrect. Choice (C) is clear and accurate in so far as it goes, but is incomplete and inadequate.

32. **(B)** Rule 3 specifically states that names of people are not to be used.

33. **(C)** In choice (A), a parallel structure would be "arrest and detention." Further, Miranda warnings are advice in themselves, not something to receive advice about. (B) is even more imprecise. Constitutional rights are not advice. (D) mixes singular and plural persons in a single sentence.

34. **(D)** A sign in the lobby read, "All applicants for the state trooper exam must check their weapons." Everyone entering the elevators for the upper floors of the municipal building must pass through a metal detector. As the man approached the elevator, the alarm began to sound. The man was not permitted to take the exam.

35. **(A)** Just as *agreement of testimony is no proof of dependability*, so agreement of testimony is no proof of undependability; they all can make the same mistake either way.

36. **(A)** Put yourself in the driver's seat, pencil in hand, and turn the paper as needed to be certain of right and left from the driver's point of view.

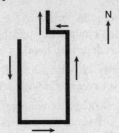

37. **(D)** The value of each roll is $3.50 × 10 = $35.00

        50 rolls @ $35 = $35.00 × 50 = $1750.00

38. **(C)** Choices (B) and (D) both report the alien kidnapping as fact. (A) reports that the old man was dropped off at the school, but not necessarily that he was found there. **(C)** is the most clear and accurate of the reports even though it omits the color of the windbreaker. In the case of unidentified persons, the color of clothing is important.

39. **(B)** Rule 1. When a suspect requests medical attention, the officer should arrange for the suspect to be promptly examined by a doctor. An officer should never assume the responsibility of deciding whether or not a suspect requires the services of a doctor.

40. **(A)** Rule 2 governs. It is apparent that the suspect requires medical attention even though there is no emergency. Medical attention is required for the suspect's wound, not for his drug addiction, therefore an ambulance should be called.

41. **(C)** A.N. Smith supervises B.B. Coen

42. **(C)** R. Coan, Jr., who was born in 1939, is a mechanic.

43. **(B)** E.M. Cope's social security number is 633-41-8076. Cope is a paramedic.

44. **(D)** Sergeant G.C. Cain was hired on 5/12/73. His social security number is 112-22-8765.

45. **(A)** Of the two troopers, the one who was born earlier is older. A.F. Cone, who was born 1/21/68, is older than F.J. Cone, whose birthdate is 11/3/72.

46. **(C)** Beware of reversed numbers. Read carefully.

47. **(C)** The second sentence lists the permissible uses of annual leave allowance.

48. **(A)** According to the last sentence of the paragraph, he *may* be required to show a doctor's note for absences of 1, 2, or 3 days.

49. **(B)** There was a turnpike crash between two trucks, one of which overturned. Cartons of cigarettes, some burst open, were scattered all over the highway. One highway patrol officer called for an ambulance for the driver of the overturned truck, who appeared to be seriously injured. Another highway patrol officer noticed that the federal tax stamps on the cigarettes were counterfeit.

50. **(D)** In choice (A), the police officers prohibit the telephone calls. In (B) it appears that prior authorization must be obtained while the officers are on duty. (C) makes it seem that the officers actually need prior authorization to go on duty.

51. **(B)** Bruce Nelson is in Group 2, and September 17 is a Thursday. On Thursdays, Group 2 works in the south quadrant.

52. **(A)** Kathy Choong is in Group 3. Group 3 takes training on Friday. September 18 is a Friday.

53. **(C)** Group 2 will be working in all four quadrants during the month of September. Demetria Kougios is in Group 2.

54. **(C)** September 9 is a Wednesday. Group 3 works in east quadrant on Wednesday, and Andy Mao is supervisor of Group 3.

55. **(D)** September 24 is a Thursday. No training is scheduled for Thursday, so the training supervisor, Herbert Talmini, has the day off. Group 3 also has Thursday off, but none of the choices is a member of that group.

56. **(D)** September 18 is a Friday. From the portion of the work schedule that we are given here, we have no way of knowing which group will work the north quadrant; we know only that it will not be one of the three groups described here.

57. **(C)** Choices (A) and (D) are wordy, childish formulations of the information. Choice (B) is incorrect because a sentence must never begin with *due to*.

58. **(B)** Reading carefully, the physical fitness screening test comes prior to the conditional offer of employment. It is reasonable to assume that there is a basis for the conditional offer, most likely a written test. (A) is therefore incorrect. (C) is ridiculous. As for (D), the physical fitness test is administered by a qualified trainer; the medical examination by a physician or qualified practitioner. Choice **(B)** is a correct interpretation of the second sentence.

59. **(C)** This is exactly what the last sentence says.

60. **(A)** This is a very generous provision, accurately restated.

61. **(B)**

62. **(D)**

63. **(B)** Choice (A) is incomplete; (C) is incomplete and inaccurate as to location of the violation; (D) is inaccurate as to where the summons was presented and residence of the violator.

64. **(C)** After step 2 comes step 3.

65. **(A)**

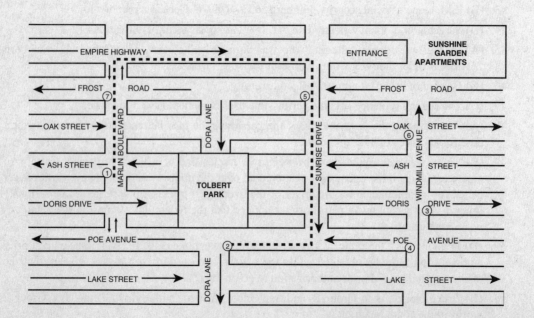

66. **(D)**

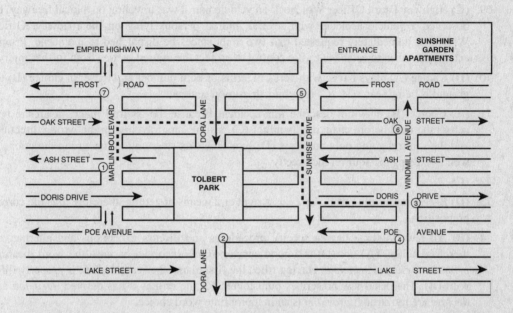

Choice (A) is incorrect because Poe Avenue is one-way westbound; (B) is impossible because Sunrise Drive and Dora Lane are parallel streets; (C) is incorrect because Frost Road is one-way westbound.

67. **(B)**

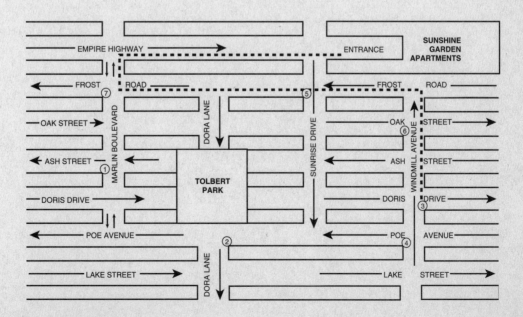

Choice (A) is incorrect because you cannot turn right from Frost Road onto Sunrise Drive without going the wrong way on a one-way street; (C) is incorrect because Windmill Avenue is one-way northbound; (D) is legal but is an unnecessarily long route.

68. **(B)** The eye patch makes for good identification because very few people wear them. The long, thin scar on the cheek would be highly visible as well. Points of identification must be distinctive or unusual, visible, and not readily subject to change.

69. **(C)** Highway Patrol Officer Wolchock on vehicle patrol was traveling on a local freeway. He observed a vehicle accident with several injured persons lying on the roadway. Officer Wolchock immediately requested that two ambulances be dispatched to the scene. Prompt action was taken to establish traffic control to protect the injured parties from further injury.

70. **(D)** Choice (A) plays havoc with verbs in terms of both number and tense; in choice (B) the ground is being searched; (C) is a childish, run-on sentence.

71. **(A)** Choice (B) does not describe this accident because the squirrel makes it all the way across the road before changing its mind; (C) has the cars traveling in the wrong directions and the squirrel going only one way; (D) sends the cars swerving in the wrong directions as well as placing the squirrel incorrectly.

72. **(C)**

73. **(D)** *Excess* means too much. *Access* is a right or a means of getting, therefore *to* is the correct preposition.

74. **(B)** All laws to some degree specify procedures and discuss exceptions and alternatives, therefore neither (A) nor (D) is a good answer. (C) is incorrect because the word meaning *primary* or *chief* is *principal*. Having filled the first blank, the second blank is properly filled with **(B).** The penal law prescribes punishment for the crimes it has defined. *Demand* and *declare* are too strong; *proclaim* is an inappropriate word choice.

75. **(D)** Obviously, if the person is arrested in the actual act of performing the crime, that person is clearly aware of the reason for the arrest and need not be informed.

Questions 76 through 84. Refer to the completed form.

REPORT OF ARREST

ARREST INFORMATION	(1) Date of arrest Aug. 14, 1996	(2) Time of arrest 10:45 P.M.	(3) Place of arrest in front of 72 Lenox St. Mt. Lawrence	(4) Station village hall Substation	(5) Arrest number 18431

DESCRIPTION OF INCIDENT

(6) Prisoner's weapon (description) Knife	(7) Date and time Aug. 14, 1996 10:30 P M

(8) Prisoner's auto (color, year, make, model, license plate number, state)
light blue, 2-door Toyota Corolla, 1991
New York X45-2CP

(9) Type of business Convenience store	(10) Location of incident (be specific) 26 Lenox Street Mount Lawrence

DESCRIPTION OF PRISONER

(11) Last name Bright	First name Peter	Middle initial NMI	(12) Date of birth April 15, 1969

(13) Sex M	(14) Race W	(15) Eyes brown	(16) Hair brown	(17) Weight 145 lb.	(18) Height 5'11"	(19) Age 27

(20) Address 72 Camptown Rd.	City Libertyville,	State NY	(21) Apt. no. 5	(22) Home phone number 841-9708

(23) Citizenship Citizen ☒ Non-Citizen ☐	(24) Place of birth Rochester, NY	(25) Marital status Single

(26) Social Security number 987-06-5432	(27) Where employed (company and address) Springwater Bottling Company 276 High Street, Libertyville, NY

(28) Nickname Fatso	(29) Scars, tattoos (describe fully and give location) Red and blue tattoo, head of Indian Chief, right forearm

DESCRIPTION OF COMPLAINANT

(30) Last name Nielsen	First name Barry	Middle initial NMI	(31) Date of birth June 17, 1957

Telephone Numbers		(34) Address	City	State
(32) Business 336-4234	(33) Home 336-6787	694 Judson Drive	Mount Lawrence, NY	

85. **(C)** According to the excerpt from the Penal Law, Officer Mahoney was indeed performing his duty when he was killed.

86. **(D)** Prior to writing the report, the officer should try to obtain a statement from the injured person or persons, that is, the officer should try to get the victim's version of the accident prior to preparing the report.

87. **(C)** This is a restatement of the last sentence.

88. **(A)** This answer is made clear in the next to the last sentence.

89. **(B)** Security staff are now checking packages being carried by employees into the state office building. This checking resulted in discovery and confiscation of a revolver on December 18. The suspect stated that he carried it to keep it away from his children. The weapon was turned over to state police officers for further investigation.

90. **(D)** Start with the first word. You can eliminate choice (B) immediately. Liking or not liking a witness should be irrelevant to an interview. At choice (A), the first word is possible, so you should look at the second. It makes no sense for the interviewer to proceed quickly if he or she is having trouble understanding the witness. (C) can be eliminated on two counts. For one, a witness is not an *it*. Proceeding cautiously in the face of disbelief would make sense if the sentence did not continue. However permitting the witness to know that his or her statements are being doubted does not lead to a fruitful interview. Read the sentence carefully, using the words from choice (D) to verify that **(D)** is indeed best.

91. **(B)** In light of Martha Goldstein's name, only (B) and (C) are correctly coded. The code at (C) gives '93 as a birth year. A person born in 1893 is most unlikely to still be driving; one born in 1993 cannot possibly be doing so.

92. **(A)** A person graduating from junior high school in 1950 would have been born in the middle 1930s. 1936 is a very reasonable birth year for John Jacobson.

93. **(C)** A 6 ft. 4 in. woman stands head and shoulders above the crowd.

94. **(C)** There are only two options for gender.

95. **(D)** A person born in the year '90, no matter which century, is unlikely to have a driver's license.

96. **(B)** This individual is 3 ft. 2 in. in height. He needs a specially equipped car, and his license must specify that he is restricted to driving a car especially designed for one his size.

97. **(D)** Both (A) and (B) are awkwardly stated. (C) is grammatical but verbose.

98. **(A)** Choice (B) is unclear as to the time frame in which the activity has gone on and may continue. (B) also involves the informant in enforcement; this is obviously irregular. (C) also neglects the ongoing nature of the activity and overstates the officer's current knowledge. (D) misidentifies John Doe.

99. **(B)**

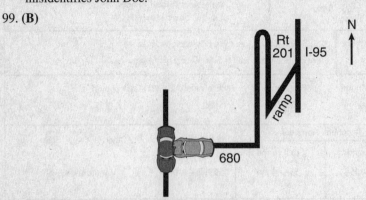

100. **(B)** 15% of 10 = 1.5; 15% of 10% = 1.5%

Answer Sheet for Model Examination 3

TEAR HERE

1. Ⓐ Ⓑ Ⓒ Ⓓ
2. Ⓐ Ⓑ Ⓒ Ⓓ
3. Ⓐ Ⓑ Ⓒ Ⓓ
4. Ⓐ Ⓑ Ⓒ Ⓓ
5. Ⓐ Ⓑ Ⓒ Ⓓ
6. Ⓐ Ⓑ Ⓒ Ⓓ
7. Ⓐ Ⓑ Ⓒ Ⓓ
8. Ⓐ Ⓑ Ⓒ Ⓓ
9. Ⓐ Ⓑ Ⓒ Ⓓ
10. Ⓐ Ⓑ Ⓒ Ⓓ
11. Ⓐ Ⓑ Ⓒ Ⓓ
12. Ⓐ Ⓑ Ⓒ Ⓓ
13. Ⓐ Ⓑ Ⓒ Ⓓ
14. Ⓐ Ⓑ Ⓒ Ⓓ
15. Ⓐ Ⓑ Ⓒ Ⓓ
16. Ⓐ Ⓑ Ⓒ Ⓓ
17. Ⓐ Ⓑ Ⓒ Ⓓ
18. Ⓐ Ⓑ Ⓒ Ⓓ
19. Ⓐ Ⓑ Ⓒ Ⓓ
20. Ⓐ Ⓑ Ⓒ Ⓓ

21. Ⓐ Ⓑ Ⓒ Ⓓ
22. Ⓐ Ⓑ Ⓒ Ⓓ
23. Ⓐ Ⓑ Ⓒ Ⓓ
24. Ⓐ Ⓑ Ⓒ Ⓓ
25. Ⓐ Ⓑ Ⓒ Ⓓ
26. Ⓐ Ⓑ Ⓒ Ⓓ
27. Ⓐ Ⓑ Ⓒ Ⓓ
28. Ⓐ Ⓑ Ⓒ Ⓓ
29. Ⓐ Ⓑ Ⓒ Ⓓ
30. Ⓐ Ⓑ Ⓒ Ⓓ
31. Ⓐ Ⓑ Ⓒ Ⓓ
32. Ⓐ Ⓑ Ⓒ Ⓓ
33. Ⓐ Ⓑ Ⓒ Ⓓ
34. Ⓐ Ⓑ Ⓒ Ⓓ
35. Ⓐ Ⓑ Ⓒ Ⓓ
36. Ⓐ Ⓑ Ⓒ Ⓓ
37. Ⓐ Ⓑ Ⓒ Ⓓ
38. Ⓐ Ⓑ Ⓒ Ⓓ
39. Ⓐ Ⓑ Ⓒ Ⓓ
40. Ⓐ Ⓑ Ⓒ Ⓓ

41. Ⓐ Ⓑ Ⓒ Ⓓ
42. Ⓐ Ⓑ Ⓒ Ⓓ
43. Ⓐ Ⓑ Ⓒ Ⓓ
44. Ⓐ Ⓑ Ⓒ Ⓓ
45. Ⓐ Ⓑ Ⓒ Ⓓ
46. Ⓐ Ⓑ Ⓒ Ⓓ
47. Ⓐ Ⓑ Ⓒ Ⓓ
48. Ⓐ Ⓑ Ⓒ Ⓓ
49. Ⓐ Ⓑ Ⓒ Ⓓ
50. Ⓐ Ⓑ Ⓒ Ⓓ
51. Ⓐ Ⓑ Ⓒ Ⓓ
52. Ⓐ Ⓑ Ⓒ Ⓓ
53. Ⓐ Ⓑ Ⓒ Ⓓ
54. Ⓐ Ⓑ Ⓒ Ⓓ
55. Ⓐ Ⓑ Ⓒ Ⓓ
56. Ⓐ Ⓑ Ⓒ Ⓓ
57. Ⓐ Ⓑ Ⓒ Ⓓ
58. Ⓐ Ⓑ Ⓒ Ⓓ
59. Ⓐ Ⓑ Ⓒ Ⓓ
60. Ⓐ Ⓑ Ⓒ Ⓓ

61. Ⓐ Ⓑ Ⓒ Ⓓ
62. Ⓐ Ⓑ Ⓒ Ⓓ
63. Ⓐ Ⓑ Ⓒ Ⓓ
64. Ⓐ Ⓑ Ⓒ Ⓓ
65. Ⓐ Ⓑ Ⓒ Ⓓ
66. Ⓐ Ⓑ Ⓒ Ⓓ
67. Ⓐ Ⓑ Ⓒ Ⓓ
68. Ⓐ Ⓑ Ⓒ Ⓓ
69. Ⓐ Ⓑ Ⓒ Ⓓ
70. Ⓐ Ⓑ Ⓒ Ⓓ
71. Ⓐ Ⓑ Ⓒ Ⓓ
72. Ⓐ Ⓑ Ⓒ Ⓓ
73. Ⓐ Ⓑ Ⓒ Ⓓ
74. Ⓐ Ⓑ Ⓒ Ⓓ
75. Ⓐ Ⓑ Ⓒ Ⓓ
76. Ⓐ Ⓑ Ⓒ Ⓓ
77. Ⓐ Ⓑ Ⓒ Ⓓ
78. Ⓐ Ⓑ Ⓒ Ⓓ
79. Ⓐ Ⓑ Ⓒ Ⓓ
80. Ⓐ Ⓑ Ⓒ Ⓓ

81. Ⓐ Ⓑ Ⓒ Ⓓ
82. Ⓐ Ⓑ Ⓒ Ⓓ
83. Ⓐ Ⓑ Ⓒ Ⓓ
84. Ⓐ Ⓑ Ⓒ Ⓓ
85. Ⓐ Ⓑ Ⓒ Ⓓ
86. Ⓐ Ⓑ Ⓒ Ⓓ
87. Ⓐ Ⓑ Ⓒ Ⓓ
88. Ⓐ Ⓑ Ⓒ Ⓓ
89. Ⓐ Ⓑ Ⓒ Ⓓ
90. Ⓐ Ⓑ Ⓒ Ⓓ
91. Ⓐ Ⓑ Ⓒ Ⓓ
92. Ⓐ Ⓑ Ⓒ Ⓓ
93. Ⓐ Ⓑ Ⓒ Ⓓ
94. Ⓐ Ⓑ Ⓒ Ⓓ
95. Ⓐ Ⓑ Ⓒ Ⓓ
96. Ⓐ Ⓑ Ⓒ Ⓓ
97. Ⓐ Ⓑ Ⓒ Ⓓ
98. Ⓐ Ⓑ Ⓒ Ⓓ
99. Ⓐ Ⓑ Ⓒ Ⓓ
100. Ⓐ Ⓑ Ⓒ Ⓓ

Model Examination 3

Time: 3½ Hours—100 Questions

Directions: Each question numbered 1 through 100 has four possible choices lettered A, B, C, and D. You are to select the answer that you deem to be correct.

1. Suppose that, while on patrol late at night, you find a woman lying in the road, apparently the victim of a hit-and-run driver. She seems to be injured seriously but you wish to ask her one or two questions in order to help locate the hit-and-run car. Of the following, the best question to ask is

    (A) In what direction did the car go?

    (B) What time did it happen?

    (C) What kind of car was it?

    (D) How many persons were in the car?

2. "Driver 1 claimed that the collision occurred because, as he approached the intersection, Driver 2 started to make a left turn suddenly and at high speed, even though the light had been red against him for 15 or 20 seconds." Suppose that you have been assigned to make a report on this accident. The position of the vehicles after the accident is indicated in the figure; the point in each case indicates the front of the vehicle. On the basis of this sketch, the best reason for concluding that Driver 1's statement is false is that

    (A) Driver 2's car is beyond the center of the intersection

    (B) Driver 2's car is making the turn on the proper side of the road

    (C) Driver 1's car is beyond the sidewalk line

    (D) Driver 1's car is on the right-hand side of the road

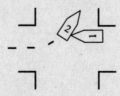

3. "If possible, the principal witnesses, especially the most trustworthy ones, should be heard before the suspect is interrogated." The most valid reason for this procedure is that

    (A) the investigator will tend to be more adequately informed when questioning the suspect

    (B) waiting to be questioned increases the pressure on the subject

    (C) trustworthy witnesses tend to become untrustworthy if kept waiting

    (D) all witnesses should be heard before the suspect

4. A state trooper must be observant of people he or she encounters while patrolling an assigned post. This attribute is most useful in law enforcement in the

    (A) detection and apprehension of criminals

    (B) fostering of good public relations

    (C) maintenance of a state of alertness in the state trooper

    (D) preparation of a state trooper for promotion

5. You are on your way to report for an assignment when you see two men fighting on the street. For you to attempt to stop the fight would be

    (A) unjustified; it is none of your business

    (B) justified; a fight between individuals may turn into a riot

    (C) unjustified; you may get hurt with the result that you will not be able to report for duty

    (D) justified; as a peace officer it is your duty to see that the public peace is kept

6. While patrolling your post you notice several people in two groups entering an old abandoned house by means of the rear entrance. The best action to take would be to

    (A) call headquarters notifying your superior of the occurrences

    (B) ignore the situation

    (C) enter the house, gun drawn

    (D) note the occurrence by an entry in your memorandum book

7. "On a dark background bloodstains are often difficult to recognize. When searching for bloodstains in such cases, one should use a flashlight, even in the daytime." Of the following, the best reason for this procedure is that

    (A) it is important to get as much light as possible

    (B) the contrast around the edges of the light is great

    (C) artificial light may make differentiation between the blood and the background possible

    (D) the movement of the flashlight will cause a moving reflection

8. Of the following kinds of wounds, the one in which there is the least danger of infection is

    (A) an abraded wound

    (B) a puncture wound

    (C) a lacerated wound

    (D) an incised wound

9. An injured person complaining about severe pains in his back should, pending arrival of medical assistance, be

   (A) moved to a more comfortable position

   (B) encouraged to lie perfectly still

   (C) put in a standing position

   (D) seated in a straight-back chair

10. One of the following deserves your primary attention when administering first aid to an injured person pending arrival of medical assistance. It is

    (A) a broken arm

    (B) severe bleeding

    (C) an irregular heartbeat

    (D) a state of hysteria

11. The statement made by a prisoner and correctly called an alibi is

    (A) "He struck me first."

    (B) "I didn't intend to hurt him."

    (C) "I was miles away from there at the time."

    (D) "I don't remember what happened."

12. A person who, after the commission of a crime, conceals the offender with the intent that the latter may escape from arrest and trial, is called

    (A) an accessory

    (B) an accomplice

    (C) a confederate

    (D) an associate

13. A sworn statement of fact is called

    (A) an affidavit

    (B) an oath

    (C) an acknowledgment

    (D) a subpoena

14. Among the following, the signature cards of a bank might be employed as a means of verifying an individual's

    (A) character

    (B) identity

    (C) financial status

    (D) employment

15. An accomplice is

(A) one who, after full knowledge that a felony has been committed, conceals same from law officers

(B) one who is liable to prosecution for the same offense with which the defendant on trial has been charged

(C) one who harbors a person charged with or convicted of a felony

(D) a person who has knowledge of a given act

In answering questions 16 through 22, make use of the following statement: "A description of persons or property wanted by this department which is to be given to the police force through the medium of a general alarm, if not distinctive, is of no value."

16. You are watching a great number of people leave a ball game. Of the persons who are described below the one whom it would be easiest to spot would be

(A) female; age 15; height 5'6"; weight 130 lbs.; long straight black hair

(B) female; age 35; height 5'4"; weight 150 lbs.; wears glasses

(C) male; age 60; height 5'7"; weight 170 lbs.; all false teeth

(D) male; age 25; height 6'3"; weight 220 lbs.; pockmarked

17. You are preparing a woman's description to be broadcast. Of the following characteristics, the one that would be of most value to the driver of a squad car is

(A) frequents movie theaters

(B) age 45 years

(C) height 6'1"

(D) smokes very heavily

18. Under the portrait parle system of identification, of the following the most important part of a description of a person is the

(A) dress, since it is the most noticeable

(B) ears, since no two are alike

(C) eyes, since they cannot be altered

(D) nose, since it is most distinctive

19. Assume that on a hot summer day you are stationed on the grass at the south bank of a busy parkway looking at eastbound traffic for a light blue Ford two-door sedan. If traffic is very heavy, the one of the following additional pieces of information that would be most helpful to you in identifying the car is that

(A) all chrome is missing from the left side of the car

(B) there is a bullet hole in the left front window

(C) the paint on the right side of the car is somewhat faded

(D) the front bumper is missing

20. Assume that you have stopped a Dodge four-door sedan that you suspect is a car that was reported as stolen the day before. The one of the following items of information that would be of greatest value in determining whether this is the stolen car is that

(A) the stolen car's license plate number was QA2356; this car's license number is U21375

(B) the stolen car's engine number was AB6231; this car's engine number is CS2315

(C) the windshield of the stolen car was not cracked; this car's windshield is cracked

(D) the stolen car had no dents; this car has numerous dents

21. You are watching a great number of people leave a sports arena after a boxing match. Of the characteristics listed below, the one that would be of greatest value to you in spotting a man wanted by the department is

(A) Height 5'3"; Weight 200 lbs.

(B) Eyes: brown; Hair: black, wavy; Complexion: sallow

(C) Mustache: when last seen in August, he wore a small black mustache

(D) Scars: thin 1/2" scar on left upper lip; Tattoos: on right forearm—"Pinto"

22. The only personal description the police have of a particular criminal was made several years ago. Of the following, the item in the description that will be most useful in identifying him at the present time is the

(A) color of his eyes

(B) color of his hair

(C) number of teeth

(D) weight

23. "Photographs of suspected persons should not be shown to a witness if the criminal himself can be arrested and placed on view for identification." The above recommendation is

(A) inadvisable; this procedure might subject the witness to future retribution by suspect

(B) advisable; a photograph cannot be used for identification purposes with the same degree of certainty as the suspect in person

(C) inadvisable; the appearance of the subject may have changed since the commission of the crime

(D) advisable; photography as an art has not achieved an acceptable degree of perfection

24. Stationed at a busy highway, you are given the description of a vehicle that has been stolen. Of the following characteristics, the one that will permit you to eliminate most easily a large number of vehicles is

(A) no spare tire

(B) make-Buick, two-door sedan

(C) color-black

(D) tires 750 × 16, white walled

25. If a sick or injured woman, to whom a male trooper is rendering aid, is unknown and the trooper has reason to believe that her clothing contains a means of identification, the trooper should

   (A) immediately search the clothing for such identification and remove any identification found therein

   (B) send for a female trooper to search the clothing for such identification

   (C) ask any female present to search the clothing for such identification

   (D) accompany her to the hospital and there seek the necessary information from hospital authorities

26. Which of the following means of avoiding identification would be most likely to meet with success?

   (A) Growing a beard

   (B) Shaving off the beard if there was one originally

   (C) Burning the fingers so as to remove the fingerprints

   (D) Changing the features by facial surgery

27. In asking a witness to a crime to identify a suspect, it is common practice to place the suspect with a group of persons and ask the witness to pick out the person in question. Of the following, the best reason for this practice is that it will

   (A) make the identification more reliable than if the witness were shown the suspect alone

   (B) protect the witness against reprisals

   (C) make sure that the witness is telling the truth

   (D) help select other participants in the crime at the same time

28. "Social security cards are not acceptable proof of identification for police purposes." Of the following, the most important reason for this rule is that the social security card

   (A) is easily obtained

   (B) states on in its face "for social security purposes—not for identification"

   (C) is frequently lost

   (D) does not contain a photograph, description, or fingerprints of the person

29. Of the following facts about a criminal the one that would be of most value in apprehending and identifying the criminal would be that he

   (A) drives a black Chevrolet sedan with chrome license plate holders

   (B) invariably uses a .38 caliber Colt blue steel revolver with walnut stock and regulation front sight

   (C) talks with a French accent and frequently stutters

   (D) usually wears three-button single-breasted "Ivy League" suits and white oxford cloth button-down collar shirts.

30. The investigator is tracing a fugitive suspect. Which of the following means of identification is the suspect least able to suppress?

(A) He suffers from spastic paralysis.

(B) His picture is available for identification.

(C) He is an habitual frequenter of a certain type of restaurant.

(D) He is a rabid baseball fan.

31. The least accurate characterization of crime is that it

(A) consists of an overt act and, in most cases, of a culpable intent

(B) is an act prohibited by a group with the power to enforce observation

(C) may be either an act of omission or commission

(D) is an act that, generally of an illegal nature, is quite possibly legal in its essence

32. The most effective method of crime prevention is in general

(A) severe punishment of malefactors

(B) probation

(C) psychiatric examination of offenders

(D) eradication of casual factors

33. Of the following, the one that is reason for believing prevention of criminal behavior to be superior to the cure of criminals as a method for handling crime problems is that with the adoption of prevention programs it is most probable that

(A) less money will be spent on jails and prisons

(B) more money will be spent on preventive programs

(C) the "born" criminal will exhibit criminal behavior anyway

(D) less money will have to be spent on such matters as recreational programs, housing, and the like

34. If it is assumed that all criminals believe in no legal restraints, then

(A) all persons who are not criminals believe in legal restraint

(B) any person who believes in no legal restraints is a criminal

(C) any person who does not believe in no legal restraints is not a criminal

(D) there would be no criminals if there were no legal restraints

35. "It is an undeniable fact that people are not born criminals." Of the following, the chief implication of the above statement is that

(A) the youth who is a juvenile delinquent becomes the adult who violates the law

(B) violations of the law are usually due to a combination of environmental factors

(C) most crimes are committed by adults

(D) criminals are not easily detected

Use the cross compass below to answer questions 36 through 40.

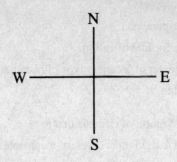

36. A state trooper driving east makes a left turn and then a right turn. He would thereafter be traveling
    (A) north
    (B) east
    (C) south
    (D) west

37. A state trooper driving north makes a left turn and then a second left turn. He would thereafter be traveling
    (A) north
    (B) east
    (C) south
    (D) west

38. A state trooper driving west makes a right turn and then a left turn. He would thereafter be traveling
    (A) north
    (B) east
    (C) south
    (D) west

39. A state trooper driving north crosses from a highway right onto a dirt road across a field traveling diagonally. He would be traveling
    (A) north by northeast
    (B) north by northwest
    (C) west by southwest
    (D) east by northeast

40. A state trooper traveling west on a limited access highway makes a right-hand exit at a "cloverleaf" intersection and heads down the exit ramp to a lower roadway crossing underneath the highway. If she continues in the same direction without crossing the lower roadway, she would be traveling

(A) north

(B) south

(C) east

(D) west

Answer questions 41 through 45 on the basis of the passage below and the Accident Report form shown on next page.

At approximately 5:00 P.M. on a foggy, rainy afternoon, Trooper Ressa arrived at the scene of an accident a few minutes after it occurred. On the basis of his observations, and from the statements of the persons involved in the accident, he decided that the accident happened this way: Mr. Goldsmith was driving his car east on Tenth Street. Tenth is a straight, one-way street that runs downhill as one goes from west to east. At the intersection of Tenth Street and Pacific Highway, Mr. Goldsmith came to a full stop for a red light. When the light turned green, he started downhill and immediately struck Mr. Bates, a forty-three-year-old high school teacher who was jogging north on Pacific. Mr. Bates was not seriously injured and admitted that he had been careless in crossing the intersection.

Trooper Ressa filled out an Accident Report form, similar to that which is shown on page 154.

41. Under the section, *Vehicle in Collision With,* Officer Ressa should have checked the box for

    (A) Pedestrian

    (B) Other Vehicle

    (C) Fixed Object

    (D) Other

42. The box that he should have checked under *Type of Traffic Control* is

    (A) Flashing Light

    (B) Other

    (C) Signal Light in Operation

    (D) Stop Sign

43. Under *Character of Road,* Officer Ressa should have checked the box for

    (A) Curve Approaching Hilltop

    (B) Straight Approaching Hilltop

    (C) Straight on Hill

    (D) Curve on Hill

44. The box that he should have checked under *Action of Pedestrian at Intersection* is

    (A) Crossing Against Signal

    (B) Crossing, No Signal

    (C) Crossing With Signal

    (D) Crossing Diagonally

ACCIDENT REPORT

Date_____   Time_____   Location of Accident_____

Vehicle in Collision With

☐ Pedestrian   ☐ Motorcycle
☐ Other Vehicle   ☐ Fixed Object
☐ Train   ☐ Bicycle
☐ Animal   ☐ Other

Type of Traffic Control

☐ Police Officer   ☐ Stop Sign
☐ Signal Light in Operation   ☐ Yield Sign
☐ Signal Light Not in Operation ☐ Other
☐ Flashing Light   ☐ None

Character of Road

☐ Straight and Level   ☐ Curve and Level
☐ Straight On Hill   ☐ Curve On Hill
☐ Straight Approaching Hilltop ☐ Curve Approaching Hilltop

Action of Pedestrian at Intersection

☐ Crossing With Signal   ☐ Crossing Diagonally
☐ Crossing Against Signal   ☐ Crossing, No Signal

Action of Vehicle at Time of Accident

☐ Going Straight Ahead   ☐ Making U-Turn
☐ Overtaking   ☐ Backing Up
☐ Making Right Turn   ☐ Starting from Parking
☐ Making Left Turn   ☐ Slowing or Stopping
☐ Parked

45. He should have checked which box under *Action of Vehicle at Time of Accident?*

(A) Starting from Parking

(B) Slowing or Stopping

(C) Going Straight Ahead

(D) Overtaking

46. During the year when July 4th falls on a Monday, the first day of June would have fallen on

(A) Tuesday

(B) Wednesday

(C) Thursday

(D) Friday

47. A state trooper, before testifying in court, notes from his memo book that he made an arrest on April 15. If he were asked to testify in court as to the day of the week that the arrest took place he could do so by

(A) determining the number of days from Good Friday

(B) determining the number of days from the second Wednesday of the month

(C) counting back from his last payday

(D) determining the day that the month began

48. If the last of November occurs on a Wednesday, November 1st will have fallen on

(A) Monday

(B) Tuesday

(C) Thursday

(D) Saturday

49. During 1987, the one of the following months that could not have contained five Mondays was

(A) January

(B) February

(C) March

(D) April

50. A state trooper, while completing his report of an altercation between two motorists, should know that during a year when the first of May falls on a Friday, the incident, which occurred on April 15, happened on

(A) Monday

(B) Tuesday

(C) Wednesday

(D) Thursday

51. A Highway Patrol car follows for 25 miles a car driven by a suspect in a crime. The suspect then veers off the road and hides. The patrol car passes the hiding place and goes 7 miles further in pursuit before the troopers realize their quarry has eluded them. They then turn around and retrace their route until the 25-mile intersection. According to this story, the troopers have traveled

    (A) 39 miles and the suspect 25 miles

    (B) 25 miles and the suspect 39 miles

    (C) 25 miles and the suspect 25 miles

    (D) 32 miles and the suspect 25 miles

52. On a road map the scale of miles reads 1 inch = 50 miles. In order to find the mileage between two towns that are three inches apart on this map and to allow for a return trip the trooper would have to

    (A) multiply by 3

    (B) multiply by 50 and then double the mileage

    (C) multiply by 3 and divide by 2

    (D) measure off the distance in inches, divide by 3, and multiply by 2

53. A Highway Patrol car travels 60 miles per hour for 10 minutes and then decreases its speed to 40 miles per hour for the next 30 minutes. How many miles would the patrol car have traveled?

    (A) 10 miles

    (B) 20 miles

    (C) 30 miles

    (D) 40 miles

54. Having chased a suspect's car for 20 minutes at 75 miles per hour, a Highway Patrol car increases its speed to 90 mph for 10 minutes. How many miles has the patrol car given chase?

    (A) 15 miles

    (B) 25 miles

    (C) 40 miles

    (D) 55 miles

55. A state trooper approaches an intersection and follows the directional signs "right turn to Cobblestone" for 20 miles. He then turns right again and drives for 30 miles. At this point he stops, studies his map and then decides to return to his original starting point. Upon his return he will have traveled

    (A) 50 miles

    (B) 100 miles

    (C) 70 miles

    (D) 80 miles

56. A state trooper is on patrol on a four-lane divided highway during a rainstorm. He approaches a bridge over a creek and discovers that the eastbound portion has broken off and fallen into the creek. The creek is swollen, the water level is very high, and the current is swift. Of the following, the first action the trooper should take is to

(A) stop traffic in both directions of the highway

(B) radio his supervisor to report this condition and to ask for help

(C) go down to the creek to examine conditions closely

(D) call the nearest local sheriff

57. A four-lane divided highway is intersected by a two-lane road. The standard red-yellow-green signal lights are at this intersection. A left turn is permitted from the center lane on the yellow signal light. If the car turns left on a green signal this action would be

(A) correct, if no traffic is coming from the other direction

(B) incorrect, since the yellow signal is not showing

(C) correct, since there is no danger involved

(D) incorrect, since left turns at this kind of intersection are always hazardous

58. A state trooper is patrolling a divided highway and drives on one part where the lights are out. The only illumination is moonlight. Upon driving through this part, he reports the conditions to his superior. He is advised that the lights cannot be turned on for the next few hours due to a local power failure. This condition is best described as

(A) hazardous; oncoming traffic may have bright headlights that are momentarily blinding

(B) not hazardous; moonlight is sufficient for driving on the highway

(C) very hazardous; highway lighting is essential for night driving

(D) somewhat hazardous; lighting from car headlights is generally sufficient for night driving

59. In lonely, uninhabited stretches of road the trooper may come upon a motorist with a disabled car. Either a flat tire or a dead battery are the most frequent causes of such disabled cars. Upon observing the situation described above, the first action for the trooper to take is to

(A) use his radio to report the occurrence and ask for assistance but continue on patrol

(B) stop to help the motorist in trouble

(C) stop only to help change a tire but not to diagnose mechanical difficulties

(D) place a white cloth on the radio antenna of the disabled car and stand there in case another motorist drives by to avoid accidents

60. Large volumes of traffic at major highway intersections, particularly after dawn and sunset, are major causes of highway congestion and lead to accidents. A state trooper assigned to highway patrol in areas including such intersections should

(A) maintain surveillance of such intersections during periods of heavy traffic

(B) avoid such intersections so as not to get caught in traffic and prevent continued patrol duties of the rest of the route

(C) approach such intersections only when assistance is requested by a motorist

(D) none of the above

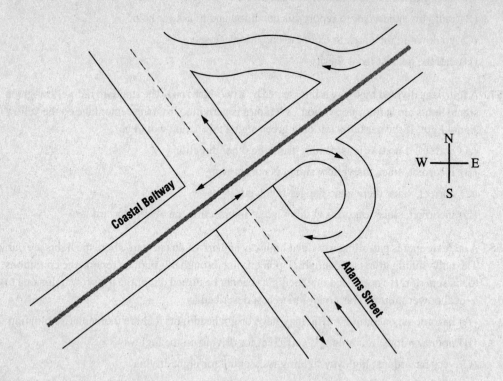

The above map for questions 61 through 63 illustrates two exit ramps from Coastal Beltway, a median divided highway on to Adams Street, a local street.

61. A car traveling southwest on the Coastal Beltway exits to Adams Street. It can then proceed only

  (A) northwest

  (B) southeast

  (C) northeast

  (D) southwest

62. A car traveling northeast on the Coastal Beltway exits to Adams Street. It can then proceed only

  (A) northwest

  (B) southeast

  (C) northeast

  (D) southwest

63. A car traveling northwest on Adams Street desires to enter Coastal Beltway. The one of the following that is correct is that

  (A) the car can enter traveling northeast

  (B) it can make a U-turn and enter the Coastal Beltway

  (C) the car cannot enter the Coastal Beltway at this junction

  (D) it can exit Adams Street by traveling southeast

In the diagrams for questions 64 and 65, symbols are used to represent vehicles and pedestrians and their movements.

- Vehicles are shown by the symbol: front ◁▭ rear.
- Pedestrians are represented by a circle: ○
- Solid lines show the path and direction of a vehicle or person *before* an accident happened:
  ────▶
- Dotted lines show the path and direction of a vehicle *after* an accident happened:
  ── ── ──▶

64. Mrs. Wagner was walking across the intersection of Elm Street and Willow Avenue when she was struck by a car approaching from her right. After hitting Mrs. Wagner, the car swerved left and ran into a tree. Which of the four diagrams below best represents the accident described?

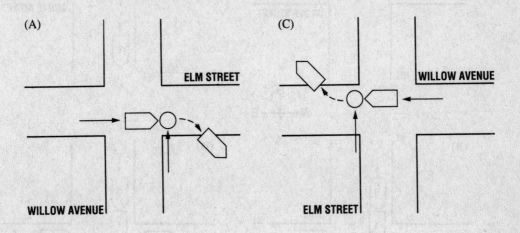

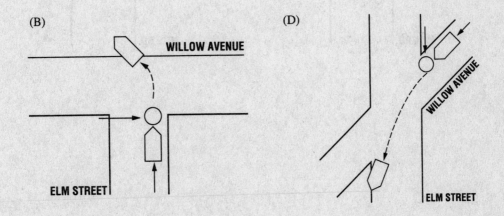

65. An automobile accident occurred at the intersection of Mill Road and Grove Street. Cars #1 and #3 were proceeding south on Mill Road and Car #2 was proceeding west on Grove Street. When Car #1 stopped quickly to avoid hitting Car #2, it was immediately struck from behind by Car #3. Car #2 continued west on Grove Street without stopping. Which of the four diagrams below best represents the accident described?

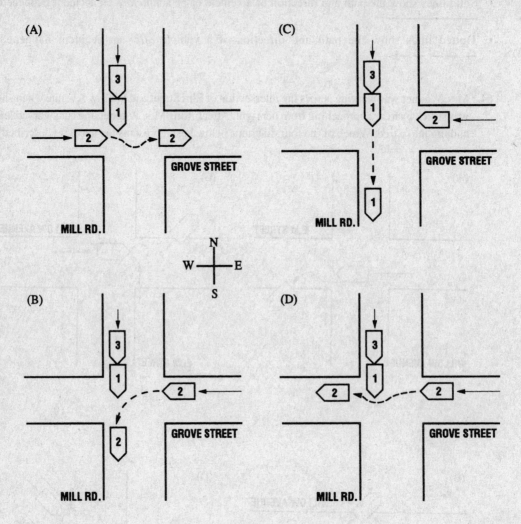

Report of stolen vehicles
October 30, 1996

Car#	Year	Make	Model	Color	Engine Identification #
1	1994	Oldsmobile	4d Sd	Gray	1G3AJ19E4EG318532
2	1988	Ford	2d Cp	Blue	5X4B021C4CT463431
3	1995	BMW	4d Sd	Olive Green	2C3TW15H5BF524352
4	1991	Chevrolet	2d Sd	White	3B4DL12F3HI256734
5	1984	Plymouth	4d Cp	Brown	2D7HT37G4KM837591
6	1988	Ford	2d Sd	Gray	5E2CK45J2LO721845
7	1985	Chrysler	4d Sd	Gray	7J5LN08T5DN643721
8	1996	Toyota	2d Cp	Red	4K8ET15A1NS297127
9	1992	Mazda	2d Cp	Blue	7L4FX54B6TW934235
10	1986	Volkswagen	4d Sd	Black	1F4MP76LFJ63251

Answer the following questions according to the above chart.

66. Which one of the following cars has an engine identification number that ends with "45"?

(A) Car 1

(B) Car 3

(C) Car 6

(D) Car 8

67. Which one of the following cars has an engine identification number containing the integer "21"?

(A) Car 2

(B) Car 5

(C) Car 8

(D) Car 9

68. Which one of the following cars has an engine identification number with the letter combination "FX"?

(A) Car 3

(B) Car 4

(C) Car 6

(D) Car 9

69. Describe the make and model of the car with an engine identification number beginning with "4K8ET."

(A) 1986 Toyota 2d Cp Red

(B) 1977 Chrysler 4d Blue

(C) 1977 Ford 2d Sd Gray

(D) 1981 Chevrolet 2d Sd White

70. The number of cars stolen that were made in the period 1988–92 is

(A) 1

(B) 2

(C) 3

(D) 4

71. Engine identification numbers in this chart are composed of

(A) 8 numbers and 9 letters

(B) 11 numbers and 6 letters

(C) 6 numbers and 9 letters

(D) 12 numbers and 4 letters

72. Which of the following cars has an engine identification number that ends with "721"?

(A) Car 2

(B) Car 5

(C) Car 7

(D) Car 9

73. Which of the following cars has an engine identification number containing the letter combination "DN"?

(A) Car 1

(B) Car 3

(C) Car 6

(D) Car 7

74. Which of the following cars has an engine identification number containing the combination "HT37"?

(A) Car 1

(B) Car 3

(C) Car 5

(D) Car 7

75. Which of the following cars has an engine identification number containing the integer "15"?

(A) Car 1

(B) Car 3

(C) Car 5

(D) Car 7

Directions: Each selection is followed by a number of questions based upon the information given in the selection. Read the selection carefully; then read each question carefully before marking your answer.

Selection for questions 76 through 79.

A summons is an official statement ordering a person to appear in court. In traffic violation situations, summonses are used when arrests need not be made. The main reason for traffic summonses is to deter motorists from repeating the same traffic violation. Occasionally motorists may make unintentional driving errors and sometimes they are unaware of the correct driving regulation. In cases such as these, the policy is to have the officer verbally inform the motorist of the violation and warn him or her against repeating it. The purpose of this practice is not to limit the number of summonses, but rather to prevent the issuing of summonses when the violation is not due to deliberate intent or to inexcusable negligence.

76. According to the preceding passage, the principal reason for issuing traffic summonses is to

    (A) discourage motorists from violating these laws again

    (B) increase the money collected by the city

    (C) put traffic violators in prison

    (D) have them serve as substitutes for police officers

77. The reason a verbal warning may sometimes be substituted for a summons is to

    (A) limit the number of summonses

    (B) distinguish between excusable and inexcusable violations

    (C) provide harsher penalties for deliberate intent than for inexcusable negligence

    (D) decrease the caseload in the courts

78. The author of the preceding passage feels that someone who violated a traffic regulation because he or she did *not* know about the regulation should be

    (A) put under arrest

    (B) fined less money

    (C) given a summons

    (D) told not to do it again

79. Using the distinctions made by the author of the preceding passage, the one of the following motorists to whom it would be most desirable to issue a summons is the one who exceeded the speed limit because he or she

    (A) did not know the speed limit

    (B) was late for an important business appointment

    (C) speeded to avoid being hit by another car

    (D) had a speedometer that was not working properly

Selection for questions 80 and 81.

All members of the police force must recognize that the people, through their representatives, hire and pay the police and that, as in any other employment, a proper employer-employee relationship must exist. Police officers must understand that the essence of a correct police attitude is a willingness to serve, but at the same time they should distinguish between service and servility, between courtesy and softness. They must be firm but also courteous, avoiding even an appearance of rudeness. They should develop a position that is friendly and unbiased, pleasant and sympathetic in their relations with the general public, but firm and impersonal on occasions calling for regulation and control. Police officers should understand that their primary purpose is to prevent violations, not to arrest people. They should recognize the line of demarcation between a police function and passing judgment, which is a court function. On the other side, a public that cooperates with the police, that supports them in their efforts, and that observes laws and regulations may be said to have a desirable attitude.

80. In accordance with this paragraph, the proper attitude for a police officer to take is

    (A) to be pleasant and sympathetic at all times

    (B) to be friendly, firm, and impartial

    (C) to be stern and severe in meting out justice to all

    (D) to avoid being rude, except in cases where the public is uncooperative

81. Assume that an officer is assigned by his superior officer to a busy traffic intersection and is warned to be on the lookout for motorists who skip the light or who are speeding. According to this paragraph, it would be proper for the officer in this assignment to

    (A) give a summons to every motorist whose car was crossing when the light changed

    (B) hide behind a truck and wait for drivers who violate traffic laws

    (C) select at random motorists who seem to be impatient and lecture them sternly on traffic safety

    (D) stand on post in order to deter violations and give offenders a summons or a warning as required

Selection for questions 82 and 83.

Proper firearms training is one phase of law enforcement that cannot be ignored. No part of the training of a police officer is more important or more valuable. The officer's life and often the lives of his fellow officers depend directly upon his skill with the weapon he is carrying. Proficiency with the revolver is not attained exclusively by the volume of ammunition used and the number of hours spent on the firing line. Supervised practice and the use of training aids and techniques help make a proficient shooter. It is essential to have a good firing range where new officers are trained and older personnel practice in scheduled firearms sessions. The fundamental points to be stressed are grip, stance, breathing, sight alignment, and trigger squeeze. Coordination of thought, vision, and motion must be achieved before the officer gains confidence in his shooting ability. Attaining this ability will make the student a better officer and enhance his value to the force.

82. A police officer will gain confidence in his shooting ability only after he has

    (A) spent the required number of hours on the firing line

    (B) been given sufficient supervised practice

    (C) learned the five fundamental points

    (D) learned to coordinate revolver movement with his sight and thought

83. Proper training in the use of firearms is one aspect of law enforcement that must be given serious consideration chiefly because it is the

   (A) most useful and essential single factor in the training of a police officer

   (B) one phase of police officer training that stresses mental and physical coordination

   (C) costliest aspect of police officer training, involving considerable expense for the ammunition used in target practice

   (D) most difficult part of police officer training, involving the expenditure of many hours on the firing line

Selection for questions 84 through 87.

Because of the importance of preserving physical evidence, the officer should not enter a scene of a crime if it can be examined visually from one position and if no other pressing duty requires his presence there. There are some responsibilities, however, that take precedence over preservation of evidence. Some examples are as follows: rescue work, disarming dangerous persons, and quelling a disturbance. The officer should learn how to accomplish these more visual tasks while at the same preserving as much evidence as possible. If he finds it necessary to enter upon the scene, he should quickly study the place of entry to learn if any evidence will suffer by his contact; then he should determine the routes to use in walking to the spot where his presence is required. Every place where a foot will fall or where a hand or other part of his body will touch should be examined with the eye. Objects should not be touched or moved unless there is a definite and compelling reason. For identification of most items of physical evidence at the initial investigation it is seldom necessary to touch or move them.

84. The one of the following titles that is the most appropriate for the above paragraph is

   (A) "Determining the Order of Tasks at the Scene of a Crime"

   (B) "The Principal Reasons for Preserving Evidence at the Scene of a Crime"

   (C) "Precautions to Take at the Scene of a Crime"

   (D) "Evidence to be Examined at the Scene of a Crime"

85. When an officer feels that it is essential for him to enter the immediate area where a crime has been committed, he should

   (A) quickly but carefully glance around to determine whether his entering the area will damage any evidence present

   (B) remove all objects of evidence from his predetermined route in order to avoid stepping on them

   (C) carefully replace any object immediately if it is moved or touched by his hands or any other part of his body

   (D) use only the usual place of entry to the scene in order to avoid disturbing any possible clues left on rear doors and windows

86. The one of the following that is the *least* urgent duty of an officer who has just reported to the scene of a crime is to

(A) disarm the hysterical victim of the crime who is wildly waving a loaded gun in all directions

(B) give first aid to a possible suspect who has been injured while attempting to leave the scene of the crime

(C) prevent observers from attacking and injuring the persons suspected of having committed the crime

(D) preserve from damage or destruction any evidence necessary for the proper prosecution of the case against the criminals

87. An officer has just reported to the scene of a crime in response to a phone call. The best of the following actions for him to take with respect to objects of physical evidence present at the scene is to

(A) make no attempt to enter the crime scene if his entry will disturb any vital physical evidence

(B) map out the shortest straight path to follow in walking to the spot where the most physical evidence may be found

(C) move such objects of physical evidence as are necessary to enable him to assist the wounded victim of the crime

(D) quickly examine all objects of physical evidence in order to determine which objects may be touched and which may not

Selection for questions 88 through 91.

Our system of criminal justice fails to reduce crime. If police, courts, and prisons functioned at the most effective level possible, they would not substantially or permanently reduce crime while conditions that breed crime persist. Mere words of prohibition, with force and the threat of force their only sanction, cannot shape human conduct in mass society.

As turbulence, doubt, and anxiety cause fear to increase, fear in turn seeks repression as a source of safety. But the result of repression is more turbulence and more crime. In frustration over the failure of law enforcement to control crime, new, quick, and cheap methods by which police and courts and prisons might be made effective are sought amid desperate hope and rising hatred. A public that believes the police alone are responsible for crime control, and therefore no other effort is needed, will vest any power in the police force that promises safety where fear of crime is great. But there is no such power.

Excessive reliance on the criminal justice system is extremely dangerous because it separates the people from the government. It is the one clear avenue to irreconcilable division in America. It puts government institutions in which people must have confidence in direct confrontation with dynamics they cannot control. When the system is abusive, society itself is unfair; government demeans human dignity. There then follows a contest of cunning between the people and the state that the state can never win.

88. The one of the following titles that most nearly expresses the main thought of this passage is

(A) "The Need for Additional Police Power"

(B) "Frustrated Law Enforcement"

(C) "Police, Courts, and Prisons—A Balancing of Power"

(D) "The Problem of Crime Control"

89. Based solely on this passage, which of the following statements is most correct?

    (A) Increasing fear is a direct result of repression.

    (B) Repression is a direct result of increasing turbulence and crime.

    (C) Turbulence, doubt, and anxiety are a direct cause of more crime.

    (D) Repression is both a result of increasing fear and a cause of greater turbulence.

90. According to this passage, the desire for improvements in the system of criminal justice in response to increasing crime

    (A) stems largely from a failure to appreciate the actual cost of crime to the community

    (B) is not likely to result in greater safety for the public

    (C) will result in a lack of confidence in the police

    (D) is caused by the resentment that is felt by certain groups in our society

91. When the author of this passage states that excessive reliance on the system of criminal justice is dangerous, he or she implies that

    (A) citizens will not accept restraints imposed by the police

    (B) division in America is a result of undue emphasis upon the rights of the individual

    (C) government institutions would be asked to perform an impossible task

    (D) police cause distrust by their failure to enforce the law diligently

Directions: Each problem in this section involves a certain amount of logical reasoning and thinking on your part, along with the usual simple computations. Read each problem carefully and choose the correct answer from the four choices that follow.

92. If the average cost of sweeping a square foot of a city street is $7.50, the cost of sweeping 100 square feet is

    (A) $75.00

    (B) $7,500.00

    (C) $750.00

    (D) $700.00

93. If a Sanitation Department scow is towed at the rate of three miles an hour, it will need how many hours to go 28 miles?

    (A) 10 hrs. 30 mins.

    (B) 12 hrs.

    (C) 9 hrs. 20 min.

    (D) 9 hrs. 15 min.

94. If a truck is 60 feet away from a sanitation worker, it is how many feet nearer to him than a truck which is 100 feet away?

    (A) 60 ft.

    (B) 40 ft.

    (C) 50 ft.

    (D) 20 ft.

95. A clerk divided his 35-hour workweek as follows: 1/5 of his time in sorting mail; 1/2 of his time in filing letters; and 1/7 of his time in reception work. The rest of his time was devoted to messenger work. The percentage of time spent on messenger work by the clerk during the week was most nearly

    (A) 6%

    (B) 10%

    (C) 14%

    (D) 16%

96. Twelve clerks are assigned to enter certain data on index cards. This number of clerks could perform the task in 18 days. After these clerks have worked on this assignment for 6 days, 4 more clerks are added to the staff to do this work. Assuming that all the clerks work at the same rate of speed, the entire task, instead of taking 18 days, will be performed in

    (A) 9 days

    (B) 12 days

    (C) 17 days

    (D) 15 days

97. Six gross of special pencils were purchased for use in a city department. If the pencils were used at the rate of 24 a week, the maximum number of weeks that the six gross of pencils would last is

    (A) 6 weeks

    (B) 12 weeks

    (C) 24 weeks

    (D) 36 weeks

98. A man worked 30 days. He paid 2/5 of his earnings for room and board, then had $1,440. What was his daily wage?

    (A) $95.00

    (B) $80.00

    (C) $85.00

    (D) $110.00

99. After gaining 50% on his original capital, a man had capital of $18,000. Find the original capital.

    (A) $12,200.00

    (B) $13,100.00

    (C) $12,000.00

    (D) $12,025.00

100. A cog wheel having 8 cogs plays into another cog wheel having 24 cogs. When the small wheel has made 42 revolutions, how many has the larger wheel made?

(A) 14

(B) 20

(C) 16

(D) 10

ANSWER KEY

1. C	21. A	41. A	61. A	81. D
2. C	22. A	42. C	62. A	82. D
3. A	23. B	43. C	63. C	83. A
4. A	24. C	44. A	64. B	84. C
5. D	25. D	45. C	65. D	85. A
6. A	26. D	46. B	66. C	86. D
7. C	27. A	47. D	67. A	87. C
8. D	28. D	48. B	68. D	88. D
9. B	29. C	49. B	69. A	89. D
10. B	30. A	50. C	70. C	90. B
11. C	31. D	51. A	71. B	91. C
12. A	32. D	52. B	72. C	92. C
13. A	33. A	53. C	73. D	93. C
14. B	34. C	54. C	74. C	94. B
15. A	35. B	55. B	75. B	95. D
16. D	36. B	56. B	76. A	96. D
17. C	37. C	57. A	77. B	97. D
18. B	38. D	58. D	78. D	98. B
19. D	39. A	59. A	79. B	99. C
20. B	40. B	60. A	80. B	100. A

EXPLANATORY ANSWERS

1. **(C)** This response to the question would be most useful in locating the vehicle.

2. **(C)** Self-explanatory in the illustration.

3. **(A)** The information supplied by the witnesses would form the basis for the main part of the interrogation.

4. **(A)** This ability will enable troopers to apprehend wanted criminals they may encounter while on patrol.

5. **(D)** A state trooper is always on duty, even on off-hours. If the trooper encounters an incident that is in violation of a law or is a disturbance of the peace, he or she should intercede just as if the incident were taking place while the trooper was on active duty.

6. **(A)** This is a suspicious incident worthy of your attention. But since there are several people involved, you will be able to do little alone. Your superior will be able to provide the assistance necessary.

7. **(C)** Self-explanatory.

8. **(D)** The wound is clean. There are no rough edges where infection can breed.

9. **(B)** It is imperative that an individual with a back injury not be moved without professional assistance.

10. **(B)** Loss of a good deal of blood can lead to a loss of life.

11. **(C)** An alibi is supposed to support the accused's plea that he or she did not commit the crime in question.

12. **(A)** An accessory is a person who, even if not present when the crime is committed, is concerned either before or after the perpetration of a felony.

13. **(A)** The answer is self-explanatory. Acknowledgment: A formal declaration before a competent authority or the official certificate of such a declaration. Oath: A solemn assertion or promise, with the invocation of God, to be a witness of the truth of what one says. Subpoena: A judicial writ requiring a person to appear as a witness at a specified time and place, under penalty of default.

14. **(B)** There is no reference to character on a bank's signature card, nor is there any financial information there. Places of employment are not kept current.

15. **(A)** An individual may be deemed to be an "accomplice" under these circumstances.

16. **(D)** The pockmarks are distinctive. Not very many people have them. All of the other physical qualities can apply to many people.

17. **(C)** Not very many females are that tall. Again, the features in the other choices can and do apply to many females.

18. **(B)** No two ears are exactly alike.

19. **(D)** Not many cars are on the road with their front bumper missing. This will make this vehicle distinctive and easily spotted.

20. **(B)** The number of an automobile engine is not easily changed, so in all likelihood this is not the stolen car, especially since only one day has passed. License plates can be substituted easily, a windshield can be readily cracked, and dents can be made to avoid identification of the vehicle.

21. **(A)** There are not many men around who weigh that much, therefore this man would tend to stand out. The identifications in choices (B) and (C) are quite common. The thin scar on the upper left lip would be difficult to recognize, and the tattoo would not be easily visible.

22. **(A)** The color of the eyes cannot be changed. Hair color is easily changed, teeth could have been lost or replaced in the interim, and of course the weight of a person is subject to change over a period of time.

23. **(B)** The answer is self-explanatory.

24. **(C)** On a busy highway, tire size and spare would be impossible to determine. Make of car is also difficult to screen quickly. Color is obvious, and many cars are not black.

25. **(D)** To avoid a future embarrassing situation, a male trooper should avoid searching a female. Since this is a sick or injured female and there is no danger of a concealed weapon, the course of action in choice **(D)** would be best.

26. **(D)** The burning of the fingers indicated in choice (C) would only call attention to the attempt. Facial surgery might be more successful.

27. **(A)** This is commonly known as a "lineup."

28. **(D)** Social Security cards do not bear any information that specifically identifies the individuals carrying them.

29. **(C)** A very small number of people stutter, and a stutterer with a French accent is unusual indeed.

30. **(A)** This type of disorder is marked by spasmodic uncontrolled physical movements.

31. **(D)** This is an incorrect statement, therefore it should be selected.

32. **(D)** If you do away with the reasons that people become criminals, you will probably do away with most crime.

33. **(A)** If a program of crime prevention is successful, there will be less need for correctional institutions.

34. **(C)** All criminals believe in "no legal restraints." Therefore, if a person does not believe in "no legal restraints," that person cannot be a criminal.

35. **(B)** Most authorities support the theory that individuals are strongly influenced by their environment and that if that environment is conducive to criminal behavior, criminal tendencies may result.

36. **(B)** Review this diagram.

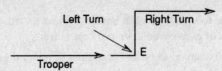

The right turn reverses direction of the left turn and keeps the trooper in the same direction as when he started.

37. **(C)** Unlike question 36, this trooper, in making a second left, goes in the opposite direction from that in which he or she started.

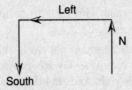

38. **(D)** This is the same result as question 36, except that the original direction is westward. Nevertheless, he finishes up in the same direction.

39. **(A)**

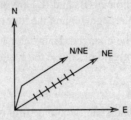

Of the choices given, (A) is the most correct. (The tracked line is shown for guidance only.)

40. **(B)**

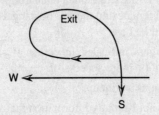

In a cloverleaf intersection, this is the path of the trooper.

41. **(A)** From the statements of the parties involved and from his own observations of the scene, it is clear that the vehicle was in collision with Mr. Bates, a pedestrian.

42. **(C)** According to the trooper's findings, the signal light had turned green when Mr. Goldsmith started downhill.

43. **(C)** According to the account, Tenth Street, on which Mr. Goldsmith was traveling, is a straight, one-way street that runs downhill as one goes from west to east.

44. **(A)** According to the account, the signal light had turned green for Mr. Goldsmith when Mr. Bates was crossing on Pacific. Therefore, Bates must have crossed against the signal.

45. **(C)** Mr. Goldsmith was going downhill on Tenth Street when the accident occurred.

46. **(B)** The first day of June will be the same day of the week as the 29th of June (look at a calendar and you'll see this). Count backward from Monday, July 4, and you will find that June 29 occurs on a Wednesday.

47. **(D)** The first of the month is by far the most reasonable starting point for determining days of the week.

48. **(B)** Use the same method as in question 46, above.

49. **(B)** 1987 was not a leap year, so February was exactly four weeks long and could not have contained five Mondays.

50. **(C)** Use the same method as in question 46, above.

51. **(A)** 25 miles + 7 miles + 7 miles = 39. Suspect has only traveled 25 miles.

52. **(B)** The answer is self-explanatory.

53. **(C)** 60 mph for 10 minutes = 10 miles
    40 mph for 30 minutes = 20 miles
    Total = 30 miles

54. **(C)** 75 mph for 20 minutes = 20/60 x 75 = 25 miles
    90 mph for 10 minutes = 10/60 x 90 = 15 miles
    Total = 40 miles

55. **(B)** Assuming that he turned around and retraced his route, the trooper traveled 100 miles.

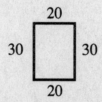

56. **(B)** A single trooper cannot stop traffic in both directions at the same time. He should stop eastbound traffic and radio for help right away.

57. **(A)** Since left turns are permitted, they are permitted on green. Left on yellow is permissive, not required.

58. **(D)** Ordinarily headlights are adequate for night driving on a highway. Lights were probably installed on this stretch for a reason, so their absence can create some problem. (A) is true but has no relation to street lighting.

59. **(A)** Part of the trooper's job is to locate motorists in distress. If he stays with this one car, others may be stranded even longer. It is sufficient to radio for help and then to continue on patrol.

60. **(A)** A primary part of the patrol function is maintaining surveillance (observation). Choices (B) and (C) would be a means of avoiding the responsibilities of highway patrol. There is no other principle of patrol other than **(A)**, so (D) is incorrect.

61. **(A)** Placing the cross compass over the map, the student will see that a vehicle traveling southwest following the arrow into the exit to Adams Street will then go northwest.

62. **(A)** The vehicle traveling northeast and exiting first turns toward the southeast but must enter Adams Street going northwest.

63. **(C)** An examination of the map shows no entrances (only exits) from the Beltway. Therefore, **(C)** is the only answer. The map does not indicate any exits after this junction. Therefore, choice (D) is wrong.

64. **(B)** Put yourself in Mrs. Wagner's place. The right and left directions will be apparent.

65. **(D)** Answer is apparent from the maps.

The table for questions 66 through 75 requires an ability to read numbers in detail. If the reader checks the table, he or she will find the answer to each question.

66. **(C)** Car 6 has an engine number that ends with "45." The others don't end with this number.

67. **(A)** Car 2 has an engine number that begins with "21." The others don't and therefore **(A)** is the only answer.

68. **(D)** Car 9 has the letter combination "FX" near the beginning of the number. Cars 3, 4, and 6 have no such letters anywhere in their engine numbers.

69. **(A)** An inspection of the table shows that Car 8 has the engine number called for by the question.

70. **(C)** Cars 2, 4, and 9 were made between 1988 and 1992.

71. **(B)** If the reader counts any set, he or she will find 11 numbers and 6 letters.

72. **(C)** Car 7 ends with "721." The others end differently.

73. **(D)** An inspection of the table shows that Car 7 has the letters "DN." The others do not have this combination.

74. **(C)** An inspection of the table shows that Car 5 has the letters and numerals "HT37."

75. **(B)** Car 3 contains the integer "15" in its engine identification number.

Answers 76 through 91 are self-explanatory.

76. **(A)**
77. **(B)**
78. **(D)**
79. **(B)**
80. **(B)**
81. **(D)**
82. **(D)**
83. **(A)**
84. **(C)**
85. **(A)**
86. **(D)**
87. **(C)**
88. **(D)**
89. **(D)**
90. **(B)**
91. **(C)**
92. **(C)** To multiply by 100 move the decimal point two places to the right.
$$\$7.50 \times 100 = \$750.00$$

93. **(C)** $28 \div 3 = 9\ 1/3$ hours (1/3 of 60 minutes is 20 minutes.)

94. **(B)** $100 - 60 = 40$

95. **(D)** $^1/_5 = 20\%$

$^1/_7 = 14^2/_7\%$

$+ \ ^1/_2 = \underline{50\%}$

$84^2/_7\%$

100%

$\underline{- \ 84^2/_7\%}$

$15 \ ^5/_7\%$ (most nearly 16%)

96. **(D)** Clerks   Days

$12 \ \times \ 18 = 216$

$12 \ \times \ 6 = 72$

$216 \ - \ 72 = 144$

Now work from 144:

$16 \ \times \ 9 = 144$

$144 \ \div \ 16 = 9$

$9 \ + \ 6 = 15$ (answer)

97. **(D)** A gross is 144.

$144 \times \ 6 = 864$

$864 \div 24 = 36$

98. **(B)** $^3/_5 = 1{,}440$

$^1/_5 = 480$

$^5/_5 = 2{,}400$

$\$2{,}400 \div 30 = \$80.00$

99. **(C)** $\$18{,}000 = 150\%$

$\$12{,}000 = 100\%$ (original capital)

100. **(A)** $^8/_{24} = ^1/_3$

$^1/_3 \times 42 = 14$

Answer Sheet for Model Examination 4

1. Ⓐ Ⓑ Ⓒ Ⓓ　　21. Ⓐ Ⓑ Ⓒ Ⓓ　　41. Ⓐ Ⓑ Ⓒ Ⓓ　　61. Ⓐ Ⓑ Ⓒ Ⓓ　　81. Ⓐ Ⓑ Ⓒ Ⓓ

2. Ⓐ Ⓑ Ⓒ Ⓓ　　22. Ⓐ Ⓑ Ⓒ Ⓓ　　42. Ⓐ Ⓑ Ⓒ Ⓓ　　62. Ⓐ Ⓑ Ⓒ Ⓓ　　82. Ⓐ Ⓑ Ⓒ Ⓓ

3. Ⓐ Ⓑ Ⓒ Ⓓ　　23. Ⓐ Ⓑ Ⓒ Ⓓ　　43. Ⓐ Ⓑ Ⓒ Ⓓ　　63. Ⓐ Ⓑ Ⓒ Ⓓ　　83. Ⓐ Ⓑ Ⓒ Ⓓ

4. Ⓐ Ⓑ Ⓒ Ⓓ　　24. Ⓐ Ⓑ Ⓒ Ⓓ　　44. Ⓐ Ⓑ Ⓒ Ⓓ　　64. Ⓐ Ⓑ Ⓒ Ⓓ　　84. Ⓐ Ⓑ Ⓒ Ⓓ

5. Ⓐ Ⓑ Ⓒ Ⓓ　　25. Ⓐ Ⓑ Ⓒ Ⓓ　　45. Ⓐ Ⓑ Ⓒ Ⓓ　　65. Ⓐ Ⓑ Ⓒ Ⓓ　　85. Ⓐ Ⓑ Ⓒ Ⓓ

6. Ⓐ Ⓑ Ⓒ Ⓓ　　26. Ⓐ Ⓑ Ⓒ Ⓓ　　46. Ⓐ Ⓑ Ⓒ Ⓓ　　66. Ⓐ Ⓑ Ⓒ Ⓓ　　86. Ⓐ Ⓑ Ⓒ Ⓓ

7. Ⓐ Ⓑ Ⓒ Ⓓ　　27. Ⓐ Ⓑ Ⓒ Ⓓ　　47. Ⓐ Ⓑ Ⓒ Ⓓ　　67. Ⓐ Ⓑ Ⓒ Ⓓ　　87. Ⓐ Ⓑ Ⓒ Ⓓ

8. Ⓐ Ⓑ Ⓒ Ⓓ　　28. Ⓐ Ⓑ Ⓒ Ⓓ　　48. Ⓐ Ⓑ Ⓒ Ⓓ　　68. Ⓐ Ⓑ Ⓒ Ⓓ　　88. Ⓐ Ⓑ Ⓒ Ⓓ

9. Ⓐ Ⓑ Ⓒ Ⓓ　　29. Ⓐ Ⓑ Ⓒ Ⓓ　　49. Ⓐ Ⓑ Ⓒ Ⓓ　　69. Ⓐ Ⓑ Ⓒ Ⓓ　　89. Ⓐ Ⓑ Ⓒ Ⓓ

10. Ⓐ Ⓑ Ⓒ Ⓓ　　30. Ⓐ Ⓑ Ⓒ Ⓓ　　50. Ⓐ Ⓑ Ⓒ Ⓓ　　70. Ⓐ Ⓑ Ⓒ Ⓓ　　90. Ⓐ Ⓑ Ⓒ Ⓓ

11. Ⓐ Ⓑ Ⓒ Ⓓ　　31. Ⓐ Ⓑ Ⓒ Ⓓ　　51. Ⓐ Ⓑ Ⓒ Ⓓ　　71. Ⓐ Ⓑ Ⓒ Ⓓ　　91. Ⓐ Ⓑ Ⓒ Ⓓ

12. Ⓐ Ⓑ Ⓒ Ⓓ　　32. Ⓐ Ⓑ Ⓒ Ⓓ　　52. Ⓐ Ⓑ Ⓒ Ⓓ　　72. Ⓐ Ⓑ Ⓒ Ⓓ　　92. Ⓐ Ⓑ Ⓒ Ⓓ

13. Ⓐ Ⓑ Ⓒ Ⓓ　　33. Ⓐ Ⓑ Ⓒ Ⓓ　　53. Ⓐ Ⓑ Ⓒ Ⓓ　　73. Ⓐ Ⓑ Ⓒ Ⓓ　　93. Ⓐ Ⓑ Ⓒ Ⓓ

14. Ⓐ Ⓑ Ⓒ Ⓓ　　34. Ⓐ Ⓑ Ⓒ Ⓓ　　54. Ⓐ Ⓑ Ⓒ Ⓓ　　74. Ⓐ Ⓑ Ⓒ Ⓓ　　94. Ⓐ Ⓑ Ⓒ Ⓓ

15. Ⓐ Ⓑ Ⓒ Ⓓ　　35. Ⓐ Ⓑ Ⓒ Ⓓ　　55. Ⓐ Ⓑ Ⓒ Ⓓ　　75. Ⓐ Ⓑ Ⓒ Ⓓ　　95. Ⓐ Ⓑ Ⓒ Ⓓ

16. Ⓐ Ⓑ Ⓒ Ⓓ　　36. Ⓐ Ⓑ Ⓒ Ⓓ　　56. Ⓐ Ⓑ Ⓒ Ⓓ　　76. Ⓐ Ⓑ Ⓒ Ⓓ　　96. Ⓐ Ⓑ Ⓒ Ⓓ

17. Ⓐ Ⓑ Ⓒ Ⓓ　　37. Ⓐ Ⓑ Ⓒ Ⓓ　　57. Ⓐ Ⓑ Ⓒ Ⓓ　　77. Ⓐ Ⓑ Ⓒ Ⓓ　　97. Ⓐ Ⓑ Ⓒ Ⓓ

18. Ⓐ Ⓑ Ⓒ Ⓓ　　38. Ⓐ Ⓑ Ⓒ Ⓓ　　58. Ⓐ Ⓑ Ⓒ Ⓓ　　78. Ⓐ Ⓑ Ⓒ Ⓓ　　98. Ⓐ Ⓑ Ⓒ Ⓓ

19. Ⓐ Ⓑ Ⓒ Ⓓ　　39. Ⓐ Ⓑ Ⓒ Ⓓ　　59. Ⓐ Ⓑ Ⓒ Ⓓ　　79. Ⓐ Ⓑ Ⓒ Ⓓ　　99. Ⓐ Ⓑ Ⓒ Ⓓ

20. Ⓐ Ⓑ Ⓒ Ⓓ　　40. Ⓐ Ⓑ Ⓒ Ⓓ　　60. Ⓐ Ⓑ Ⓒ Ⓓ　　80. Ⓐ Ⓑ Ⓒ Ⓓ　　100. Ⓐ Ⓑ Ⓒ Ⓓ

TEAR HERE

Model Examination 4

Directions: Each question has four suggested answers, lettered (A), (B), (C), and (D). Decide which one is the best answer, and on the sample answer sheet, locate the question number and darken the area corresponding to your answer choice.

Questions 1 through 15 are to be answered on the basis of the description of the police action that follows. You will have ten minutes to read and study the description. Then you will have to answer the 15 questions about the incident without referring back to the description of the incident.

State Police Officers Smith and Jones were working a midnight to 8 A.M. tour of duty. It was a Saturday morning in the month of July and the weather was clear. At about 4:30 A.M., they received a radio call reporting a burglary in progress at 777 Seventh Street, the address of an appliance store.

Upon their arrival at the scene, the troopers could not find any evidence of a break-in. However, as they continued their investigation, they heard noises coming from the rear of the building. As they raced to the rear of the building, they saw four people alighting from the roof, by way of a ladder, and climbing over a fence that leads to the rear of a warehouse. The troopers climbed over the fence and observed two of the people running into an alleyway on the west side of the warehouse and the other two people running into a parking lot on the east side of the warehouse.

Smith, using a walkie-talkie, called for assistance and proceeded to give chase after the two persons who entered the alley. The description of these two individuals was as follows: One was a white male with long blond hair, wearing light pants, a blue shirt, and white sneakers, and carrying what appeared to be a portable TV set. The other was also a white male, with short dark hair, wearing dungarees, a white T-shirt, and cowboy boots, and carrying what appeared to be a portable cassette-stereo-radio.

Jones continued to give chase to the two individuals who had entered the parking lot. The description of these two individuals was as follows: one was a Hispanic male with long dark hair, wearing dark pants, a yellow shirt, and dark shoes, and carrying what appeared to be a video recorder. The other was a black male with a bald head, wearing dungarees, a white T-shirt, and white sneakers, and carrying what appeared to be a baseball bat and portable TV set.

As Smith emerged from the alley onto the sidewalk, he again observed the two individuals he had been chasing. They were entering a dark blue Chevrolet with license plates beginning with the letters AKG. The vehicle drove west on Seventh Street. The male with the long blond hair appeared to be driving.

As Jones reached the parking lot, he observed the two individuals he was pursuing speed off in a white station wagon, heading west on Seventh Street. The license plates could not be discerned. Officer Jones found a broken portable TV set in the parking lot.

Smith broadcast this additional information, and both officers then quickly returned to their radio car to conduct a search of the area.

Do not refer back to the description while answering questions 1 through 15.

1. Officers Smith and Jones responded to a "burglary in progress" call at approximately

   (A) midnight

   (B) 8:00 A.M.

   (C) 4:30 P.M.

   (D) 4:30 A.M.

2. The suspects in the burglary gained entrance to the store by

   (A) breaking a front window

   (B) breaking a rear window

   (C) breaking in from an adjoining warehouse

   (D) using a ladder to get to the roof

3. The suspects, when fleeing from the burglary

   (A) all ran into an alleyway

   (B) all ran into a parking lot

   (C) all ran into a warehouse

   (D) went in different directions

4. The white male with the long blond hair was carrying what appeared to be a

   (A) portable TV set

   (B) portable cassette-stereo-radio

   (C) video recorder

   (D) portable cassette player

5. The Hispanic male was carrying what appeared to be a

   (A) video recorder

   (B) portable cassette-stereo-radio

   (C) portable TV set

   (D) portable cassette player

6. The white male with the short hair was carrying what appeared to be a
    (A) portable TV set
    (B) portable cassette-stereo-radio
    (C) video recorder
    (D) portable cassette player

7. The suspect wearing cowboy boots was the
    (A) white male with long blond hair
    (B) black male
    (C) Hispanic male
    (D) white male with short hair

8. The suspect wearing light pants and a blue shirt was the
    (A) black male
    (B) white male with long blond hair
    (C) Hispanic male
    (D) white male with short hair

9. The suspect wearing dark pants and a yellow shirt was the
    (A) white male with long blond hair
    (B) black male
    (C) white male with short hair
    (D) Hispanic male

10. When the suspects were fleeing, the two white males entered a
    (A) blue station wagon with unknown license plates
    (B) white station wagon with license plates beginning with the letters AKG
    (C) blue Chevrolet with license plates beginning with the letters AKG
    (D) white Chevrolet with unknown license plates

11. From reading the description of the incident, one could assume
    (A) that Seventh Street is one-way westbound
    (B) that Seventh Street is a two-way street
    (C) that Seventh Street is one-way eastbound
    (D) none of the above

12. Upon entering the parking lot, Jones found a broken portable TV set that had apparently been dropped by the
    (A) white male with blond hair
    (B) white male with dark hair
    (C) black male
    (D) Hispanic male

13. The black male was

    (A) bald and wearing dark pants, a yellow shirt, and dark shoes

    (B) bald and wearing dungarees, a white T-shirt, and white sneakers

    (C) wearing dungarees, a white T-shirt, and cowboy boots and had dark hair

    (D) bald and wearing light pants and a blue shirt

14. The suspect who was carrying the baseball bat was also carrying what appeared to be a

    (A) portable TV set

    (B) video recorder

    (C) portable cassette-stereo-radio

    (D) portable cassette player

15. A description of the suspects was broadcast to other police units so that they could assist in searching the area. This was done by

    (A) both Jones and Smith as they both had walkie-talkies

    (B) Trooper Jones as he had a walkie-talkie

    (C) Trooper Smith as he had a walkie-talkie

    (D) both troopers upon returning to their radio car

16. In the investigation of a homicide case, it is desirable to have photographs taken of the body in its original condition and position. Of the following, the best reason for this practice is that the photographs

    (A) show the motive for the homicide and thus indicate likely suspects

    (B) indicate if the corpse has been moved in any way

    (C) form a permanent record of the body and the scene of the crime

    (D) reveal the specific method used in committing the homicide

17. A state trooper hears two shots fired and proceeds in the direction of the shots. He comes upon an intoxicated man who is angrily screaming at a woman. The trooper notices that the handle of a pistol is protruding from the man's pocket and orders him to surrender the pistol. The man apparently ignores the order and continues screaming at the woman. For the trooper now to fire a warning shot over the man's head would be

    (A) bad; it is quite possible that the man is so intoxicated that he did not clearly hear or understand the trooper's order

    (B) bad; the trooper should realize that an intoxicated person is not entirely responsible for his actions

    (C) good; the warning shot will impress the man with the seriousness of the situation

    (D) good; since the man had already fired twice, the trooper should take no further chances

18. The practice of writing down confessions while a suspect is being questioned is

    (A) bad, chiefly because the time taken to put a confession into written form may prove to be a waste of time since it may later be declared to be inadmissible as evidence in court

    (B) bad, chiefly because this may cause the suspect to withhold information when he or she knows that the confession is being recorded

    (C) good, chiefly because the suspect cannot claim at a later date that the information was obtained by force

    (D) good, chiefly because the suspect is thereby given more time to gather his or her thoughts and give the information wanted by the police

19. An escaped prisoner has been wounded and is lying flat on his stomach with his head turned to one side. The one of the following directions from which a state trooper should approach the prisoner in order to make it most difficult for the prisoner to fire quickly and accurately at the police officer is from the side

    (A) directly behind the prisoner's head

    (B) facing the top of the prisoner's head

    (C) facing the prisoner's face

    (D) facing the prisoner's heels

20. A gas main explosion has caused some property damage. Examination by an emergency repair crew clearly indicates that no further explosions will occur. Nevertheless, rumors are circulating that more explosions and greater damage are going to occur. This situation has resulted in a high degree of fear among local residents. The best of the following actions for a state trooper on duty at the scene to take *first* would be to

    (A) ignore the rumors since they are false and no real danger exists

    (B) inform the people of the true circumstances of the emergency

    (C) question several people at the scene in an attempt to determine the source of the rumors

    (D) order everyone to leave the area quickly and in an orderly fashion

21. A state trooper finds a young child wandering about a residential neighborhood. After unsuccessfully questioning the child as to the location of his home, the trooper phones police headquarters and is informed that no child meeting the description given by the officer has been reported missing. The officer decides to make inquiries about the child in the immediate area before taking any other action. The action is advisable chiefly because

    (A) the child's parents probably know of his whereabouts since no report of the missing child has been received at headquarters

    (B) the child has probably been away from home only a short time since no report of the missing child has been received at headquarters

    (C) the child is less likely to become emotionally disturbed if he remains in his own neighborhood

    (D) young children, when lost, never wander more than a short distance from home

22. While a trooper in plain clothes is following and watching a suspect in a homicide case, the trooper becomes convinced that the suspect realizes he is being watched. The suspect's identity is known to the police, but he is also known to have changed his place of residence frequently during the past few months. The trooper does not have sufficient evidence to arrest the suspect at this time. Of the following, the best action for the trooper to take is to

(A) approach the suspect, inform him that he is being followed, and demand an explanation of his suspicious past conduct

(B) continue to follow the suspect until an opportunity is presented for the officer to telephone for a replacement

(C) continue to follow the suspect since he will probably commit an illegal act eventually

(D) discontinue following the suspect and attempt to gain evidence by other means

23. Probationary State Police Officers A and B are given a special assignment by the sergeant. Officer B does not fully understand some of the instructions given by the sergeant concerning the carrying out of the assignment. Of the following, it would be best for Officer B to

(A) proceed with those parts of the assignment he understands and ask for an explanation from the sergeant when he can go no further

(B) observe Officer A's work carefully in order to determine how the assignment is to be carried out

(C) ask the sergeant to explain that portion of the instructions that he does not fully understand before starting the assignment

(D) suggest to Officer A that he supervise the operation since he probably understands the sergeant's instruction better

24. A state police officer responds at night to a telephone complaint that a prowler has been observed at a particular location. The officer arrives at the location and notices someone who appears to fit the description of the prowler previously given by the complainant. In approaching the individual, it would be best for the police officer to

(A) consider this individual to be a potentially dangerous criminal

(B) avoid taking any precautionary measures since there is no way of knowing whether any offense has been committed

(C) consider that this individual is probably harmless and is only a "Peeping Tom"

(D) fire a warning shot over the man's head

25. A state police officer has been asked by a merchant on his post to recommend the best make of burglar alarm for his store. The chief reason why the police officer should *not* make any specific recommendation is that

(A) he does not have enough technical knowledge of the operation of burglar alarms

(B) the merchant may interpret the officer's recommendation as an official police department endorsement

(C) such a recommendation would imply that the police are incapable of protecting the merchant's property

(D) he is not likely to know the prices of the various makes and models available

26. Two state police officers in a radio patrol car stop a car that they recognize as having been reported stolen. The police officers immediately separate the two occupants of the car and proceed to question them apart from each other. Of the following, the most important reason for questioning them separately is to

(A) give each suspect an opportunity to admit guilt out of the presence of the other suspect

(B) prevent the suspects from agreeing on an explanation of their presence in the car

(C) prevent the errors that may arise when attempting to record in a notebook two separate statements being made at the same time

(D) determine which of the two suspects actually planned the theft of the car

27. A state trooper is informed by the manager of a supermarket that an object that appears to be a homemade bomb has been discovered in his market. His *first* action should be to

(A) go to the market and make sure that everyone leaves it immediately

(B) go to the market, examine the bomb, and then decide what action should be taken

(C) question the manager in detail in an effort to determine whether this really is a bomb

(D) telephone the bomb squad for instructions as to how the bomb should be rendered harmless

28. The most reasonable advice that a state police officer can give to a merchant who asks what he should do if he receives a telephone call from a person he doesn't recognize regarding an alleged emergency at his store after ordinary business hours is that the merchant should go to the store and, if officers are not at the scene, he should

(A) continue past the store and call the police for assistance

(B) continue past the store, and return and enter it if there doesn't appear to be an emergency

(C) enter the store and ascertain whether the alleged emergency exists

(D) enter the store only if there is no one apparently loitering in the vicinity

29. Whenever a crime has been committed, the criminal has disturbed the surroundings in one way or another by his or her presence. The *least* valid deduction for the police to make from this statement is that

(A) clues are thus present at all crime scenes

(B) even the slightest search at crime scenes will turn up conclusive evidence

(C) the greater the number of criminals involved in a crime, the greater the number of clues likely to be available

(D) the completely clueless crime is rarely encountered in police work

30. An off-duty state police officer was seated in a restaurant when two men entered, drew guns, and robbed the cashier. The officer made no attempt to prevent the robbery or to apprehend the criminals. Later he justified his conduct by stating that an officer, when off duty, is a private citizen with the same duties and rights of all private citizens. The officer's conduct was

(A) wrong; a police officer must act to prevent crimes and apprehend criminals at all times

(B) right; the police officer was out of uniform at the time of the robbery

(C) wrong; he should have obtained the necessary information and descriptions after the robbers left

(D) right; it would have been foolhardy for him to intervene when outnumbered by armed robbers

31. A state police officer is the first one to arrive at the scene of a murder. The suspect offers to make a statement concerning the crime. The police officer refuses to accept the statement. The officer's action is

   (A) good; interrogation of suspects should be performed by experienced detectives

   (B) poor; the suspect may later change his mind and refuse to make any statement

   (C) good; the officer will be too busy maintaining order at the scene to be able to accept the statement

   (D) poor; a statement made by the suspect would quickly solve the crime

Answer questions 32 through 41 on the basis of the following legal definitions.

BURGLARY is committed when a person enters a building to commit a crime therein.

LARCENY is committed when a person wrongfully takes, obtains, or withholds the property of another.

ROBBERY is the forcible stealing of property. If a person, while committing a larceny, uses or threatens the *immediate* use of force, the crime changes from larceny to robbery.

SEXUAL ABUSE is committed when a person subjects another person to sexual contact without the second person's consent or when a person has sexual contact with another person less than 17 years of age. (A person less than 17 years of age cannot legally consent to any sexual conduct.) "Sexual contact" may be defined as touching the sexual or other intimate parts of a person to achieve sexual gratification.

SEXUAL MISCONDUCT is committed when a male has sexual intercourse with a consenting female who is at least 13 years of age but less than 17 years of age.

HARASSMENT is committed when a person intends to harass, annoy, or alarm another person and does so by striking, shoving, kicking, or otherwise subjecting the other person to physical contact.

ASSAULT is committed when a person unlawfully causes a physical injury to another person.

32. James Kelly enters the home of Mary Smith with the intention of taking Mary's portable TV set. While Kelly is in the apartment, Mary wakes up and attempts to retrieve her TV set from Kelly. Kelly punches Mary in the face and flees with the TV set. Kelly can be charged with

   (A) burglary and larceny

   (B) burglary only

   (C) robbery and larceny

   (D) burglary and robbery

33. John Brown enters a department store with the intention of doing some shopping. Brown has a .38 caliber revolver in his coat pocket and also has a criminal conviction for armed robbery. As he passes the jewelry counter, he notices an expensive watch lying on the showcase. He checks to see if anyone is watching him, and, when he feels that he is not being observed, he slips the watch into his pocket and leaves the store. Brown could be charged with

   (A) larceny

   (B) burglary and larceny

   (C) burglary and robbery

   (D) robbery

34. Tom Murphy enters a crowded subway car. He positions himself behind a woman and starts to touch her buttocks with his hand. The woman becomes very annoyed and starts to move away. As she does so, Murphy reaches into her pocketbook and removes $10. He then exits the train at the next station. Murphy could be charged with

    (A) robbery, larceny, and sexual misconduct

    (B) burglary, robbery, and sexual abuse

    (C) burglary, larceny, and sexual misconduct

    (D) larceny and sexual abuse

35. Ed Saunders entered the apartment of Jane Robers with the intent to sexually abuse her. However, Robers was not at home and Saunders left the apartment. Saunders could be charged with

    (A) sexual abuse

    (B) sexual misconduct

    (C) burglary

    (D) none of the above as a crime did not take place because Robers was not at home

36. Frank Taylor entered the apartment of his 16-year-old girlfriend, Doris, to have sexual intercourse with her. Doris consented to this sexual conduct and they engaged in intercourse. Taylor could be charged with

    (A) burglary

    (B) sexual misconduct

    (C) both burglary and sexual misconduct

    (D) no crime as Doris consented to the activity

37. Brian Jones asks his 17-year-old girlfriend, Mary, if she would like to go to a motel and have sexual intercourse. She agrees and they go to the motel. Jones could be charged with

    (A) burglary

    (B) sexual misconduct

    (C) both burglary and sexual misconduct

    (D) no crime as she consented to the activity

38. Bill is at a party at Joan's house. An argument ensues between two of the guests. Bill overhears Helen make a derogatory comment about him. He walks up to Helen and demands she "apologize or else." Helen refuses to apologize; Bill slaps her in the face and then rushes from the apartment. Bill could be charged with

    (A) assault

    (B) burglary and assault

    (C) harassment

    (D) burglary and harassment

39. Joe is on his way to work. He is in a very bad mood. As he enters the warehouse where he works, he slips and falls to the floor. This only escalates his foul mood. As he is getting up, he sees a fellow worker who had made some unkind remarks to him two days before. Joe picks up a piece of board that is lying on the floor, walks up to the other worker, and hits him across the arm. This causes the other worker to suffer a broken arm. Joe could be charged with

    (A) assault

    (B) burglary and assault

    (C) harassment

    (D) none of the above as Joe was emotionally upset

40. Jim enters a school through a rear window at 2:00 A.M. He wants to take a movie projector that he knows is kept in a specific room. He enters the room, takes the projector, and starts to leave when he is confronted by a security guard. The guard attempts to grab Jim; however, Jim slips away. As a guard again attempts to apprehend him, Jim swings the projector, striking the guard in the face. The guard falls to the floor unconscious and suffers a broken nose. Jim could be charged with

    (A) burglary, larceny, and robbery

    (B) robbery, larceny, and assault

    (C) burglary, larceny, and assault

    (D) burglary, robbery, and assault

41. Sue invites Tom to her apartment for dinner. After dinner, Tom decides that he would like to have a sexual encounter with Sue. She attempts to discourage his advances. Tom then proceeds to hold her down on the couch and to fondle her breasts and touch her private parts. When Sue starts to scream, Tom rushes from the apartment. Tom could be charged with

    (A) burglary and sexual abuse

    (B) burglary and sexual misconduct

    (C) sexual abuse

    (D) no crime as Sue invited him to her apartment

42. It is important that the police give proper attention to the investigation of apparently minor, as well as major, complaints made by citizens. Of the following, the one that is the *most* valid reason for doing so is that

    (A) minor complaints may be of great importance in the mind of the complainant

    (B) minor complaints are more readily disposed of

    (C) minor complaints may be an indication of a serious police problem

    (D) police efficiency is determined by the attitude shown towards citizen complaints

43. Hearsay evidence may be defined as testimony by one person that another person told him or her about a criminal act that that other person had witnessed. Hearsay evidence is usually *not* admissible in a criminal trial mainly because

    (A) hearsay evidence is consistently biased and deliberately distorted

    (B) hearsay evidence is usually not relevant to the issues of the case

    (C) such evidence is usually distorted by both the original witness and the person to whom the observations were stated

    (D) the actual witness to the criminal act is not being examined under oath

44. "Arrests should not be given too much weight in the appraisal of a police officer's performance since a large number of arrests does not necessarily indicate that a good police job is being done." This statement is

    (A) true; factors other than the number of arrests made must also be considered in judging police effectiveness

    (B) false; the basic job of the police is to suppress crime and the surest measure of this is the number of arrests made

    (C) true; arrest figures are not indicative in any way of a police officer's efficiency

    (D) false; although some police officers are in a better position to make arrests than others, the law of averages should operate to even this out

45. "Arson is a particularly troublesome crime for the police." Of the following statements, the one that is the *most* important reason why this is so is that

    (A) arsonists usually seek the protection of darkness for their crimes

    (B) arson occurs so infrequently that the police lack a definite approach for combating it

    (C) important evidence is frequently destroyed by the fire itself

    (D) witnesses find it difficult to distinguish arsonists from other criminals

46. "Undoubtedly, the police have an important contribution to make to the welfare of youth." Of the following, the principal reason for this is that

    (A) effectiveness is a result of experience and the police have had the longest experience in youth work

    (B) no other agency can make use of the criminal aspects of the law as effectively as the police

    (C) the police are in a strategic position to observe children actually or potentially delinquent and the conditions contributing thereto

    (D) welfare agencies lack an understanding of the problems of youth

47. An apparently senile man informs a police officer that he is returning from a visit to his daughter and that he is unable to find his way back home because he has forgotten his address. Of the following courses of action, the *first* one that should be taken by the officer is to

    (A) question the man in an effort to establish his identity

    (B) request the police missing persons section to describe any person recently reported as missing

    (C) suggest that the man return to his daughter for travel directions to his home

    (D) telephone a description of the man to the precinct station house

48. The one of the following that is the most accurate statement concerning the proper attitude of a state trooper toward persons in his or her custody is that the officer should

   (A) ignore any serious problems of those in custody if they have no bearing on the charges preferred

   (B) not inform the person who has been arrested of the reason for the arrest

   (C) not permit a person in custody to give vent to feelings at any time

   (D) watch a brooding or silent person more carefully than one who noisily threatens suicide

49. A pawnshop dealer has submitted to the police an accurate and complete description of a wristwatch that he recently purchased from a customer. The one of the following factors that would be most important in determining whether this wristwatch was stolen is the

   (A) degree of investigative perseverance demonstrated by the police

   (B) exactness of police records describing stolen property

   (C) honesty and neighborhood reputation of the pawnbroker

   (D) time interval between the purchase of the wristwatch by the pawnbroker and the report made to the police

50. A police officer at the scene of a serious vehicular accident requests two witnesses to the accident not to speak to each other until each one has given a statement to the officer concerning the accident. The most likely reason for this request by the police officer is that if the witnesses were allowed to speak to each other at this time they might

   (A) become involved in a violent quarrel over what actually happened

   (B) change their opinion so that identical statements to the police would result

   (C) discuss the possibility of a bribe offer to either of them by one of the operators involved in the accident

   (D) have their original views of the accident somewhat altered by hearing each other's view of the accident

51. "Tests have shown that sound waves set up by a siren have a greater intensity ahead than at either side or at the rear of a police car." On the basis of this quotation, it would be most reasonable for the operator of a police car, when responding to the scene of an emergency and using the siren, to expect that a motorist approaching an intersection from

   (A) a side street may not stop his vehicle as soon as a more distant motorist directly ahead of the police car

   (B) directly ahead may not stop his vehicle as soon as a more distant motorist approaching from the rear of the police car

   (C) directly ahead may not stop his vehicle as soon as a more distant motorist approaching from the side of the police car

   (D) the rear of the police car may stop his vehicle before the less distant motorist approaching from a side street

52. A police officer is guarding the entrance of an apartment in which a homicide occurred. While awaiting the arrival of the detectives assigned to the case, the officer is approached by a newspaper reporter who asks to be admitted. The police officer refuses to admit the reporter. The officer's action is

    (A) wrong; the police should cooperate with the press

    (B) right; the reporter might unintentionally destroy evidence if admitted

    (C) wrong; experienced newspaper reporters can be trusted to act intelligently in situations such as this

    (D) right; this reporter should not be given an advantage over other reports

53. A phone call is received at police headquarters indicating that a burglary is now taking place in a large loft building. Several radio motor patrol teams are dispatched to the scene. In order to prevent the escape of the burglars, the two police officers arriving first at the building, knowing that there is at least one entrance on each of the four sides of the building, should first

    (A) station themselves at diagonally opposite corners outside of the building

    (B) enter the building and proceed to search for the criminals

    (C) station themselves at the most likely exit from the building

    (D) enter the building and remain on the ground floor attempting to keep all stairways under observation

54. Soon after being appointed a police officer, you decide that some of the rules and regulations of the police department are unwise. It would be best for you to

    (A) carry out these rules and regulations regardless of your opinion

    (B) make any changes that you decide are necessary

    (C) not do your job until some changes are made

    (D) disregard these rules and regulations and use your own good judgment

55. In most cases, a written report about a serious accident is better than an oral report mainly because a written report

    (A) includes more of the facts

    (B) can be referred to later

    (C) takes less time to prepare

    (D) is more accurate

56. Officers assigned to regular posts for an extended period of time should try to establish friendly relations with the people in the area. For officers to follow this procedure is generally

    (A) advisable, mainly because the officers will be more likely to get the cooperation of the residents when needed

    (B) inadvisable, mainly because it will take the officers' attention away from their regular duties

    (C) advisable, mainly because it will help officers to impress their superior officers

    (D) inadvisable, mainly because the people may be encouraged to take advantage of this friendliness to commit minor violations

Assume that a police officer at a certain location is equipped with a two-way radio to keep him in constant touch with his security headquarters. Radio messages and replies are given in code form, as follows:

	J	P	M	F	B
Radio Code for Type of Situation					
Radio Code for Action to Be Taken	o	r	a	z	q
Radio Response for Action Taken	1	2	3	4	5

Assume that each of the above capital letters is the radio code for a particular type of situation, that the small letter below each capital letter is the radio code for the action a police officer is directed to take, and that the number directly below each small letter is the radio response the police officer should make to indicate what action was actually taken.

> **Directions:** In each of the following questions, 57 through 62, the code letter for the action directed (column 2) and the code number for the action taken (column 3) should correspond to the capital letters in column 1.
>
> If only column 2 is different from column 1, mark your answer (A).
> If only column 3 is different from column 1, mark your answer (B).
> If both column 2 and column 3 are different from column 1, mark your answer (C).
> If both columns 2 and 3 are the same as column 1, mark your answer (D).

Sample Question:

Column 1	Column 2	Column 3
JPFMB	orzaq	12453

The code letters in column 2 are correct, but the numbers "53" in column 3 should be "35." Therefore, the correct answer is **(B)**.

	Column 1	Column 2	Column 3
57.	PBFJM	rqzoa	25413
58.	MPFBJ	zrqoa	32541
59.	JBFPM	oqzra	15432
60.	BJPMF	qaroz	51234
61.	PJFMB	rozaq	21435
62.	FJBMP	zoqra	41532

Answer questions 63 through 71 solely on the basis of the following narrative and assistance report. The report contains 20 numbered boxes. First read the narrative and the information given concerning the form and then study the form thoroughly before answering the questions.

A state trooper is required to prepare an assistance report whenever an occurrence that requires that a person receive medical aid or assistance comes to the trooper's attention. However, if a person is sick at his or her own residence, an assistance report is not required. The officer then need only make a logbook entry.

It was 9:30 A.M., Sunday, June 14. State Troopers Whelan and Murphy of the 2nd Precinct, riding in patrol car 1294, received a radio call of an injury at the northwest corner of Seventh Avenue and 83rd Street. The location of the injury was within the confines of the 3rd Precinct; however, the 3rd Precinct did not have any cars available to respond.

Upon arriving at the scene, Whelan and Murphy found a white male, approximately 28 years of age, lying on the sidewalk. The man was bleeding moderately from a cut on the forehead. When questioned by the officers, the man identified himself as John Mandello, and he stated that someone ran up behind him and pushed him to the ground, causing him to strike his head on the sidewalk. The person who pushed him to the ground also took a wallet containing $100 from his rear left pocket. Trooper Whelan informed Mr. Mandello that an ambulance was on the way. Mr. Mandello stated that he would take care of the injury himself and did not want any medical assistance.

Trooper Whelan canceled the ambulance and proceeded to take the information to be included in the report. As he was doing so, he noticed that the corner traffic light was not working.

Just as Whelan was finished getting the information, he and Trooper Murphy heard what sounded like brakes screeching and cars colliding. The two ran around the corner and saw a car on the southeast corner sidewalk of 82nd Street and Seventh Avenue. They also observed a van, lying on its side, in the intersection of 82nd Street and Seventh Avenue. Murphy ran back to his car and put in a call for an additional car to handle traffic conditions. The accident had occurred within the confines of the Village of Monroe.

Whelan checked the car that was on the sidewalk. The car, after colliding with the van, apparently mounted the sidewalk and went through the front windows of a men's clothing store, setting off the burglar alarm. The driver was lying on the front seat with moderate bleeding from a cut on his head and had what appeared to be a broken arm. The driver of the car was identified as Joe Serrano, a white male, 29 years of age, residing at 384 Lincoln Place.

Murphy went to the van and, with the help of several passersby, pulled the driver out. The driver was unconscious. A search of the unconscious van driver's wallet identified him as Juan Rodriguez, a Hispanic male, 24 years of age, residing at 98 Fourth Avenue.

An ambulance from Washington Hospital arrived at the scene. The ambulance attendant, John Francis, administered first aid to both drivers who were then removed to Washington Hospital.

Further investigation produced two witnesses to the accident. The first witness was Mary Randolph of 876 First Avenue; the second was Helen Sweeney of 684 Broadway. The witnesses stated to Trooper Whelan that the traffic light at the intersection of 82nd Street and Seventh Avenue was not working.

Mr. Thomas Serrano of 384 Lincoln Place, Apt. 4E, phone 287-8777, was notified that his brother, Joe, was admitted to Washington Hospital. The admission number for Joe Serrano was 18764.

No friends or relatives of Juan Rodriguez could be notified that he was admitted to Washington Hospital. His admission number was 18763.

Box #1 will indicate the date that the report is being prepared. If the occurrence happened on a date that is different from the date of the report, the date of occurrence will be listed under "Remarks," box #17. The reasons for the delay in reporting the incident will also be noted under "Remarks," box #17.

Box #8 will give the specific location of the occurrence, i.e., 374 First Street, Apt. 1D; Front of 374 First Street on sidewalk; NW corner of 86th Street and First Avenue.

Box #39 will indicate, to the best of your knowledge, the illness or injury sustained, i.e., cut on forehead, dizziness, etc. The official doctor's or hospital's diagnosis, if available, will be listed under "Remarks," box #17.

Box #10 will list the precinct of the site of the incident and the precinct report number.

Check the appropriate circumstance in box #11.

ASSISTANCE REPORT

1. Date	2. Last name First name M.I.	3. Age	4. Sex	5. Color

6. Time	7. Residence (including street address, apt. # & Zip Code)

8. Location of occurrence (including street address, apt. # & Zip Code)

9. Illness or injury	10. Precinct and report number

11. Check:	12. Taken to: Name of
sick mentally ill injured dead	hospital ( ) morgue ( )

13. Admission number	14. Name of doctor or ambulance attendant

15. Person notified	Relationship

16. Witnesses

17. Remarks

18. Additional required reports (Check appropriate boxes, if any)

        Crime report   Morgue report
        Vehicle accident report   Street injury report

19. Other agency notifications

20. Reporting Officer

  Rank   Name   Number   Precinct

Check the appropriate disposition in box #12. If a person is treated at his or her home and is not removed to another location, no report is required. If a person is removed to a hospital or morgue, check the appropriate box and list the name of the hospital or morgue. If the person refuses medical assistance, write "refused assistance" in box #12. If a person is treated at another location other than his or her home and is not removed to a hospital or morgue, state such facts under "Remarks," box #17.

The hospital admission number is listed in box #13 only if a relative or a friend cannot be notified that the person is being admitted to the hospital.

Box #14 will indicate the name of the doctor or ambulance attendant who treated the individual.

Box #15 will list the name and address of the friend or relative who was notified of the person's admission to the hospital. The relationship of the person notified to the person admitted will also be listed, i.e., friend, wife, brother, etc.

Box #16 will indicate the names and addresses of any witnesses.

Box #17 will contain a short description of the incident.

In box #18, check the appropriate box for any additional forms that may be needed. Check *crime report* if medical assistance was made necessary as a result of a criminal act. Check *vehicle accident report* if the incident involved a motor vehicle accident. Check *morgue report* if the individual involved dies. Check *street injury report* if the person was injured as a result of a defect in a street or sidewalk.

Box #19 will list the names of any other city agencies that may have to be notified, i.e., damaged or broken traffic or street lights—Traffic Department; potholes in the street or broken sidewalks—Department of Highways; broken or damaged fire hydrants or water mains—Department of Water Supply, etc.

Box #20 will contain the rank, name, and command of the Police Officer making the report.

Questions 63 through 66 are to be answered solely on the basis of the information relating to the case of John Mandello.

63. An assistance report
    (A) would not be required because Mr. Mandello refused medical assistance
    (B) would not be required; only a police officer's log entry would be necessary
    (C) would be required, and the precinct that would be listed in box #10 would be the 2nd Precinct
    (D) would be required, and the precinct number that would be listed in box #20 would be the 2nd Precinct

64. In box #9, the trooper would
    (A) enter the official hospital diagnosis when it became available
    (B) enter the description of the illness or injury in his own words
    (C) make a reference to see box #17, "Remarks," for the official diagnosis
    (D) enter "refused medical assistance"

65. In box #18, the trooper would check the box(es) for

(A) street injury report, because Mr. Mandello was injured when his head struck the sidewalk

(B) street injury report, because the injury was incurred when Mr. Mandelo's head struck the sidewalk, and crime report, because he was apparently the victim of a robbery

(C) crime report only

(D) no additional report would be required because Mr. Mandello refused medical assistance

66. In box #19, the trooper would

(A) enter Traffic Department

(B) enter Department of Highways

(C) enter both Traffic Department and Department of Highways

(D) make no entry as no additional agency would have to be notified

Answer questions 67 through 71 based on the information given regarding Joe Serrano and Juan Rodriguez.

67. Box #13 would be

(A) filled in only in the case of Mr. Serrano

(B) filled in only in the case of Mr. Rodriguez

(C) filled in in the cases of both Mr. Serrano and Mr. Rodriguez

(D) left blank in both cases

68. The official hospital diagnoses of Mr. Serrano's injuries were a laceration of the forehead and a fracture of the right arm. This information would

(A) be listed in box #17, "Remarks"

(B) be listed in box #9, "Illness or Injury"

(C) be listed in box #14 next to the doctor's name

(D) not be listed in the report

69. In box #18, the additional report(s) that would be required is (are)

(A) a crime report

(B) a street injury report

(C) a vehicle accident report

(D) a vehicle accident report and a crime report

70. Based on the information given by the witnesses, box #19 would contain the name(s) of which other agency or agencies?

(A) Traffic Department

(B) Traffic Department and Highway Department

(C) Highway Department

(D) Building Department

71. In preparing the assistance report

    (A) the caption "Sick" would be checked in box #11

    (B) the relationship of the person notified in the case of Mr. Serrano would be "father" and would be entered in box #15

    (C) the location of the occurrence would be the intersection of 83rd Street and Seventh Avenue and would be entered in box #8

    (D) the name John Francis would be entered in box #14

Answer questions 72 through 75 on the basis of the information given in the following passage.

The public often believes that the main job of a uniformed officer is to enforce laws simply by arresting people. In reality, however, many of the situations that an officer deals with do not call for the use of the power of arrest. In the first place, an officer spends much of his or her time *preventing* crimes from happening by spotting potential violations or suspicious behavior and taking action to prevent illegal acts. In the second place, many of the situations in which officers are called on for assistance involve elements like personal arguments, husband and wife quarrels, noisy juveniles, or emotionally disturbed persons. The majority of these problems do not result in arrests and convictions, and often they do not even involve illegal behavior. In the third place, even in situations where there seems to be good reason to make an arrest, an officer may have to exercise very good judgment. There are times when making an arrest too soon could touch off a riot, or could result in the detention of a minor offender while major offenders escape, or could cut short the gathering of necessary on-the-scene evidence.

72. The passage implies that most citizens

    (A) will start to riot if they see an arrest being made

    (B) appreciate the work that law enforcement officers do

    (C) do not realize that making arrests is only a small part of law enforcement

    (D) never call for assistance unless they are involved in a personal argument or a husband and wife quarrel

73. According to the passage, one way in which law enforcement officers can prevent crimes from happening is by

    (A) arresting suspicious characters

    (B) letting minor offenders go free

    (C) taking action on potential violations

    (D) refusing to get involved in husband and wife fights

74. According to the passage, which of the following statements is *not* true of situations involving emotionally disturbed persons?

    (A) It is a waste of time to call on law enforcement officers for assistance in such situations.

    (B) Such situations may not involve illegal behavior.

    (C) Such situations often do not result in arrests.

    (D) Citizens often turn to law enforcement officers for help in such situations.

75. The last sentence in the passage mentions "detention of minor offenders." Of the following, which best explains the meaning of the word "detention" as used here?

(A) Sentencing someone

(B) Indicting someone

(C) Calling someone before a grand jury

(D) Arresting someone

Answer questions 76 through 79 on the basis of the information given in the following passage.

Automobile tire tracks found at the scene of a crime constitute an important link in the chain of physical evidence. In many cases, these are the only clues available. In some areas, unpaved ground adjoins the highway or paved streets. A suspect will often park his or her car off the paved portion of the street when committing a crime, sometimes leaving excellent tire tracks. Comparison of the tire track impressions with the tires is possible only when the vehicle has been found. However, the initial problem facing the police is the task of determining what kind of car probably made the impressions found at the scene of the crime. If the make, model, and year of the car that made the impressions can be determined, it is obvious that the task of elimination is greatly lessened.

76. The one of the following that is the most appropriate title for this passage is

(A) "The Use of Automobiles in the Commission of Crimes"

(B) "The Use of Tire Tracks in Police Work"

(C) "The Capture of Criminals by Scientific Police Work"

(D) "The Positive Identification of Criminals Through Their Cars"

77. When searching for clear signs left by the car used in the commission of a crime, the most likely place for the police to look would be on the

(A) highway adjoining unpaved streets

(B) highway adjacent to paved streets

(C) paved streets adjacent to a highway

(D) unpaved ground adjacent to a highway

78. Automobile tire tracks found at the scene of a crime are of value as evidence in that they are

(A) generally sufficient to trap and convict a suspect

(B) the most important link in the chain of physical evidence

(C) often the only evidence at hand

(D) circumstantial rather than direct

79. The primary reason that the police try to determine the make, model, and year of the car involved in the commission of a crime is to

(A) compare the tire tracks left at the scene of the crime with the type of tires used on cars of that make

(B) determine if the mud on the tires of the suspected car matches the mud in the unpaved road near the scene of the crime

(C) reduce, to a large extent, the amount of work involved in determining the particular car used in the commission of a crime

(D) alert the police patrol forces to question the occupants of all automobiles of this type

Answer questions 80 through 83 on the basis of the information given in the following passage:

When stopping vehicles on highways to check for suspects or fugitives, the police use an automobile roadblock whenever possible. This consists of three cars placed in prearranged positions. Car 1 is parked across the left lane of the roadway with the front diagonally facing toward the center line. Car 2 is parked across the right lane, with the front of the vehicle also toward the center line, in a position perpendicular to car 1 and appropriately 20 feet to the rear. Continuing another 20 feet to the rear along the highway, car 3 is parked in an identical manner to car 1. The width of the highway determines the angle or position in which the autos should be placed. In addition to the regular roadblock signs, and the use of flares at night only, there is an officer located at both the entrance and exit to direct and control traffic from both directions. This type of roadblock forces all approaching autos to reduce speed and zigzag around the police cars. Officers standing behind the parked cars can most safely and carefully view all passing motorists. Once a suspect is inside the block, it becomes extremely difficult to crash out.

80. Of the following, the most appropriate title for this passage is

(A) "The Construction of an Escape-Proof Roadblock"

(B) "Regulation of Automobile Traffic Through a Police Roadblock"

(C) "Safety Precautions Necessary in Making an Automobile Roadblock"

(D) "Structure of a Roadblock to Detain Suspects or Fugitives"

81. When setting up a three-car roadblock, the relative positions of the cars should be such that

(A) the front of car 1 is placed diagonally to the center line and facing car 3

(B) car 3 is placed parallel to the center line and its front faces the right side of the road

(C) car 2 is placed about 20 feet from car 1 and its front faces the left side of the road

(D) car 3 is parallel to and about 20 feet away from car 1

82. Officers can observe occupants of all cars passing through the roadblock with greatest safety when

(A) warning flares are lighted to illuminate the area sufficiently at night

(B) warning signs are put up at each end of the roadblock

(C) they are stationed at both the exit and the entrance of the roadblock

(D) they take up positions behind cars in the roadblock

83. The type of automobile roadblock described in the passage is of value in police work because

   (A) a suspect is unable to escape its confines by using force
   (B) it is frequently used to capture suspects with no danger to police officers
   (C) it requires only two officers to set up and operate
   (D) vehicular traffic within its confines is controlled as to speed and direction

Answer questions 84 through 86 on the basis of the information given in the following passage.

When police officers search for a stolen car, they first check for the color of the car, then for make, model, year, body damage, and finally license number. The first five checks can be made from almost any angle, while the recognition of the license number is often not immediately apparent. The serial number and motor number, though less likely to be changed than the easily substituted license number, cannot be observed in initial detection of the stolen car.

84. According to the passage, the one of the following features that is *least* readily observed in checking for a stolen car in moving traffic is the

   (A) license number
   (B) serial number
   (C) model
   (D) make

85. The feature of a car that cannot be determined from most angles of observation is the

   (A) make
   (B) model
   (C) year
   (D) license number

86. Of the following, the feature of a stolen car that is most likely to be altered by a car thief shortly after the car is stolen is the

   (A) license number
   (B) motor number
   (C) color
   (D) minor body damage

Answer questions 87 and 88 on the basis of the information given in the following passage.

A survey has shown that crime prevention work is most successful if the officers are assigned on rotating shifts to provide around-the-clock coverage. An officer may work for days at a time and then be switched to nights. The prime object of the night work is to enable the officer to spot conditions inviting burglars. Complete lack of, or faulty locations of, night lights and other conditions that may invite burglars, which might go unnoticed during the daylight hours, can be located and corrected more readily through night work. Night work also enables the officer to check local hangouts of teenagers, such as where a teenage dance is held every Friday night. Detectives also join patrol officers cruising in radio patrol cars to check on teenagers loitering late at night and to spot-check local bars for teenagers.

87. The most important purpose of assigning officers to night shifts is to make is possible for them to

    (A) correct conditions that may not be readily noticed during the day

    (B) discover the location of and replace missing and faulty night lights

    (C) locate criminal hangouts

    (D) notice things at night that cannot be noticed during the daytime

88. The type of shifting of officers that best prevents crime is to have

    (A) day-shift officers rotated to night work

    (B) rotating shifts provide sufficient officers for coverage 24 hours daily

    (C) an officer work around the clock on a 24-hour basis as police needs arise

    (D) rotating shifts to give officers varied experience

Answer questions 89 through 91 on the basis of the information given in the following passage.

In addition to making the preliminary investigation of crimes, police patrol officers should serve as eyes, ears, and legs for the detective division. The patrol division may be used for surveillance, to serve warrants and bring in suspects and witnesses, and to perform a number of routine tasks for the detectives which will increase the time available for tasks that require their special skills and facilities. It is to the advantage of individual detectives, as well as of the detective division, to have patrol officers working in this manner. More cases are cleared by arrest, and a greater proportion of stolen property is recovered when, in addition to the detective regularly assigned, a number of patrol officers also work on the case. Detectives may stimulate the interest and participation of patrol officers by keeping them informed of the presence, identity or description, hangouts, associates, vehicles, and method of operation of each criminal known to be in the community.

89. According to this passage, a patrol officer should

    (A) assist the detective in certain routine functions

    (B) be considered for assignment as a detective on the basis of patrol performance

    (C) leave the scene once a detective arrives

    (D) perform as much of the detective's duties as time permits

90. According to this passage, patrol officers should aid detectives by

    (A) accepting from detectives assignments that give promise of recovering stolen property

    (B) making arrests of witnesses for the detectives' interrogation

    (C) performing all special investigative work for detectives

    (D) producing for questioning individuals who may aid the detectives in investigation

91. According to this passage, detectives can keep patrol officers interested by

    (A) ascertaining that patrol officers are doing investigative work properly

    (B) having patrol officers directly under their supervision during an investigation

    (C) informing patrol officers of the value of their efforts in crime prevention

    (D) supplying the patrol officers with information regarding known criminals in the community

Answer questions 92 and 93 on the basis of the information given in the following passage.

The medical examiner may contribute valuable data to the investigator of fires that cause fatalities. By careful examination of the bodies of any victims, the examiner not only establishes cause of death, but may also furnish, in many instances, answers to questions relating to the identity of the victim and the source and origin of the fire. The medical examiner is of greatest value to law enforcement agencies because he or she is able to determine the exact cause of death through an examination of tissue of the apparent arson victims. Thorough study of a burned body or even of parts of a burned body will frequently yield information that will help to clarify problems confronting the arson investigator and the police.

92. According to the passage, the most important task of the medical examiner in the investigation of arson is to obtain information concerning the

 (A) identity of arsonists

 (B) cause of death

 (C) identity of victims

 (D) source and origin of fires

93. The central thought of the passage is that the medical examiner aids in the solution of crimes of arson when

 (A) a person is burned to death

 (B) identity of the arsonist is unknown

 (C) the cause of the fires is unknown

 (D) trained investigators are not available

Directions: Each of the following sentences may or may not be correct as written. Below each sentence you will find four different ways of writing the italicized part. If you think the sentence is correct as written, choose answer A, which is always the same as the italicized part. If you think one of the other choices makes a better sentence, mark the letter of your choice.

94. Edna burst into the room shouting, "Why *was Marilyn and he* permitted to go?"

 (A) was Marilyn and he

 (B) was Marilyn and him

 (C) was Marilyn and his

 (D) were Marilyn and he

95. The teacher, *with all her students, was* late for the train

 (A) with all her students, was

 (B) with all her students was

 (C) with all her students, were

 (D) with all her students; was

96. Watching the takeoff, the small boy waved his arms *as if he were a plane himself.*

    (A) as if he were a plane himself

    (B) as if he was a plane himself

    (C) like he was a plane hisself

    (D) like he was a plane himself

97. How much *has fuel costs raised* during the past year?

    (A) has fuel costs raised

    (B) have fuel costs raised

    (C) has fuel costs risen

    (D) have fuel costs risen

98. *It was all so different than I expected.*

    (A) It was all so different than I expected.

    (B) It was all so different from what I expected.

    (C) It was all different and not expected.

    (D) It was all different than what I had expected.

99. Some gardeners put dead leaves or straw between the rows of seedlings so that the ground doesn't dry out and *you don't have to weed as much.*

    (A) you don't have to weed as much

    (B) they don't have to weed as much

    (C) they don't have weeding as much as before

    (D) your weeding is less

100. *Pat went to Jones Beach with his girlfriend wearing a blue and white bathing suit.*

    (A) Pat went to Jones Beach with his girlfriend wearing a blue and white bathing suit.

    (B) Pat went to Jones Beach, wearing a blue and white bathing suit, with his girlfriend.

    (C) Pat, wearing a blue and white bathing suit, went to Jones Beach with his girlfriend.

    (D) To Jones Beach, wearing a blue and white bathing suit, went Pat with his girlfriend.

ANSWER KEY

1. D	21. B	41. C	61. D	81. C
2. D	22. B	42. C	62. A	82. D
3. D	23. C	43. D	63. D	83. D
4. A	24. A	44. A	64. B	84. B
5. A	25. B	45. C	65. C	85. D
6. B	26. B	46. C	66. A	86. A
7. D	27. A	47. A	67. B	87. D
8. B	28. A	48. D	68. A	88. B
9. D	29. B	49. B	69. C	89. A
10. C	30. A	50. D	70. A	90. D
11. D	31. B	51. A	71. D	91. D
12. C	32. D	52. B	72. C	92. B
13. B	33. A	53. A	73. C	93. A
14. A	34. D	54. A	74. A	94. D
15. C	35. C	55. B	75. D	95. A
16. C	36. C	56. A	76. B	96. A
17. A	37. D	57. D	77. D	97. D
18. B	38. C	58. C	78. C	98. B
19. A	39. A	59. B	79. C	99. B
20. B	40. D	60. A	80. D	100. C

EXPLANATORY ANSWERS

1. **(D)** Refer to the third sentence of the description.
2. **(D)** The officers observed the suspects alighting from the roof by way of ladder.
3. **(D)** The two white males ran into an alleyway, and the black male and Hispanic male ran into a parking lot.
4. **(A)** This information is included in the description of the white male with long blond hair.
5. **(A)** This information is included in the description of the Hispanic male.
6. **(B)** This information is included in the description of the white male with short hair.
7. **(D)** This information is included in the description of the white male with short hair.
8. **(B)** This information is included in the description of the white male with long blond hair.
9. **(D)** This information is included in the description of the Hispanic male.
10. **(C)** This is the description of the vehicle in which the two white males fled.
11. **(D)** The description states only that the escape vehicles fled west on Seventh Street. There is no information as to what type of street Seventh Street is.
12. **(C)** Both the black male and Hispanic male entered the parking lot. However, it was the black male who was carrying what appeared to be a portable TV set.
13. **(B)** This information is included in the description of the black male.
14. **(A)** This information is included in the description of the black male.
15. **(C)** The description refers only to Officer Smith using a walkie-talkie and broadcasting information.

16. **(C)** Photographs form a permanent record of how the crime scene appeared when the police arrived. These pictures can be used at a criminal trial to show how the crime scene looked.

17. **(A)** There is no *immediate* danger to the officer or to the woman since the gun is in the man's pocket. Therefore, it is not necessary or proper for the officer to fire a shot. The office should repeat his order before taking any further action.

18. **(B)** If the suspect observes that notes are being taken, he or she may freeze up or not talk as freely because he knows that what he or she is saying will become part of the permanent record.

19. **(A)** The prisoner would either have to roll over or turn his head completely around to see the officer in order to shoot accurately. The time required for this type of movement would allow the officer to take cover or to fire the first shot.

20. **(B)** Ignoring the rumors or not supplying the true circumstances of the emergency as soon as they are available only increases the fear people may have and may result in a possible panic situation.

21. **(B)** If a child had been missing for an extended period of time, police headquarters usually would have received information concerning the child.

22. **(B)** If the plainclothes officer were to stop following the suspect now, the suspect would be difficult to locate again since he is known to have changed residences frequently.

23. **(C)** If a police officer doesn't fully understand the instructions given by a supervisor, the officer should immediately ask for clarification from the person giving the instructions so that he or she can carry out the assignment properly.

24. **(A)** A police officer should always be alert and on guard until the nature of the situation in which he or she is involved is made completely clear.

25. **(B)** Police officers and police departments should never recommend a specific product or business. Endorsements tend to indicate favoritism and police officers should always be impartial.

26. **(B)** Suspects and witnesses should always be questioned separately so that the description that one person gives does not influence the description given by any other persons at the scene.

27. **(A)** If there is the slightest chance that the object could be a bomb, all persons should be removed from the location for safety reasons.

28. **(A)** The call could be a set-up for robbing both the owner and his store. If there were a real emergency, the police would most likely be on the scene.

29. **(B)** In most cases it takes a *thorough* search of the crime scene to uncover the clues left by the criminal. Most clues in and of themselves are not conclusive. However, when used collectively, they form the foundation for proving the guilt or innocence of the suspect.

30. **(A)** He was wrong. The principle here is that a police officer has a duty to protect the public at all times, even when off duty.

31. **(B)** A statement should be taken as soon as the suspect offers to make one. The suspect may feel an immediate need to tell someone what happened. A delay in taking the statement may cause the suspect to remain silent about the matter.

32. **(D)** The situation fits both the definition of burglary (to enter a building to commit a crime) and of robbery (stealing by force—in this case, the punch in the face).

33. **(A)** John Brown can be charged with larceny only as there was no intent to commit a crime when he entered the store and there was no force used.

34. **(D)** The charges are sexual abuse (touching of the buttocks) and larceny (taking $10 from the pocketbook). No force was used to remove the money, thus eliminating the charge of robbery.

35. **(C)** To charge a person with burglary, it must only be shown that the building was entered with the intention of committing a crime therein. (In this case, the crime was sexual abuse.) Despite the fact that Saunders was not successful in committing the crime he intended, the intention was there.

36. **(C)** Taylor's intention for entering the apartment was to have sexual intercourse with his 16-year-old girlfriend, a crime because she is younger than 17 years of age. He could be charged with burglary (intent to commit a crime) and sexual misconduct (sexual intercourse with a female less than 17 years of age).

37. **(D)** Mary is 17 years old and gave her consent.

38. **(C)** There was neither any intention to commit a crime when Bill entered the building nor was there any injury incurred. For the charge to be assault, there must be some kind of injury.

39. **(A)** Joe had no intent to commit a crime before he entered the warehouse. He caused an injury to a fellow worker, a broken arm, by his actions; therefore, the charge of assault could be preferred. Emotional disturbance is not a valid excuse for such actions.

40. **(D)** The charges are burglary (entering the school with the intention of taking a movie projector), robbery (using force on the security guard to take the projector), and assault (causing an injury, the broken nose, to the security guard).

41. **(C)** Because Tom used force to touch Sue's private parts, he could be charged with sexual abuse. Since there was no intention to commit the crime prior to his entering her apartment, the possibility of a burglary charge is eliminated.

42. **(C)** Minor complaints, when properly investigated, can show a pattern of conduct that could lead to a major problem for the police.

43. **(D)** With the exception of a few narrowly defined situations, the courts demand that actual witnesses be examined under oath.

44. **(A)** A police officer does a multitude of things other than arrest people. The officer responds to sick, injured, and emotionally disturbed people calling for help. He or she handles vehicle accidents, family disputes, lost children, traffic problems, and so on. The officer's effectiveness should be based on how the officer handles the entire spectrum of his or her duties rather than on the number of arrests he or she makes in a given period of time.

45. **(C)** Fire destroys valuable clues that are usually found at a crime scene. Investigation is made considerably more difficult as a result.

46. **(C)** When the police observe potential delinquent-producing conditions, they can take immediate action to correct them.

47. **(A)** By questioning the man first, the officer may be able to ascertain who he is and where he lives and thereby return him to his home without any further delay.

48. **(D)** A suspect who broods silently may be feeling very humiliated and depressed and may indeed be suicidal.

49. **(B)** Police descriptions must be accurate in order to match the article to complainant. For example, just listing the watch as a yellow metal man's wristwatch would fit thousands of complaints of lost or stolen watches.

50. **(D)** Witnesses and suspects should always be separated when being questioned or giving statements so that the statement one makes does not influence what the others might say.

51. **(A)** This information is stated clearly in the quotation itself.

52. **(B)** Until a crime scene is properly searched and investigated, no one other that those assigned directly to the case should be allowed to enter the area because of the likelihood that valuable evidence will be destroyed.

53. **(A)** By stationing themselves in this manner, the two officers would be able to observe all four sides of the building.

54. **(A)** In order to function effectively, police departments have specific rules and regulations that must be followed. Individual police officers must follow the rules; they cannot change or disregard these rules because they think they are unwise or unnecessary. All changes will be made by the chiefs of the respective departments.

55. **(B)** With the passage of time, accurate mental recall of an incident decreases. Written reports should always be prepared for future reference, especially if the case may go to court.

56. **(A)** Once the people in the neighborhood get to *know* the police officer who is regularly assigned, they are more likely to cooperate. People don't generally cooperate with strangers, even if the stranger is a police officer

57. **(D)** All the letters in column 2 and all the numbers in column 3 are in sequence with the capital letters in column 1.

58. **(C)** When compared to column 1, the letters (column 2) *z, q, o,* and *a* and the numbers (column 3) *5* and *4* are out of sequence.

59. **(B)** When compared to column 1, all the letters in column 2 are in their proper sequence; however, the numbers *2* and *3* in column 3 are out of sequence.

60. **(A)** When compared to column 1, all the numbers in column 3 are in their proper sequence; however, the letters *a* and *o* in column 2 are out of sequence.

61. **(D)** When compared to column 1, all the letters in column 2 and all the numbers in column 3 are in proper sequence.

62. **(A)** When compared to column 1, all the numbers in column 3 are in proper sequence; however, the letters *r* and *a* in column 2 are out of sequence.

63. **(D)** The person is treated at a location other than his home. If he were treated at home, a report would not be required. The reporting officer is from the 2nd Precinct.

64. **(B)** The directions for box #9 state that the officer will enter the nature of the illness or injury to the best of his or her knowledge.

65. **(C)** Mr. Mandello was the victim of a robbery; therefore, a crime report is required. A street injury report is not required because he was not injured as a result of a defect in the sidewalk.

66. **(A)** As he was taking the information from the assistance report, Officer Whelan noticed that the corner streetlight was not working.

67. **(B)** An admission number is required only when a relative or friend can't be notified that a person was admitted to a hospital. This is true only in the case of Mr. Rodriguez.

68. **(A)** The directions for preparing the report state that the official diagnosis will be listed in box #17, "Remarks."

69. **(C)** Only a vehicle accident report is required. There was no crime involved and the accident was not caused by a defect in the roadway, thus eliminating a street injury report.

70. **(A)** The witnesses state that the traffic light was not working, therefore the Traffic Department should be notified.

71. **(D)** John Francis was the ambulance attendant who responded. The victims were not sick; they were injured. Mr. Serrano's brother, not his father, was notified as to his injury in an accident that occurred on Seventh Avenue and 82nd Street.

72. **(C)** Refer to the first sentence of the passage.

73. **(C)** Refer to the third sentence of the passage.

74. **(A)** It is stated in the fourth sentence that many of the situations in which police assistance is required involved emotionally disturbed persons.

75. **(D)** A police officer arrests; the courts sentence, indict, or call people before a grand jury.

76. **(B)** The passage talks exclusively about tire tracks. No mention is made of autos being used in the commission of crimes, of scientific police work, or of positive identification through cars.

77. **(D)** Refer to the third and fourth sentences of the passage.

78. **(C)** Refer to the second sentence of the passage.

79. **(C)** Refer to the last sentence of the passage.

80. **(D)** The paragraph doesn't state that the type of roadblock mentioned is escape-proof, but it does state that the roadblock described will force all approaching vehicles to reduce speed and make it extremely difficult for vehicles to crash out of the roadblock.

81. **(C)** Refer to the fourth sentence of the passage. If the car is parked in the right lane with its front facing the center line, the front is necessarily facing the left side of the road.

82. **(D)** Refer to the next-to-the-last sentence of the passage.

83. **(D)** Refer to the eighth sentence of the passage.

84. **(B)** Refer to the last sentence of the passage.

85. **(D)** Refer to the second sentence of the passage.

86. **(A)** Refer to the last sentence of the passage. The changing of color or the repairing of body damage could not be accomplished in a short period of time.

87. **(D)** Certain conditions that might go unnoticed by day are visible at night, especially lighting problems. Officers notice these on the night shift; building owners thus alerted make the corrections.

88. **(B)** Refer to the first sentence of the passage.

89. **(A)** The first sentence of the passage states that the patrol officer "should serve as eyes, ears, and legs for the detective division." No statement in the passage makes any mention of police officers being considered for assignment to the detective division, leaving the scene when detectives arrive, or performing detectives' duties.

90. **(D)** Refer to the second sentence of the passage.

91. **(D)** Refer to the last sentence of the passage.

92. **(B)** Refer to the third sentence of the passage.

93. **(A)** Refer to the first sentence of the paragraph. The medical examiner deals with dead human bodies, not with trying to identify arson suspects or with determining the causes of a fire.

94. **(D)** *Marilyn and he* is the compound subject of the plural verb *were*.

95. **(A)** The singular teacher is the subject of the sentence. The students represent additional information but are not part of the subject.

96. **(A)** The statement contrary to fact (the boy is not an airplane) correctly takes the subjunctive *were*.

97. **(D)** The correct tense of the verb to use in this sentence is the present perfect. *Costs* are plural. The construction here is "fuel costs have risen."

98. **(B)** The correct form is *different from*.

99. **(B)** Don't change persons midsentence. The sentence is about gardeners, not about *you*. (C) does not change persons but is awkwardly stated.

100. **(C)** Who was wearing a blue and white bathing suit? Only this choice makes it clear.

Answer Sheet for Model Examination 5

1. Ⓐ Ⓑ Ⓒ Ⓓ   26. Ⓐ Ⓑ Ⓒ Ⓓ   51. Ⓐ Ⓑ Ⓒ Ⓓ   76. Ⓐ Ⓑ Ⓒ Ⓓ   101. Ⓐ Ⓑ Ⓒ Ⓓ

2. Ⓐ Ⓑ Ⓒ Ⓓ   27. Ⓐ Ⓑ Ⓒ Ⓓ   52. Ⓐ Ⓑ Ⓒ Ⓓ   77. Ⓐ Ⓑ Ⓒ Ⓓ   102. Ⓐ Ⓑ Ⓒ Ⓓ

3. Ⓐ Ⓑ Ⓒ Ⓓ   28. Ⓐ Ⓑ Ⓒ Ⓓ   53. Ⓐ Ⓑ Ⓒ Ⓓ   78. Ⓐ Ⓑ Ⓒ Ⓓ   103. Ⓐ Ⓑ Ⓒ Ⓓ

4. Ⓐ Ⓑ Ⓒ Ⓓ   29. Ⓐ Ⓑ Ⓒ Ⓓ   54. Ⓐ Ⓑ Ⓒ Ⓓ   79. Ⓐ Ⓑ Ⓒ Ⓓ   104. Ⓐ Ⓑ Ⓒ Ⓓ

5. Ⓐ Ⓑ Ⓒ Ⓓ   30. Ⓐ Ⓑ Ⓒ Ⓓ   55. Ⓐ Ⓑ Ⓒ Ⓓ   80. Ⓐ Ⓑ Ⓒ Ⓓ   105. Ⓐ Ⓑ Ⓒ Ⓓ

6. Ⓐ Ⓑ Ⓒ Ⓓ   31. Ⓐ Ⓑ Ⓒ Ⓓ   56. Ⓐ Ⓑ Ⓒ Ⓓ   81. Ⓐ Ⓑ Ⓒ Ⓓ   106. Ⓐ Ⓑ Ⓒ Ⓓ

7. Ⓐ Ⓑ Ⓒ Ⓓ   32. Ⓐ Ⓑ Ⓒ Ⓓ   57. Ⓐ Ⓑ Ⓒ Ⓓ   82. Ⓐ Ⓑ Ⓒ Ⓓ   107. Ⓐ Ⓑ Ⓒ Ⓓ

8. Ⓐ Ⓑ Ⓒ Ⓓ   33. Ⓐ Ⓑ Ⓒ Ⓓ   58. Ⓐ Ⓑ Ⓒ Ⓓ   83. Ⓐ Ⓑ Ⓒ Ⓓ   108. Ⓐ Ⓑ Ⓒ Ⓓ

9. Ⓐ Ⓑ Ⓒ Ⓓ   34. Ⓐ Ⓑ Ⓒ Ⓓ   59. Ⓐ Ⓑ Ⓒ Ⓓ   84. Ⓐ Ⓑ Ⓒ Ⓓ   109. Ⓐ Ⓑ Ⓒ Ⓓ

10. Ⓐ Ⓑ Ⓒ Ⓓ   35. Ⓐ Ⓑ Ⓒ Ⓓ   60. Ⓐ Ⓑ Ⓒ Ⓓ   85. Ⓐ Ⓑ Ⓒ Ⓓ   110. Ⓐ Ⓑ Ⓒ Ⓓ

11. Ⓐ Ⓑ Ⓒ Ⓓ   36. Ⓐ Ⓑ Ⓒ Ⓓ   61. Ⓐ Ⓑ Ⓒ Ⓓ   86. Ⓐ Ⓑ Ⓒ Ⓓ   111. Ⓐ Ⓑ Ⓒ Ⓓ

12. Ⓐ Ⓑ Ⓒ Ⓓ   37. Ⓐ Ⓑ Ⓒ Ⓓ   62. Ⓐ Ⓑ Ⓒ Ⓓ   87. Ⓐ Ⓑ Ⓒ Ⓓ   112. Ⓐ Ⓑ Ⓒ Ⓓ

13. Ⓐ Ⓑ Ⓒ Ⓓ   38. Ⓐ Ⓑ Ⓒ Ⓓ   63. Ⓐ Ⓑ Ⓒ Ⓓ   88. Ⓐ Ⓑ Ⓒ Ⓓ   113. Ⓐ Ⓑ Ⓒ Ⓓ

14. Ⓐ Ⓑ Ⓒ Ⓓ   39. Ⓐ Ⓑ Ⓒ Ⓓ   64. Ⓐ Ⓑ Ⓒ Ⓓ   89. Ⓐ Ⓑ Ⓒ Ⓓ   114. Ⓐ Ⓑ Ⓒ Ⓓ

15. Ⓐ Ⓑ Ⓒ Ⓓ   40. Ⓐ Ⓑ Ⓒ Ⓓ   65. Ⓐ Ⓑ Ⓒ Ⓓ   90. Ⓐ Ⓑ Ⓒ Ⓓ   115. Ⓐ Ⓑ Ⓒ Ⓓ

16. Ⓐ Ⓑ Ⓒ Ⓓ   41. Ⓐ Ⓑ Ⓒ Ⓓ   66. Ⓐ Ⓑ Ⓒ Ⓓ   91. Ⓐ Ⓑ Ⓒ Ⓓ   116. Ⓐ Ⓑ Ⓒ Ⓓ

17. Ⓐ Ⓑ Ⓒ Ⓓ   42. Ⓐ Ⓑ Ⓒ Ⓓ   67. Ⓐ Ⓑ Ⓒ Ⓓ   92. Ⓐ Ⓑ Ⓒ Ⓓ   117. Ⓐ Ⓑ Ⓒ Ⓓ

18. Ⓐ Ⓑ Ⓒ Ⓓ   43. Ⓐ Ⓑ Ⓒ Ⓓ   68. Ⓐ Ⓑ Ⓒ Ⓓ   93. Ⓐ Ⓑ Ⓒ Ⓓ   118. Ⓐ Ⓑ Ⓒ Ⓓ

19. Ⓐ Ⓑ Ⓒ Ⓓ   44. Ⓐ Ⓑ Ⓒ Ⓓ   69. Ⓐ Ⓑ Ⓒ Ⓓ   94. Ⓐ Ⓑ Ⓒ Ⓓ   119. Ⓐ Ⓑ Ⓒ Ⓓ

20. Ⓐ Ⓑ Ⓒ Ⓓ   45. Ⓐ Ⓑ Ⓒ Ⓓ   70. Ⓐ Ⓑ Ⓒ Ⓓ   95. Ⓐ Ⓑ Ⓒ Ⓓ   120. Ⓐ Ⓑ Ⓒ Ⓓ

21. Ⓐ Ⓑ Ⓒ Ⓓ   46. Ⓐ Ⓑ Ⓒ Ⓓ   71. Ⓐ Ⓑ Ⓒ Ⓓ   96. Ⓐ Ⓑ Ⓒ Ⓓ   121. Ⓐ Ⓑ Ⓒ Ⓓ

22. Ⓐ Ⓑ Ⓒ Ⓓ   47. Ⓐ Ⓑ Ⓒ Ⓓ   72. Ⓐ Ⓑ Ⓒ Ⓓ   97. Ⓐ Ⓑ Ⓒ Ⓓ   122. Ⓐ Ⓑ Ⓒ Ⓓ

23. Ⓐ Ⓑ Ⓒ Ⓓ   48. Ⓐ Ⓑ Ⓒ Ⓓ   73. Ⓐ Ⓑ Ⓒ Ⓓ   98. Ⓐ Ⓑ Ⓒ Ⓓ   123. Ⓐ Ⓑ Ⓒ Ⓓ

24. Ⓐ Ⓑ Ⓒ Ⓓ   49. Ⓐ Ⓑ Ⓒ Ⓓ   74. Ⓐ Ⓑ Ⓒ Ⓓ   99. Ⓐ Ⓑ Ⓒ Ⓓ   124. Ⓐ Ⓑ Ⓒ Ⓓ

25. Ⓐ Ⓑ Ⓒ Ⓓ   50. Ⓐ Ⓑ Ⓒ Ⓓ   75. Ⓐ Ⓑ Ⓒ Ⓓ   100. Ⓐ Ⓑ Ⓒ Ⓓ   125. Ⓐ Ⓑ Ⓒ Ⓓ

TEAR HERE

Model Examination 5

Time: 3¹/₂ Hours—125 Questions

Directions: Each question numbered 1 through 81 has four possible choices lettered A, B, C, and D. You are to select the answer that you deem to be correct.

1. In addressing a class of recruits, an instructor remarked: "Carelessness and failure are twins." The one of the following that most nearly expresses the meaning of this statement is

   (A) negligence seldom accompanies success

   (B) incomplete work is careless work

   (C) conscientious work is never attended by failure

   (D) a conscientious person never makes mistakes

2. In lecturing on the law of arrest, an instructor remarked: "To go beyond is as bad as to fall short." The one of the following that most nearly expresses the meaning of this statement is

   (A) never undertake the impossible

   (B) extremes are not desirable

   (C) look before you leap

   (D) too much success is dangerous

3. In recent years, the age group 16 through 25 showed the greatest number of arrests for

   (A) grand larceny from highways and vehicles

   (B) burglary

   (C) rape

   (D) homicide

4. The two leading causes of traffic accidents involving pedestrians are
   (A) crossing a street against the light and crossing past a parked car
   (B) crossing a street at a point other than the crossing and crossing against the light
   (C) crossing a street at a point other than the crossing and running off the sidewalk
   (D) crossing a street against the light and failing to observe whether cars are making right or left turns

5. A "modus operandi" file will be most valuable to a new state trooper as a means of showing the
   (A) method used by criminals
   (B) various bureaus and divisions of the police department
   (C) number and nature of vehicular accidents
   (D) forms used by the police department

6. A state trooper is frequently advised to lie down before returning fire if a person is shooting at him or her. This is primarily because
   (A) a smaller target will thus be presented to the assailant
   (B) he or she can return fire more quickly while in the prone position
   (C) the assailant will think the trooper has been struck and cease firing
   (D) it will indicate that the trooper is not the aggressor

7. In making arrests during a large riot, it is the practice for troopers to take the ringleaders into custody as soon as possible. This is primarily because
   (A) the police can obtain valuable information from them
   (B) they deserve punishment more than the other rioters
   (C) rioters need leadership and, without it, will disperse more quickly
   (D) arrests of wrongdoers should always be in order of their importance

8. As you are patrolling your post, you observe two men running toward a parked automobile in which a driver is seated. You question the three men and you note the license number. You should
   (A) let them go if you see nothing suspicious
   (B) warn them not to be caught loitering again
   (C) arrest them because they have probably committed a crime
   (D) take them back with you to the place from which the two men came

9. Assume that you are a state trooper. A woman has complained to you about a man's indecent exposure in front of her house. As you approach the house, the man begins to run. You should
   (A) shoot to kill as the man may be a dangerous maniac
   (B) shout at the man to halt
   (C) summon other troopers in order to apprehend him
   (D) question the woman regarding the man's identity

10. You are patrolling a parkway in a radio car with another trooper. A maroon car coming from the opposite direction signals you to stop and the driver informs you that he was robbed by three men speeding ahead of him in a black sedan. Your radio car cannot cross the center abutment. You should

    (A) request the driver to make a report to the nearest precinct as your car cannot cross over to the other side

    (B) make a U-turn in your radio car and give chase on the wrong side of the parkway

    (C) fire warning shots in the air to summon other troopers

    (D) flash headquarters over your radio system

11. On patrol, you notice that a man is limping hurriedly, leaving a trail of blood behind him. You question him and his explanation is that he was hurt accidentally while he was watching a man clean a gun. You should

    (A) let him go as you have no proof that his story is not true

    (B) take him to the nearest hospital and question him again after treatment

    (C) ask him whether the man had a license for his gun

    (D) ask him to lead you to the man who cleaned his gun so that you may question him further about the accident

12. Which of the following situations, if observed by you while on highway patrol, should you consider *most* suspicious and deserving of further investigation?

    (A) A shabbily dressed person is driving a new Mercedes Benz.

    (B) A 1987 Chrysler has been parked without lights outside an apartment house for several hours.

    (C) A light is on in the rear of a one-family luxurious residence.

    (D) Two well-dressed men are standing at a bus stop at 2 A.M. and arguing heatedly.

13. In addition to cases of submersion involving blocked breathing, artificial respiration is a recommended first aid procedure for

    (A) sunstroke

    (B) chemical poisoning

    (C) electrical shock

    (D) apoplexy

14. An injury to muscle or tendon brought about by severe exertion and resulting in pain and stiffness is called a

    (A) strain

    (B) sprain

    (C) bruise

    (D) fracture

15. The delivery of an arrested person, upon giving security for his appearance at the time and place designated to submit to the jurisdiction and judgment of the court, is known as

   (A) bail

   (B) habeas corpus

   (C) parole

   (D) probation

16. Jones was charged with the murder of Smith. Brown, Jones's landlord, testified at the trial that Jones had in his home a well-equipped laboratory that contained all the necessary chemicals for producing the poison that an autopsy showed caused Smith's death. Brown's testimony constitutes what is called

   (A) corroborative evidence

   (B) opinion evidence

   (C) hearsay evidence

   (D) circumstantial evidence

17. The procedure whereby a defendant is brought before a magistrate, informed of the charge against him, and asked how he pleads thereto, is called

   (A) arraignment

   (B) indictment

   (C) presentment

   (D) inquisition

18. It is customary for state police to keep records of lost or stolen automobile license plates. Of the following, the best reason for this practice is to

   (A) permit the prompt issuance of new plates

   (B) keep a record of all outstanding license plates in use

   (C) prevent cars from being stolen

   (D) capture or detain any person found using or attempting to use any of these plates

19. "A criminal will become either a thief, an assailant, or a sexual offender, never an all-around criminal." Of the following, an important reason for these basic differences in criminal behavior is probably that

   (A) to be an all-around criminal requires more intelligence than the average criminal has

   (B) crime syndicates have gained control over certain branches of crime and have made it difficult for a beginner to break in

   (C) criminal acts are an expression of the criminal's whole personality

   (D) most crimes are committed on the spur of the moment and without previous thought

20. One of the chief reasons why fingerprints are of great value in helping to identify people is that

    (A) criminals always leave fingerprints at the scene of a crime, whether they know it or not

    (B) no two persons have the same fingerprint pattern

    (C) fingerprint patterns change as people grow older

    (D) nationality, religion, and race can be determined by fingerprint patterns

21. It is *least* accurate to state of fingerprints that

    (A) it is possible to fingerprint even a dead person

    (B) the value of fingerprints left at the scene of a crime does not vary with the distinctness of the fingerprint impressions

    (C) no fingerprints of different persons have ever been found to be alike

    (D) the prime value of fingerprints lies in their effectiveness in identifying people

22. Of the following, the one that is *least* a purpose of fingerprinting procedure is the

    (A) identification of deceased persons

    (B) identification of the guilty

    (C) protection of the innocent

    (D) recognition of first offenders

23. It is suggested that a suspect should not be permitted to walk in or about the scene of a crime where fingerprints may be present until a thorough search has been made for such evidence. This suggested procedure is

    (A) good; the suspect, if permitted to walk about the scene, would smear all fingerprints that might be found by police investigators

    (B) bad; the return of a suspect to the scene of a crime provides an opportunity to obtain additional fingerprints from the suspect

    (C) good; if the suspect handled any objects at the scene, the value of any original fingerprints, as evidence, might be seriously impaired

    (D) bad; the return of a suspect to the scene of a crime provides an opportunity to identify objects that had been handled during the commission of the crime

24. According to a manual of procedure of a state police department, the delivery, for laboratory examination, of any article required as evidence must be made by the member of the force finding or coming into the possession of such evidence. Of the following, the most likely reason for this procedure is that it

    (A) assists in the establishment of the authenticity of the evidence

    (B) encourages a more careful search of the crime scene for all physical evidence that may be related to the crime

    (C) ensures that the evidence will be properly marked or tagged for future identification

    (D) prevents the undue delay that might result from a delivery through official channels

25. A certain trooper brought a bullet to a scientific crime laboratory for examination. The officer produced the bullet from his pocket and with it money and a penknife that were his personal property. The officer had carried the bullet for several days in his pocket in this manner. His action in this case is

    (A) not proper, since the value of ballistics analysis of the bullet has probably been largely decreased

    (B) intelligent, since his technique of preserving the bullet practically eliminates the possibility of losing the bullet

    (C) intelligent, since no harm has been done and the entire matter has been handled without the undue expenditure of time or effort

    (D) not proper, because evidence of this type necessarily decreases in value if carried on one's person for more than a maximum of 24 hours

26. Of the following, the most accurate characterization of the value of the scientific laboratory to a police force is that the laboratory is

    (A) a supplement to the work of the police officer

    (B) destined eventually to replace the police officer

    (C) a device, especially useful in detective work, without which police officers could hope to solve only a small percentage of crimes committed

    (D) useful as an instrument for the prevention of crime but likely to be grossly fallible as a device to help solve crimes actually committed

27. The use of truth serum (scopolamine)

    (A) is specifically authorized

    (B) is specifically outlawed

    (C) is regarded as a violation of the privilege against self-incrimination

    (D) needs no statutory sanction

28. Poroscopy is

    (A) the science of identification through the sweat pores

    (B) the science of microscopic hair analysis

    (C) a term applied to art or literature of an obscene nature

    (D) the science of determining the mineral content of soil

29. Suppose you are checking an alphabetical card reference file to locate information about a "George Dyerly." After checking all the "D's" you can find a card only for a "George Dyrely." Of the following the best action for you to take is to

    (A) check the balance of the file to see if the card you are interested in has been misfiled

    (B) check the data on the card to see if it relates to the same person in whom you are interested

    (C) correct the spelling of the name on your records and reports to conform to the spelling on the card

    (D) reject this reference file as a source of information regarding this person

30. A businessperson requests advice concerning good practice in the use of a safe in the office. The one of the following points that should be stressed most in the use of safes is that

(A) a safe should not be placed where it can be seen from the street

(B) the combination should be written down and carefully hidden in the office

(C) a safe located in a dark place is more tempting to a burglar than one which is located in a well-lighted place

(D) factors of size and weight alone determine the protection offered by a safe

31. In general, a police officer dealing with teenagers should

(A) establish two-way communication with them

(B) show them that he or she can solve their problems

(C) force them to respect the law

(D) avoid face-to-face contact

Completion of Forms

Directions: Questions 32 through 36 test your ability to fill out forms correctly. An incident is described requiring that a police form be filled out. Read the questions that apply to the form. For each question, choose the one best answer (A, B, C, or D) and blacken the space after its letter on the separate answer sheet.

Answer questions 32 through 36 on the basis of the passage below and the Report of Aid Given form shown on the next page.

Troopers Margaret Firestone and Harry Davis are partners on patrol. They see a man lying on his back on the southwest corner of Capital Highway. Trooper Firestone leaves the patrol car to look at him more closely. The man is dressed in clean clothes and seems to have stopped breathing. Trooper Firestone bends over him, makes a quick inspection, and tells Trooper Davis to send for an ambulance. She begins to administer mouth-to-mouth resuscitation. At this point the man becomes fully conscious and states that this has happened before. He insists that all he needs is a glass of water. He does not want to go to the hospital, nor does he want to be driven home. Trooper Davis gets a glass of water for the man from a nearby store. The man refuses to give his name and will not wait for the ambulance. He drinks the water, thanks the officers for their help, and walks north on Second where he disappears from view.

32. Under *Identification,* the correct entry for Place is

(A) Capital Highway

(B) Second and Seventh

(C) corner of Sixth Avenue and Second Street

(D) Second Avenue North, East Sixth Street

33. Since the man refused to give his name, Trooper Firestone should check the box for

(A) Other, under *Aid Given*

(B) Unknown, under *Identification*

(C) Other, under *Disposition of Case*

(D) Unknown, under *Nature of Illness or Injury*

34. Under *Nature of Problem,* the correct box to check is

(A) Injured

(B) Ill

(C) Neglected

(D) Destitute

REPORT OF AID GIVEN

Identification

Date _____   Time _____   Place _____

Name of Person Aided _____ ☐ Unknown

Nature of Problem

☐ Abandoned   ☐ Destitute   ☐ Ill

☐ Neglected   ☐ Lost   ☐ Injured

Nature of Illness or Injury

☐ Mental   ☐ Physical   ☐ Unknown

Aid Given

☐ Artificial Respiration   ☐ Food or Water

☐ Control of Bleeding   ☐ Clothing or Blankets

☐ Temporary Splint   ☐ Other

Disposition of Case

☐ Taken Home   ☐ Left in Custody of Friend or Relative

☐ Removed to Hospital   ☐ Taken to Morgue

☐ Left at Place of Occurrence   ☐ Other

Name of Officer Reporting _____

35. The correct boxes to check under *Aid Given* are

(A) Food or Water and Other

(B) Food or Water and Clothing or Blankets

(C) Artificial Respiration and Food or Water

(D) Artificial Respiration and Other

36. Under *Disposition of Case*, Officer Firestone should check the box for

(A) Removed to Hospital

(B) Left in Custody of Friend or Relative

(C) Other

(D) Left at Place of Occurrence

Assume that you are a state trooper. A duty roster (see below) has been posted in the barracks. Answer the following questions, 37–46, only on the basis of this duty roster.

TROOPER'S NAME	MON.	TUES.	WED.	THURS.	FRI.	SAT.	SUN.
T. Adams	A	D	A	A	A	A	A
R. Brown	D	B	A	C	B	B	B
B. Carlos	C	C	C	C	C	C	D
R. Donaldson	A	C	D	A	C	C	C
A. Edwards	B	B	D	A	A	A	A
C. Frederickson	B	D	A	A	C	C	C
H. Galway	A	A	C	C	D	A	A
L. Isaacson	B	B	B	B	D	B	B
D. Jackson	A	A	A	D	C	A	A
R. Karlsen	C	C	D	A	A	A	A
M. Latimer	B	B	B	B	D	B	B
P. Goldberg	C	C	D	B	B	B	B
L. Mulvaney	A	D	A	A	A	A	A

CODE: A = 8:30 A.M.—4:30 P.M.
B = 4:30 P.M.—12:30 A.M.
C = 12:30 A.M.—8:30 A.M.
D = Day Off

37. The troopers who have only one tour during the week are

(A) Adams and Carlos

(B) Karlsen and Mulvaney

(C) Galway and Latimer

(D) Edwards and Galway

38. The one of the following troopers who shifts from Tour A to Tour C is

(A) Isaacson

(B) Jackson

(C) Karlsen

(D) Goldberg

39. The troopers assigned exclusively to the B tour are

(A) Isaacson and Latimer

(B) Brown and Edwards

(C) Goldberg and Brown

(D) Edwards and Frederickson

40. The one of the following troopers who shifts only from Tour C to Tour B is

(A) Latimer

(B) Brown

(C) Galway

(D) Goldberg

41. The one of the following troopers who is assigned on all three tours during the week is

(A) Donaldson

(B) Brown

(C) Karlsen

(D) Galway

42. The one of the following troopers who is assigned exclusively to the A tour is

(A) Galway

(B) Frederickson

(C) Mulvaney

(D) Latimer

43. The following pairs of troopers who could be assigned as partners on highway patrol each day of the week are

(A) Galway and Jackson

(B) Edwards and Frederickson

(C) Latimer and Goldberg

(D) Adams and Mulvaney

44. The following pairs of troopers who could be assigned as partners on highway patrol each day of the week are

(A) Carlos and Galway

(B) Isaacson and Latimer

(C) Donaldson and Jackson

(D) Latimer and Mulvaney

45. The one of the following troopers who is assigned exclusively to the C tour is

(A) Donaldson

(B) Carlos

(C) Goldberg

(D) Galway

46. The one of the following who could have the least regular sleeping hours is

(A) Karlsen

(B) Goldberg

(C) Brown

(D) Edwards

Arithmetic Questions Based on Mileage

47. On a certain map a distance of 10 miles is represented by $\frac{1}{2}$ inch. If two towns are $3\frac{1}{2}$ inches apart on this map, then the actual distance in miles between the two towns is

(A) 35 miles

(B) 65 miles

(C) 70 miles

(D) 80 miles

48. If a highway patrol car averages 18 miles to a gallon of gasoline, how many gallons of gasoline will be needed on a trip of 369 miles?

(A) $20\frac{1}{2}$ gallons

(B) 28 gallons

(C) 15 gallons

(D) 12 gallons

49. A distance of 25 miles is represented by $2\frac{1}{2}$ inches. On the map, 1 inch is therefore

(A) 5 miles

(B) 10 miles

(C) 15 miles

(D) 20 miles

50. On a road map, $\frac{1}{4}$ inch represents 8 miles of actual road distance. How many miles apart are two towns that are represented by points $2\frac{1}{8}$ inches apart on the map?

(A) 32 miles

(B) 64 miles

(C) 68 miles

(D) 72 miles

51. A family is planning a trip of 4,000 miles. Later they increase the estimated mileage by 25%. They plan to average 250 miles per day. How many days will the trip take?

    (A) 20 days

    (B) 40 days

    (C) 60 days

    (D) none of these

Calendar/Procedure Questions

52. A state trooper, while completing his report of a multi-car accident, should know that during a year when the first of November falls on a Saturday an accident that occurred on October 13th happened on

    (A) Monday

    (B) Tuesday

    (C) Wednesday

    (D) Thursday

53. If the last day of June occurs on a Sunday, June 1st will have fallen on

    (A) Monday

    (B) Tuesday

    (C) Saturday

    (D) Thursday

54. If during a given year Christmas was celebrated on a Thursday, the first of the month of December would have fallen on

    (A) Monday

    (B) Tuesday

    (C) Wednesday

    (D) Thursday

55. A state trooper, before testifying in court, notes from his memorandum book that he had made an arrest on November 6th. If he were asked to testify in court as to the day of the week that the arrest took place he could do so by

    (A) determining the number of days from election day

    (B) determining the number of days from the third Thursday in the month

    (C) counting back from his last payday

    (D) determining the day that month began

56. During the year of 1985, one month contained all of the days of the week four times each. The month was

    (A) March

    (B) September

    (C) February

    (D) October

57. A highway has two lanes, one in each direction. The lanes are separated by a broken white line. Cars are permitted to pass when there is a broken line. On a solid line, passing is forbidden. Further on, the solid line occurs as the highway climbs a hill. The solid line is necessary to prevent

    (A) cars passing each other in the face of oncoming traffic that cannot be seen

    (B) motorists attempting to pass slow-moving vehicles

    (C) truck drivers crawling up a hill blocking traffic

    (D) cars in the right lane being unable to drive onto the shoulder of the road in an emergency

58. Many states have laws to control and penalize motorists who drive while intoxicated (DWI). Such laws are most effective in instances where

    (A) troopers stop and check all vehicles

    (B) all DWI operators are given jail sentences

    (C) traffic restrictions are enforced strictly

    (D) enforcement is combined with publicity about the dangers of DWI

59. A state trooper is patrolling a busy highway and passes a small pickup truck driven by a person who appears to be a young girl. The trooper is concerned because

    (A) the girl could get in trouble

    (B) motor vehicles should not be driven by underage persons who may not be licensed operators

    (C) drivers of other vehicles may be distracted by this pickup truck

    (D) the truck could be involved in an accident

60. Large, slow-moving vehicles, such as garbage collection or building material trucks, often cause passenger car drivers to become impatient and irritable. The best one of the following practices that a trooper should enforce to avoid trouble in these situations is

    (A) keep slow-moving vehicles in one right lane

    (B) order all slow-moving vehicles off the highway onto side roads

    (C) give slow-moving vehicle operators court summonses

    (D) all of the above

61. Posted symbols used as highway signs are placed not only for the convenience of motorists but also for safety precautions. A double zigzag line near the top of a hill indicates

    (A) a steep, straight incline upon descent from the top

    (B) a curve at descent from the hill with an obstructed view of oncoming traffic

    (C) an intersecting road at the top of the hill

    (D) an intersection at the bottom of the hill with an obstructed view of oncoming traffic

62. At a certain highway intersection, left and right turns are permitted in any direction at all hours on the green signal light. Right turns only are permitted on the red signal light. In patrolling through this intersection, the highway patrol trooper should mainly be concerned with

    (A) left turns against the red signal light
    (B) right turns on the green signal light
    (C) traffic volume during the night hours
    (D) traffic volume during daylight hours

63. State troopers on highway patrol must stop to assist motorists involved in accidents that may have resulted in personal injury. The major concern of the highway patrol is to

    (A) keep traffic moving as efficiently as possible
    (B) call for emergency medical assistance
    (C) see that motorists involved have each other's license numbers and insurance companies
    (D) all of the above

64. A state trooper assigned to highway patrol passes two motorists who appear to be arguing over some body damage to their vehicles. Traffic is restricted to one lane moving slowly past the scene. The most important action for the trooper to take is to

    (A) stop the argument
    (B) direct traffic so motorists do not stop to observe the scene
    (C) call for assistance to direct traffic and move the vehicles
    (D) arrest the motorists

65. Automobile accidents unfortunately often result in serious injury. The one of the following that is the primary duty of the state trooper, is to

    (A) render first aid
    (B) call for emergency medical service assistance immediately
    (C) contact relatives of the injured
    (D) direct traffic at the site of the accident

66. A state trooper is on highway patrol on a median-barrier-divided highway and observes two cars that appear to be in a high-speed chase but are in the lanes going in the opposite direction. The trooper should

    (A) jump the barrier to follow the two cars
    (B) speed in the same direction he has been following until he finds a legal crossing through the median barrier
    (C) radio for other police vehicles to investigate
    (D) ignore the situation

Answer questions 67 through 76 on the basis of the diagram shown below.

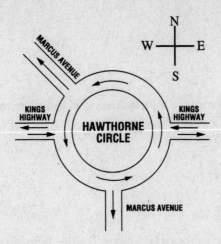

67. In the traffic circle illustrated above, vehicles traveling from east to west must

(A) drive north around the circle

(B) drive south around the circle

(C) cross Marcus Avenue south and proceed thereon

(D) drive completely around the circle

68. In the traffic circle illustrated above, Marcus Avenue

(A) flows from east to west

(B) flows from north to south

(C) flows south and northwest

(D) is a dead-end road

69. The traffic circle illustrated above provides a safe passage for vehicles chiefly because

(A) the circle separates traffic going in different directions thus avoiding left and right turns at a right-angle intersection

(B) it provides a means of exit from Kings Highway

(C) it can allow for maximum traffic speed

(D) Highway patrols can observe traffic from various stationary positions

70. A disadvantage of the traffic circle illustrated above is that

(A) distance traveled is modified by time saved

(B) traffic flow within the circle is one-way

(C) to get to Marcus Avenue south from Kings Highway going west, a vehicle would have to drive almost $3/4$ of the road around the circle

(D) traffic volume can modify traffic patterns

71. To go east along Kings Highway, vehicles coming from the west travel around the circle
    (A) south and east
    (B) north and west
    (C) north and east
    (D) south and west

72. In examining the above map, a vehicle driver could consider traveling around the circle to reverse direction on Kings Highway by driving
    (A) clockwise
    (B) counterclockwise
    (C) either direction
    (D) none of the above

73. In examining the above map of the Hawthorne Traffic Circle, it is most reasonable to conclude that
    (A) U-turns are forbidden
    (B) U-turns are feasible but unnecessary
    (C) there are two dead-end streets
    (D) none of the above

74. Marcus Avenue vehicles can travel
    (A) one-way northwest
    (B) one-way south
    (C) both northwest and south from the circle
    (D) in two-way traffic in either direction

75. A vehicle driving east on Kings Highway and desiring to enter Marcus Avenue South must drive in the traffic circle
    (A) southeast
    (B) southwest
    (C) northeast
    (D) northwest

76. Reversing traffic around the traffic circle would necessitate reversal of direction on
    (A) Marcus Avenue
    (B) Kings Highway
    (C) Marcus Avenue north only
    (D) None of the above

For questions 77 through 81, refer to the direction indicator below:

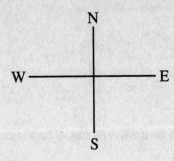

77. A vehicle proceeding diagonally north and veering right is said to be traveling
   (A) northeast
   (B) northwest
   (C) southeast
   (D) none of the above

78. A vehicle proceeding diagonally northwest and veering right is said to be traveling
   (A) northwest
   (B) north by northwest
   (C) north by northeast
   (D) north

79. A vehicle proceeding east and veering right diagonally toward the southeast is said to be traveling
   (A) east by northeast
   (B) east by southeast
   (C) south by southeast
   (D) north by northeast

80. In describing a location as south and west of a right-angle intersection, a trooper would be required to indicate
   (A) southbound road with a right turn at the closest intersection to the destination
   (B) southbound road with a left turn at the closest intersection to the destination
   (C) westbound road with a left turn at the closest intersection to the destination
   (D) southwest path that is available only to pedestrians

81. In describing a location as north and west of a right angle intersection a trooper would be required to indicate a
   (A) northbound road with a right turn at the closest intersection to the destination
   (B) northbound road with a left turn at the closest intersection to the destination
   (C) westbound road with a right turn at the closest intersection to the destination
   (D) westbound road with an alternate northbound road in an easterly diagonal direction

Directions: This part of the test consists of several reading passages, each followed by a number of statements. Analyze each statement on the basis of the material given. Then, mark your answer sheet A, B, C, or D.

Mark it (A) if the statement is entirely true.

Mark it (B) if the statement is entirely false.

Mark it (C) if the statement is partially false and partially true.

Mark it (D) if the statement cannot be judged on the basis of the facts given in the excerpt.

Questions 82 through 86 are to be answered based on the contents of the following paragraph.

A prisoner, who, being confined in a prison, or being in lawful custody of an officer or other person, escapes from such prison or custody, is guilty of a felony if such custody or confinement is upon a charge, arrest, commitment, or conviction for a felony, and of a misdemeanor if such custody or confinement is upon a charge, arrest, commitment or conviction for a misdemeanor. A prisoner confined in a state prison for a term less than for life, who attempts, although unsuccessfully, to escape from such prison, is guilty of a felony.

82. An unsuccessful attempt at escape from custody is not generally punishable.

83. A captured state convict serving less than a life sentence is reimprisoned for life upon recapture.

84. A prisoner having been arrested on a misdemeanor charge is guilty of a felony if he makes a successful attempt at escape but is later recaptured.

85. A person charged with a misdemeanor being held in legal custody is guilty of a misdemeanor in the event of an escape from custody.

86. A prisoner not under a life sentence confined to a state prison is deemed guilty of a felony if he or she makes a successful attempt at escape and is subsequently recaptured; but if the attempt is unsuccessful, the prisoner is guilty of a misdemeanor.

Questions 87 through 91 are to be answered on the basis of the contents of the following paragraph.

A person, who, with intent to effect or facilitate the escape of a prisoner, whether the escape is effected or attempted or not, enters a prison, or conveys to a prisoner any information, or sends into a prison any disguise, instrument, weapon, or other thing, is guilty of a felony if the prisoner is held upon a charge, arrest, commitment, or conviction for a felony; and of a misdemeanor if the prisoner is held upon a charge, arrest, commitment, or conviction of a misdemeanor.

87. A person sending a misdemeanant a weapon with intent to effect that person's escape is liable to arrest under the charge of felony.

88. Entering a state prison for the sole purpose of conveying information to a prisoner is not legally punishable.

89. The attempt by a third party to effect the escape of a state prisoner is not punished as severely as an actual attempt by the prisoner.

90. Any attempt on the part of an outside person to facilitate the escape of a felon is punishable as a felony.

91. The act of conveying a disguise to a prisoner is in itself punishable as either a misdemeanor or a felony.

Questions 92 through 96 are to be answered on the basis of the following paragraph.

A sheriff, or other officer or person, who allows a prisoner, lawfully in his custody, in any action or proceedings, civil or criminal, or in any prison under his charge or control, to escape or go at large, except as permitted by law, or connives at or assists such escape, or omits an act or duty whereby such escape is occasioned, or contributed to, or assisted is: 1. If he corruptly and willfully allows, connives at, or assists the escape, guilty of a felony; 2. In any other case, guilty of a misdemeanor. Any officer who is convicted of the offense specified, forfeits his office, and is forever disqualified to hold any office, or place of trust, honor, or profit, under the constitution or laws of this state.

92. If a prisoner escapes from a guard through no fault of the latter, the guard is not liable to any action.

93. A prison guard assisting the escape of a felon is himself open to a charge constituting felony.

94. A person having legal custody over a prisoner, who unlawfully permits his freedom, is liable to forfeiture of his office if the charge against the prisoner is criminal but is not so liable if civil.

95. A guard who through negligence in his duty permits a prisoner to escape is not open to a criminal charge.

96. A sheriff illegally permitting a prisoner in a civil action, not under a charge of felony, to go at large may be punished as a misdemeanant.

Questions 97 through 101 are to be answered on the basis of the following paragraph.

A person who gives or offers a bribe to any executive officer, or to a person elected or appointed to become an executive officer, of this state with intent to influence that person in respect to any act, decision, vote, opinion, or other proceedings as such officer, is punishable by imprisonment in a state prison not exceeding ten years or by a fine not exceeding ten years or by a fine not exceeding five thousand dollars, or by both.

97. An elected executive officer may not generally be punished for accepting a small bribe.

98. An appointed executive officer convicted of accepting a bribe may be punished by either fine or imprisonment.

99. Bribing of an executive officer with intent to influence the officer's vote is deemed a criminal act and, in certain instances, may be punishable by life imprisonment.

100. The length of a sentence to which a person is liable upon conviction for offering a bribe to an executive officer is limited to ten years.

101. An executive officer accepting a bribe is equally guilty as the person offering the bribe, though the punishment is not as severe.

Questions 102 through 106 are to be answered on the basis of the following paragraph.

A Commissioner of Correction, warden or other officer or prison guard, employed at any of the prisons who: 1. Shall be directly or indirectly interested in any contract, purchase or sale, for, by or on account of such prison; or 2. Accepts a present from a contractor or contractor's agent, directly or indirectly, or employs the labor of a convict or another person employed in such prison on any work for the private benefit of such commissioner, warden or guard, is guilty of a misdemeanor, except that the warden shall be entitled to employ prisoners for necessary household services.

102. A guard who employs the labor of prisoners in his or her own interests is guilty of a misdemeanor, except that such labor may be so employed indirectly.

103. Only a Commissioner of Correction may accept a small present from a contractor, and then only indirectly.

104. In no case may a prison guard be directly interested in a contract in which the prison is a party.

105. It is illegal to employ the labor of a convict in any case.

106. A warden may only indirectly be interested in the sale of merchandise on account of the prison at which he or she is employed.

> **Directions:** This test of your ability to comprehend what you read consists of a number of different passages. One or more questions are based on each passage. Questions consist of incomplete statements about a passage. Each incomplete statement is followed by four choices lettered A, B, C, and D. Mark your answer sheet with the letter of that choice which best conveys the meaning of the passage and which best completes the statement.

Questions 107 through 114 are based on the following excerpt from an annual report of a police department. This material should be read first and then referred to in answering these questions, which are to be answered solely on the basis of the material herein contained.

Legal Bureau

One of the more important functions of this bureau is to analyze and furnish the department with pertinent information concerning federal and state statutes and local laws which affect the department, law enforcement, or crime prevention. In addition, all measures introduced in the state legislature and the city council, which may affect this department, are carefully reviewed by members of the Legal Bureau and where necessary, opinions and recommendations thereon are prepared.

Another important function of this office is the prosecution of cases in the Criminal Court. This is accomplished by assignment of attorneys who are members of the Legal Bureau to appear in those cases which are deemed to raise issues of importance to the department or questions of law which require technical presentation to facilitate proper determination; and also in the cases where request is made for such appearances by a magistrate, some other official of the city, or a member of the force. Attorneys are regularly assigned to prosecute all cases in the Supreme Court.

Proposed legislation was prepared and sponsored for introduction in the state legislature and, at this writing, one of these proposals has already been enacted into law and five others are presently on the Governor's desk awaiting executive action. The new law prohibits the sale or possession of a hypodermic syringe or needle by an unauthorized person. The bureau's proposals awaiting executive action pertain to: an amendment to the Code of Criminal Procedure prohibiting desk officers from taking bail in gambling cases or in cases mentioned in Section 552, Code of Criminal Procedure; including confidence men and swindlers as jostlers in the Penal Law; prohibiting the sale of switchblade knives of any size to children under 16 and bills extending the licensing period of gunsmiths.

The following is a report of the activities of the Bureau during Year 2 as compared with Year 1:

	Year 2	Year 1
Memoranda of law prepared	83	68
Legal matters forwarded to Corporation Counsel	122	144
Letters requesting legal information	756	807
Letters requesting departmental records	139	111
Matters for publication	26	17
Court appearances of members of bureau	4,678	4,621
Conferences	94	103
Lectures at Police Academy	30	33
Reports on proposed legislation	255	194
Deciphering of codes	79	27
Expert testimony	31	16
Notices to court witnesses	81	55
Briefs prepared	22	18
Court papers prepared	258	

107. One of the functions of the Legal Bureau is to
    (A) review and make recommendations on proposed federal laws affecting law enforcement
    (B) prepare opinions on all measures introduced in the state legislature and the city council
    (C) furnish the department with pertinent information concerning all new federal and state laws
    (D) analyze all laws affecting the work of the department

108. The one of the following that is not a function of the Legal Bureau is
    (A) law enforcement and crime prevention
    (B) prosecution of all cases in Supreme Court
    (C) prosecution of cases in Criminal Court
    (D) lecturing at the Police Academy

109. Members of the Legal Bureau frequently appear in Criminal Court for the purpose of
    (A) defending members of the department
    (B) raising issues of importance to the department
    (C) prosecuting all offenders arrested by the members of the department
    (D) facilitating proper determination of questions of law requiring technical presentation

110. The Legal Bureau sponsored a bill that would

    (A) extend the licenses of gunmen

    (B) prohibit the sale of switchblade knives to children of any size

    (C) place confidence men and swindlers in the same category as jostlers in the Penal Law

    (D) prohibit desk officers from admitting gamblers, confidence men, and swindlers to bail

111. From the report it is not reasonable to infer that

    (A) fewer briefs were prepared in Year 2

    (B) the preparation of court papers was a new activity assumed in Year 2

    (C) the Code of Criminal Procedure authorizes desk officers to accept bail in certain cases

    (D) the penalty for jostling and swindling is the same

112. According to the report, the activity showing the greatest increase in Year 2 as compared with Year 1 was

    (A) matters for publication

    (B) reports on proposed legislation

    (C) notices to court witnesses

    (D) memoranda of law prepared

113. According to the report, the activity showing the greatest percentage of increase in Year 2 as compared with Year 1 was

    (A) court appearances of members of the Bureau

    (B) giving expert testimony

    (C) deciphering of codes

    (D) letters requesting departmental records

114. According to the report, the percentage of bills prepared and sponsored by the Legal Bureau which were passed by the State Legislature and sent to the Governor for approval was

    (A) approximately 3.1%

    (B) approximately 2.6%

    (C) approximately .5%

    (D) not capable of determination from the data given

Answer questions 115 through 118 on the basis of the following statement.

Disorderly conduct, in the abstract, does not constitute any crime known to law; it is only when it tends to a breach of the peace, under the circumstances detailed in section 1458 of the Consolidation Act, that it constitutes a minor offense cognizable by the judge, and when it in fact threatens to disturb the peace, it is a misdemeanor as well under section 675 of the Penal Code as at common law, and not within the jurisdiction of the judge, but of the Criminal Court.

115. Of the following, the most accurate statement on the basis of the preceding paragraph is that

    (A) an act that merely threatens to disturb the peace is not a crime

    (B) disorderly conduct, by itself, is not a crime

    (C) some types of disorderly conduct are indictable

    (D) a minor offense may or may not be cognizable

116. Of the following, the least accurate statement on the basis of the preceding paragraph is that

    (A) disorderly conduct that threatens to disturb the peace is within the jurisdiction of the judge

    (B) disorderly conduct that "tends to a breach of the peace" may constitute a minor offense

    (C) Section 1458 of the Consolidation Act discusses a "breach of the peace"

    (D) disorderly conduct that "tends to a breach of the peace" is not the same as that which threatens to disturb the peace

117. The preceding paragraph does not clarify the difference between

    (A) jurisdiction of a judge and jurisdiction of the Criminal Court

    (B) disorderly conduct as a crime and disorderly conduct not as a crime

    (C) what "tends to a breach of the peace" and what threatens to disturb the peace

    (D) a minor offense and a misdemeanor

118. Of the following generalizations, the one that is best illustrated by the preceding paragraph is that

    (A) acts that in themselves are not criminal may become criminal as a result of their effect

    (B) abstract conduct may, in and of itself, be criminal

    (C) criminal acts are determined by results rather than by intent

    (D) an act that is criminal to begin with may not be criminal if it fails to have the desired effect

Questions 119 and 120 pertain to the following section of the Penal Code.

Section 1942. A person who, after having been three times convicted within this state, of felonies or attempts to commit felonies, or under the law of any other state, government or country, of crimes which if committed within this state would become felonious, commits a felony, other than murder, first or second degree, or treason, within this state, shall be sentenced upon conviction of such fourth, or subsequent, offense to imprisonment in a state prison for an indeterminate term, the maximum term provided for first offenders for the crime for which the individual has been convicted, but, in any event, the minimum term upon conviction for a felony as the fourth or subsequent offense, shall not be less than fifteen years, and the maximum thereof shall be his natural life.

119. Under the terms of the quoted portion of section 1942 of the Penal Law, a person must receive the increased punishment therein provided if

    (A) he is convicted of a felony and has been three times previously convicted of felonies

    (B) he has been three times previously convicted of felonies, regardless of the nature of his present conviction

    (C) his fourth conviction is for murder, first or second degree, or treason

    (D) he has previously been convicted three times of murder, first or second degree, or treason

120. Under the terms of the quoted portion of section 1942 of the Penal Law, a person convicted of a felony for which the penalty is imprisonment for a term not to exceed ten years, and who has been three times previously convicted of felonies in this State, shall be sentenced to a term the minimum of which shall be:

    (A) ten years

    (B) fifteen years

    (C) indeterminate

    (D) his natural life

In answering questions 121 to 125, the following definitions of crimes should be applied, bearing in mind that all elements contained in the definitions must be present in order to charge a person with that crime.

BURGLARY is the breaking and entering of a building with intent to commit some crime therein.

EXTORTION is the obtaining of property from another, with his consent, induced by a wrongful use of force or fear, or under color of official right.

LARCENY is the taking and carrying away of the personal property of another with intent to deprive or defraud the owner of the use and benefit of such property.

ROBBERY is the unlawful taking of the personal property of another from his person or in his presence, by force or violence or by putting him in fear of injury, immediate or future, to his person or property.

121. If A entered B's store during business hours, tied B to a chair, and then helped himself to the contents of B's cash register, A should, upon arrest, be charged with

    (A) burglary

    (B) extortion

    (C) larceny

    (D) robbery

122. If A broke the panel of glass in the window of B's store, stepped in and removed some merchandise from the window, he should, upon arrest, be charged with

    (A) burglary

    (B) extortion

    (C) larceny

    (D) robbery

123. If A, after B had left for the day, found the door of B's store open, walked in, took some merchandise and then left through the same door, he should, upon arrest, be charged with

    (A) burglary

    (B) extortion

    (C) larceny

    (D) robbery

124. If A, by threatening to report B for failure to pay to the city the full amount of sales tax he had collected from various customers, induced B to give him the contents of his cash register, A should, upon arrest, be charged with

(A) burglary

(B) extortion

(C) larceny

(D) robbery

125. If A, on a crowded train, put his hand into B's pocket and removed B's wallet without his knowledge, A should, upon arrest, be charged with

(A) burglary

(B) extortion

(C) larceny

(D) robbery

ANSWER KEY

1. A	26. C	51. A	76. D	101. D
2. B	27. D	52. A	77. A	102. C
3. B	28. A	53. C	78. B	103. B
4. B	29. B	54. A	79. B	104. A
5. A	30. C	55. D	80. A	105. B
6. A	31. A	56. C	81. B	106. B
7. A	32. A	57. A	82. B	107. D
8. A	33. B	58. D	83. D	108. A
9. B	34. B	59. B	84. B	109. D
10. D	35. C	60. A	85. A	110. C
11. B	36. C	61. B	86. C	111. D
12. A	37. A	62. A	87. B	112. B
13. C	38. B	63. B	88. D	113. C
14. A	39. A	64. C	89. B	114. D
15. A	40. D	65. B	90. A	115. B
16. D	41. B	66. C	91. B	116. A
17. A	42. C	67. A	92. D	117. D
18. D	43. D	68. C	93. A	118. A
19. C	44. B	69. A	94. C	119. A
20. B	45. B	70. C	95. B	120. B
21. B	46. C	71. A	96. A	121. D
22. D	47. C	72. B	97. D	122. A
23. C	48. A	73. A	98. D	123. C
24. A	49. B	74. C	99. B	124. B
25. A	50. C	75. A	100. A	125. C

EXPLANATORY ANSWERS

1. **(A)** The preamble of the question states that carelessness leads to failure. Choice (A) says essentially the same thing, that being negligent seldom leads to success. Incomplete work is not necessarily careless work. Conscientious work, on the other hand, does not ensure success. Conscientious workers make errors although they probably make fewer than workers who are not conscientious.

2. **(B)** The lecturer is saying that it is nearly always best to follow the required procedures and not to go beyond. Very often doing too much causes as many difficulties as doing too little.

3. **(B)** This age group has a large number of drug addicts, and the need for money to acquire drugs leads to burglaries.

4. **(B)** These are the two leading causes of pedestrian involvement in traffic accidents.

5. **(A)** A "modus operandi" file classifies criminals by the methods they use to commit crimes, e.g. criminals who tend to burglarize homes of women living alone are filed together. When such a crime is committed, the police will look in that part of the file for likely suspects.

6. **(A)** This answer explains itself.

7. **(A)** The ringleaders started the riot and knowing how it got started could help bring it to an end.

8. **(A)** Based on the facts presented in the question there is nothing further for the trooper to do. The trooper's suspicion was aroused, an investigation was made, and nothing turned up.

9. **(B)** A shout to stop delivered in an authoritative manner could very well do the trick. This would be the first step to take, to be followed by a call for assistance to apprehend him if he does not respond favorably.

10. **(D)** This is an occasion when assistance is needed; call for it. The course of action in choice (A) would permit the car to get away. Choice (B) would create a dangerous situation, and choice (C) would only be effective if other troopers were in the area.

11. **(B)** Initially medical treatment is most important. Further investigation should follow medical care.

12. **(A)** Of the four situations only this one would seem to be suspicious. The other three situations are really quite ordinary.

13. **(C)** Artificial respiration is called for whenever breathing has stopped. This is often the case during electrical shock.

14. **(A)** A bruise is an abrasion. A sprain involves stretching or dislocating a joint unnaturally, and a fracture involves a broken bone.

15. **(A)** The preamble of the question states the legal definition of "bail."

16. **(D)** Purely circumstantial. No evidence has been brought forward that Jones committed the murder, only that Jones might have had the wherewithal to do so.

17. **(A)** The arraignment represents the first step in the trying of an accused.

18. **(D)** This procedure often leads to the location of stolen vehicles and the apprehension of wanted criminals. Many jurisdictions now use a computer to expedite the process.

19. **(C)** Criminals are essentially specialists. The type of crime that a criminal tends to commit is a manifestation of his or her personality. The criminal who tends to commit sexual crimes does not generally feel a compulsion to commit other types of crimes. The same for the burglar and the thief, etc. There are occasions when a rapist will commit a larceny at the same time as the rape, but the primary tendency will be towards rape, and that act is an expression of the personality of the perpetrator.

20. **(B)** A set of fingerprints is unique, and no two people have the same fingerprints. They are not subject to change or to being changed, therefore, they are an excellent means of identification.

21. **(B)** This is a negative question and, therefore, you should select the choice that contains a statement that is the least accurate of the choices given. Many fingerprints left at the scene of a crime are not valuable because they are smudged, are too light to read accurately, etc.

22. **(D)** This is not the primary objective of a fingerprint system. All of the other choices contain objectives of a sophisticated fingerprint system. This again is a negative question requiring the choice of an item that is the least correct of the items given.

23. **(C)** Choice (C) is a much better reason for this procedure because there would be no positive way of saying that the fingerprints were made at the time of the commission of the crime and not at a later date.

24. **(A)** The officer will then be in a position to testify that what he or she found at the scene of the crime was brought to the laboratory for analysis.

25. **(A)** The surface of the bullet would probably be altered by the articles in the officer's pocket.

26. **(C)** Many crimes are solved in the police laboratory through scientific means that bring to light facts that cannot be determined by the naked eye.

27. **(D)** The law neither sanctions nor prohibits its use.

28. **(A)** The arrangement of the sweat pores on the skin's surface is unique and is not subject to change. However, the science of poroscopy is not used much today in police work because fingerprints are much more useful in the identification of criminals.

29. **(B)** There is the chance the name was misspelled either on the card or on your records.

30. **(C)** A thief will assume that the concealed safe contains more valuable items than the safe left out in the open. Also, a passerby may spot someone trying to break into a safe.

31. **(A)** Two-way communication should be established to show that the officer is there not only to enforce the laws but also to help people. The officer may not be able to solve a citizen's problems, but he/she should be able to refer them to sources where they may be able to receive help. Two-way communication is the most effective means of dealing with all persons.

Answers 32–36: no explanations necessary.

32. **(A)**

33. **(B)**

34. **(B)**

35. **(C)**

36. **(C)**

37. **(A)** Troopers Adams and Carlos are the only ones who have one tour listed next to their names. Therefore, (A) is the only answer. Karlsen, Galway, and Edwards each have two tours. Mulvaney and Latimer have one tour but are partners with others who have two tours; therefore, the other options would not be correct.

38. **(B)** Jackson shifts from Tour A to Tour C on Friday. Isaacson is entirely on Tour B. Karlsen goes from C to A, and Goldberg from C to B.

39. **(A)** An inspection of the table shows only Isaacson and Latimer on the B tour during the entire week. Goldberg goes from C to B on Thursday. Brown shifts from B to A, C, and then B. Edwards shifts from B to A on Thursday, and Frederickson shifts from B to A and C.

40. **(D)** Goldberg is the only trooper of those listed shifting from Tour C to Tour B. Latimer is only on Tour B, Brown is on all three tours, and Galway goes from Tour A to Tour C.

41. **(B)** As noted in the explanation for question 39, Brown is assigned to all three tours. Donaldson, Karlsen, and Galway have two each.

42. **(C)** Of all of the choices given, Mulvaney is the only one assigned the A tour during the entire week. Galway is on the A and C tours. Frederickson is on all three, and Latimer is on the B tour for the entire week.

43. **(D)** Adams and Mulvaney are assigned to Tour A each day of the week and therefore could be assigned as partners for the week. Galway, Jackson, Goldberg, Edwards, and Frederickson change tours. Latimer is on Tour B.

44. **(B)** Isaacson and Latimer are both assigned to Tour A each day of the week. Mulvaney and Latimer are on different tours, as are Carlos and Galway. Donaldson and Jackson shift tours during the week.

45. **(B)** Of those given, Carlos is the only one assigned to the C tour. Donaldson, Goldberg, and Galway shift tours during the week.

46. **(C)** Trooper Brown has all three tours during the week, therefore his sleeping hours change Tuesday, Wednesday, and Friday. Karlsen has only two duty tours with a day off between. The same with Goldberg and Edwards.

47. **(C)** 10 miles = $^{1}/_{2}$ inch
    20 miles = 1 inch
    60 miles = 3 inches
    Therefore 3 $^{1}/_{2}$ inches = 70 miles

48. **(A)** Divide 369 by 18. Answer is 20 $^{1}/_{2}$ gallons.

49. **(B)** $\dfrac{25}{2\,^{1}/_{2}} = \dfrac{25}{^{5}/_{2}} = 25 \times \dfrac{2}{5} = \dfrac{50}{5} = 10$

50. **(C)** $^{1}/_{4}$ inch = 8 miles
    1 inch = 8 x 4 = 32 miles
    2 inches = 32 x 2 = 64 miles
    $^{1}/_{8}$ inch = $^{1}/_{2}$ of $^{1}/_{4}$ inch
    Therefore $^{1}/_{8}$ inch = 4 miles
    Total for 2 $^{1}/_{8}$ inches = 68 miles

51. **(A)** 25% of 4,000 = 1,000
    Total mileage is 5,000
    5,000 divided by 250 = 20 days

52. **(A)** October

12	(13)					
19	20	21	22	23	24	25
26	27	28	29	30	31	(1)
S	M	T	W	Th	F	(S)

53. **(C)**

						(1)
2						
9						
16						
23	24	25	26	27	28	29
30						
S	M	T	W	Th	F	(S)

54. **(A)**

	(1)	2	3	4		
				11		
				18		
				25		
S	(M)	T	W	Th	F	S

55. **(D)** Election day date varies depending on which date falls on the first Tuesday after the first Monday in November. (B) Third Thursday is far ahead of the 6th of November. (C) Back from his last payday would be indeterminate depending on the day of the court testimony. (D) is the current and logical calculation. If November 1st falls on a Saturday, the sixth day would be Thursday, i.e., 6 days thereafter.

56. **(C)** February has 28 days. Each week contains 7 days. 28 is evenly divisible by 4.

57. **(A)** The use of a solid line dividing a highway, with traffic in both directions, prevents cars from passing each other by driving in the lane for traffic going in the opposite direction. This avoids head-on collisions. Choices (B) and (C) are not relevant, and choice (D) is not affected by the lines.

58. **(D)** Publicity as a form of education is often used to aid law enforcement. (A) is incorrect because of the word "all."

59. **(B)** All states have a minimum age for driving vehicles. Choices (A), (C), and (D) are speculative.

60. **(A)** This is the most common practice. Choice (B) would be impossible to enforce. There is no law against slow-moving vehicles, (C). For these reasons, choice (D) is inoperative.

61. **(B)** A zigzag line logically would mean a curve or curves. There would be no need for a zigzag line if the road were straight.

62. **(A)** Of the four options given, option (A) is the only one that is forbidden by the terms of the question and is a general prohibition to motorists.

63. **(B)** No explanation necessary.

64. **(C)** Two conditions are stated in the question, i.e. the motorists arguing and the slow-moving traffic. Since the trooper cannot handle both, he would be wise to call for assistance.

65. **(B)** The primary duty of the trooper is to ensure that victims get medical treatment as soon as possible. All the other choices, though important, are secondary considerations.

66. **(C)** The trooper cannot jump his vehicle over a median barrier without considerable risk to himself, his vehicle, and others. If he continues in the same direction, even at high speed, he would still lose time. Since he cannot ignore such an obvious suspicious occurrence, his best action is to use his radio.

67. **(A)** Note the arrows in the circle. If you enter the circle from the right of the map you will be going from east to west. See now that the arrow goes northerly to get around the circle.

68. **(C)** This can be determined from looking at the map. Marcus Avenue leaves the circle at the bottom of the map going south and at the top of the map going northwest.

69. **(A)** is clearly the answer as shown on the map by the arrows within the circle.

70. **(C)** Note the question asks for a disadvantage. If you look at the right of the map, you will see the arrow going from east to west. Upon entering the circle it can only go north, then west and southeast. Thus a vehicle would have to drive 3/4 of the road around the circle.

71. **(A)** This question is the opposite of question 70. If you look at the left side of the map and at the cross compass, you will find Kings Highway going east. Upon entering the circle, a vehicle must "turn down south" and then "up east."

72. **(B)** This question is self-explanatory. If you imagine this map placed on a clock face, the arrows will go opposite to the direction of the minute hand.

73. **(A)** is clearly the answer since traffic in the circle is only going one way. Since a dead-end street has no means of exit, choice (C) is false; all streets enter or leave this circle. Choice (B) is false since the traffic goes in one direction around the circle.

74. **(C)** This question can be explained by referring to question 68 and its explanation.

75. **(A)** Looking at the map on the left side, you will see the arrow going east. Then the vehicle would enter the traffic circle southerly and go around for a short distance easterly to exit at Marcus Avenue South.

76. **(D)** This question is understandable when the map is placed on a clock; reversal of traffic would mean a clockwise direction. Since all streets are either two-way or exit from the circle, there is no need to change direction on any accessible street.

Explanation for Compass Direction Questions

In answering questions on compass directions, the reader should imagine that facing forward is north, the right hand is east, the left is west, and the rear is south. In a circular view, the compass may be depicted as shown here.

The directions in between the four points are stated in terms of the nearest quarter direction. Thus going from north to east the compass runs: north by northeast, northeast, east by northeast, east.

Diagonally opposite northeast is southwest.

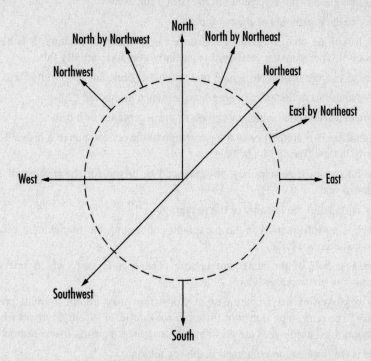

77. **(A)** Note introduction—veering right moves toward the east.

78. **(B)** See diagram—the right of northwest is north by northwest as indicated.

79. **(B)** If the reader faces north and then turns right, he will be facing east. Continuing to turn right the direction is east by southeast.

80. **(A)** Following the circular diagram given above, the vehicle would go south and then make a right turn to go west.

81. **(B)** Northwest is shown on the above diagram as a leftward direction from north of the center of the circle.

82. **(B)** This statement is entirely false. The extent of the punishment is directly related to the crime for which the arrest was made. If the prisoner was arrested for a felony, an attempt to escape is a felony.

83. **(D)** No such statement is made in the paragraph.

84. **(B)** On the contrary. Refer to the last part of the first sentence in the paragraph.

85. **(A)** The last part of the first sentence in the paragraph conveys this thought.

86. **(C)** The statement is true as far as successful escape is concerned but is not true as far as an unsuccessful escape is concerned. In the case of an unsuccessful escape, the prisoner would be guilty of a felony.

87. **(B)** The statement is entirely false. Refer to the latter part of the paragraph.

88. **(D)** This paragraph in part concerns itself only with the conveyance of information which would assist the prisoner to escape.

89. **(B)** On the contrary, one who assists a prisoner guilty of a felony to escape is guilty of a felony.

90. **(A)** A true statement according to the paragraph.

91. **(B)** Only if an attempt at escape is made. The act of conveying the disguise in itself is insufficient to be charged with a crime.

92. **(D)** This condition is not referred to in the paragraph at all.

93. **(A)** Refer to the fourth line of the paragraph.

94. **(C)** It is true if the charge against the prisoner is of a criminal nature. It is also true if the action is civil. Therefore the statement is partially true and partially false.

95. **(B)** Refer to that part of the paragraph that reads, "or omits an act of duty," etc.

96. **(A)** Refer to the sixth line of the paragraph, sentence numbered "2."

97. **(D)** There is no reference in the paragraph to the acceptance of a bribe.

98. **(D)** Again there is no reference in the paragraph to the acceptance of a bribe. The paragraph refers only to the offering of a bribe.

99. **(B)** The maximum time one may be sentenced to prison for the bribing of an executive officer is ten years.

100. **(A)** This is stated in the last line of the paragraph.

101. **(D)** There is no information in the paragraph concerning the punishment of an executive officer who accepts a bribe.

102. **(C)** The first half of the statement is true. The second part, which refers to indirect employment of prisoners, is false.

103. **(B)** No employee of the Department of Correction may accept a small present from a contractor. The paragraph does not differentiate one level of employment from the other. Top to bottom, all employees are prohibited from accepting gifts from contractors.

104. **(A)** This is the implication contained in the regulation.

105. **(B)** The regulation states that it is illegal to utilize the labor of a convict for private benefit only.

106. **(B)** A warden may not have an interest in the sale of merchandise produced or used in the prison directly or indirectly.

107. **(D)** This is stated in the last sentence of the first paragraph.

108. **(A)** There is no implication in the reading that the Legal Bureau has any responsibility in law enforcement or crime prevention.

109. **(D)** This is stated in the second sentence of the second paragraph.

110. **(C)** Refer to the last part of the third paragraph.

111. **(D)** There is nothing in the question in support of this contention.

112. **(B)** Matters for publication 9.

    Reports on proposed legislation 61.

    Notices to court witnesses 26.

    Memoranda of law prepared 15.

113. **(C)** Court appearances of members 1.2%.

    Giving expert testimony 9.4%.

    Deciphering codes 19.3%.

    Letters requesting departmental records 2.5%.

114. **(D)** This information is not contained anywhere in the report.

115. **(B)** At the beginning of the paragraph.

116. **(A)** Disorderly conduct that threatens to disturb the peace is a misdemeanor and is within the jurisdiction of the Criminal Court.

117. **(D)** The paragraph gives examples of minor offense and misdemeanor but does not define either one.

118. **(A)** This inference is supported in the very beginning of the paragraph.

119. **(A)** This is true according to the paragraph even though the convictions had taken place for crimes committed in other states.

120. **(B)** Refer to the last part of the paragraph.

121. **(D)** A took B's property in B's presence by force using violence (tying B to a chair).

122. **(A)** A broke into B's store taking B's property when B was not present.

123. **(C)** The act of "breaking and entering" was not involved.

124. **(B)** A obtained B's property with B's consent. However, the consent was forthcoming only because A instilled appropriate fear in B's mind.

125. **(C)** A took B's property without B's consent. A's intention was to deprive B of the use of B's property. A's plan for the use of the property is not an element in the crime.

PART THREE

Skill Building

How to Sharpen Reading Comprehension Skills

State Trooper candidates must be able to read quickly and carefully and with comprehension. The two essential ingredients for successful performance on reading tests are speed and comprehension. This chapter will explain the different kinds of comprehension questions and provide reading passages that will help to sharpen your skills. For the best results, follow the simple steps below:

1. Read the section "Planning a Strategy" to learn about the different kinds of reading comprehension questions.

2. Read the section "Reading: Quick Tips" to pick up valuable information on how to increase your reading speed and how to use the principles of paragraph construction to improve your comprehension.

3. Review the section "Sample Questions With Full Explanations." This section contains the kinds of reading comprehension questions most likely to appear on your examination. Each question is fully explained with the reasons for discarding incorrect choices and the justifications for the correct answers.

4. You can practice what you have learned in this chapter with the questions in the following chapter. The chapter contains 47 reading comprehension questions taken from actual examinations.

PLANNING A STRATEGY

Hints

1. Read the passage quickly but carefully enough to get the main idea and major supporting details.

2. Read each question and decide which kind it is. *Always* consider each possible answer before making a choice.

3. Eliminate obviously wrong responses immediately. If possible, check confusing answer choices in the passage text.

The Questions

The reading comprehension questions on your examination will usually be one of three kinds. Sample questions of each kind follow.

Main Idea

The question, whether an act repugnant to the Constitution can become the law of the land, is a question deeply interesting to the United States; but, happily, not of an intricacy proportioned to its interest. It seems only necessary to recognize certain principles, supposed to have been long and well established, to decide it. That the people have an original right to establish, for their future government, such principles as, in their opinion, shall most conduce to their own happiness, is the basis on which the whole American fabric has been erected. The exercise of this original right is a very great exertion; nor can it, nor ought it to, be frequently repeated. The principles, therefor, so established, are deemed fundamental; and as the authority from which they proceed is supreme, and can seldom act, they are designed to be permanent.

The best title for the paragraph would be

(A) Principles of the Constitution

(B) The Root of Constitutional Change

(C) Only People Can Change the Constitution

(D) Methods of Constitutional Change

This selection deals with the basis for possible changes in the Constitution. Therefore, the correct answer is **(B)**.

Details

"Another explanation of the persistence of the criminal is found in the existence of criminality or near-criminality in the general society." The statement *least* consistent with this question is

(A) not all criminals are apprehended and sentenced for their crimes

(B) advertisements of many commodities are often fraudulent in their claims

(C) the reformation of the offender would be much simpler if society contained more persons of the near criminal type

(D) many business concerns are willing to purchase stolen goods

Choice **(C)** is in direct opposition to the quotation. It is therefore *least* consistent with the quotation.

Inference

An inference is a conclusion made from something that is implied. The answer to an inference question will not be found in the passage and is therefore the most difficult type of reading comprehension question to answer. You must read carefully and think logically in order to draw the correct conclusion from the information given.

The facts, as we see them, on drug use and the dangerous behavior caused by drugs are that some people get into trouble while using drugs, and some of those drug users are dangerous to others. Sometimes a drug is a necessary element in order for a person to commit a crime, although it may not be the cause of his or her criminality. On the other hand, the use of a drug sometimes seems to be the only convenient excuse by means of which the observer can account for the undesirable behavior.

The author apparently feels that

(A) the use of drugs always results in crime

(B) drugs and crime are only sometimes related

(C) drug use does not always cause crime

(D) drugs are usually an element in accidents and suicides

The author states that drugs are sometimes a necessary element in a crime, but at other times are just an excuse for criminal behavior. Therefore, **(B)** is the correct answer.

READING: QUICK TIPS
Words to Know

Main ideas are the most important thoughts in a paragraph or selection. The main idea is often stated in a topic sentence.

Supporting details are the major thoughts used to explain and expand the main idea.

Skimming is a speed-reading technique that is used to extract the main idea and supporting details from a selection.

Scanning is the method used to locate specific information in a selection.

For speed and accuracy in reading and answering comprehension questions, practice and use these skimming and scanning techniques.

To Answer Main Idea and Inference Questions:

1. Use your index finger as a guide and a pacer. Read the selection through quickly.
2. As you move your finger across each line, concentrate on looking at three or four word phrases, not at one word at a time. Try not to "say" the words in your mind as you go.
3. Follow your finger only with your eyes, not with your whole head.
4. Your purpose is to locate the topic sentence, the main idea, and the major supporting details. This information should enable you to answer most main idea and inference questions.

To Answer Detail Questions:

1. Take a key word from the question you want to answer and "lock" it in your mind.
2. Using your index finger as a guide, scan the lines for that word.
3. *Do not read when you scan!* You are simply looking for the key word.
4. When you find the word, *stop!* The answer to your question will usually be in the same sentence.
5. Read the entire sentence carefully before choosing an answer.

The most important ingredients in successful reading performance are accuracy and speed. Both require lots of practice. The tips you have just read should noticeably improve your accuracy and speed if you practice them conscientiously.

SAMPLE QUESTIONS WITH FULL EXPLANATIONS

Answer questions 1 through 5 on the basis of the information given in the following passage. Circle the letter of the answer you choose.

If we are to study crime in its widest social setting, we will find a variety of conduct which, although criminal in the legal sense, is not offensive to the moral conscience of a considerable number of persons. Traffic violations, for example, do not brand the offender as guilty of moral offense. In fact, the recipient of a traffic ticket is usually simply the subject of some good-natured joking by friends. Although there may be indignation among certain groups of citizens against gambling and liquor law violations, these activities are often tolerated, if not openly supported, by the more numerous residents of the community. Indeed, certain social and service clubs regularly conduct gambling games and lotteries for the purpose of raising funds. Some communities regard violations involving the sale of liquor with little concern in order to profit from increased license fees and taxes paid by dealers. The thousand and one forms of political graft and corruption which infest our urban centers only occasionally arouse public condemnation and official action.

1. According to the passage, all types of illegal conduct are
    (A) condemned by all elements of the community
    (B) considered a moral offense, although some are tolerated by a few citizens
    (C) violations of the law, but some are acceptable to certain elements of the community
    (D) found in a social setting and therefore not punishable by law

2. According to the passage, traffic violations are generally considered by society to be
    (A) crimes requiring the maximum penalty set by the law
    (B) more serious than violations of the liquor laws
    (C) offenses against the morals of the community
    (D) relatively minor offenses requiring minimum punishment

3. According to the passage, a lottery conducted for the purpose of raising funds for a church
    (A) is considered a serious violation of the law
    (B) may be tolerated by a community that has laws against gambling
    (C) may be conducted under special laws demanded by the more numerous residents of a community
    (D) arouses indignation in most communities

4. On the basis of the passage, the most likely reaction in the community to a police raid on a gambling casino would be
    (A) more an attitude of indifference than interest in the raid
    (B) general approval of the raid
    (C) condemnation of the raid by most people
    (D) demand for further action, since this raid is not sufficient to end gambling

5. The one of the following that best describes the central thought of this passage and would be most suitable as a title would be

   (A) "Crime and the Police"

   (B) "Public Condemnation of Graft and Corruption"

   (C) "Gambling Is Not Always a Vicious Business"

   (D) "Public Attitude Toward Law Violations"

Answer questions 6 through 8 on the basis of the information given in the following passage:

The law enforcement agency is one of the most important agencies in the field of juvenile delinquency prevention. This is so, however, not because of the social work connected with this problem, for this is not a police matter, but because the officers are usually the first to come in contact with the delinquent. The manner of arrest and detention makes a deep impression on the delinquent and affects his or her lifelong attitude toward society and toward the law. The juvenile court is perhaps the most important agency in this work. Contrary to general opinion, however, it is not primarily concerned with putting children into correctional schools. The main purpose of the juvenile court is to save the child and to develop his or her emotional makeup so that he or she can grow up to be a decent and well-balanced citizen. The system of probation is the means by which the court seeks to accomplish these goals.

6. According to the passage, police work is an important part of a program to prevent juvenile delinquency because

   (A) social work is no longer considered important in juvenile delinquency prevention

   (B) police officers are the first to have contact with the delinquent

   (C) police officers jail the offender in order to be able to change his or her attitude toward society and the law

   (D) it is the first step in placing the delinquent in jail

7. According to the passage, the chief purpose of the juvenile court is to

   (A) punish the child for the offense

   (B) select a suitable correctional school for the delinquent

   (C) use available means to help the delinquent become a better person

   (D) provide psychiatric care for the delinquent

8. According to the passage, the juvenile court directs the development of delinquents under its care chiefly by

   (A) placing the child under probation

   (B) sending the child to a correctional school

   (C) keeping the delinquent in prison

   (D) returning the child to his or her home

9. "Prostitution is a crime, but one meets it at every corner." The clearest implication of this statement is

   (A) some laws are ignored

   (B) prostitution is a serious offense

   (C) the principal purpose of any law is to catch a lawbreaker

   (D) prostitution is quite uncommon

10. "Discipline should be education; instead it is little more than application of the theory of spanking to adults" means most nearly

    (A) whipping is a good way to handle a man who beats his wife

    (B) a thieving banker should be imprisoned for life

    (C) those who commit crimes exhibit a marked lack of self-control

    (D) reeducation is really a kind of discipline

11. "Crimes against the person are apt to be more spectacular than other types of crime and, consequently, space is accorded them in the public press out of proportion to their actual frequency." This means most nearly that

    (A) there has been a notable increase in crimes against the person

    (B) the newspapers pay more attention to robberies than to cases of fraud

    (C) the newspapers pay no attention to crimes against property

    (D) crimes against property are not as serious as crimes against the person

ANSWER KEY - READING COMPREHENSION

1. C	4. A	6. B	8. A	10. D
2. D	5. D	7. C	9. A	11. B
3. B				

EXPLANATORY ANSWERS - READING COMPREHENSION

1. **(C)**

   (A) Not true; the passage indicates that certain violations of laws are more or less accepted by the citizenry, e.g., traffic violations, liquor laws, etc.

   (B) Not true; the passage indicates that traffic violators are usually not deemed guilty of a moral offense.

   (C) Exactly what the passage implies; this choice is correct.

   (D) Nothing in the passage indicates that this is true.

2. **(D)**

   (A) Nothing in the passage indicates this. In fact, traffic violators are usually only subjected to good-natured joking by their friends.

   (B) The implication in the passage is that violators of liquor laws are probably frowned upon more than traffic violators.

   (C) The passage states exactly the opposite.

   (D) This is the exact inference of the passage and is the correct choice.

3. **(B)**

   (A) There is nothing in the passage to indicate this.

   (B) This is the correct choice as supported by the contents of the passage.

   (C) There is nothing in the passage to support this choice.

   (D) The passage supports the opposite point of view.

4. **(A)**

   (A) This is the correct choice.

   (B) Not correct; the community, in general, would not approve of a raid on an activity that it favors.

   (C) Not correct; the community's reaction would be that the police could better busy themselves on other areas of crime prevention.

   (D) There is nothing in the passage to support this choice.

5. **(D)**

   (A) Not suitable; this title is too broad. The passage deals specifically with certain kinds of crime.

   (B) The passage makes the point that the public does not always condemn crime and corruption.

   (C) This title is too narrow since other crimes are discussed in addition to gambling.

   (D) The correct choice; this title describes the main focus of the passage.

6. **(B)**

(A) The passage states exactly the opposite; social work is a very important part of any juvenile delinquency program.

(B) The correct choice; a police officer's attitude during this initial encounter is of great importance.

(C) Not true; in fact, the passage states that probation is preferred to accomplish these goals.

(D) Not true; the passage emphasizes that the solution to the problem is not placing the delinquent in a jail or correctional school but helping to modify his or her attitudes by means of a probation program.

7. **(C)**

(A) The passage stresses reform rather than punishment.

(B) The passage states that the chief purpose of the juvenile court is to change the attitude of the juvenile offender, not to institutionalize him or her.

(C) This is the implication of the passage and therefore the correct choice.

(D) Psychiatric care is not mentioned directly although it may be implied in the passage. In any case, it is neither a main means of reformation nor the chief purpose of the juvenile court.

8. **(A)**

(A) The correct choice; refer to the last sentence of the passage.

(B) The juvenile court prefers probation as a means of effecting change in delinquents.

(C) Not true; the final sentence makes it quite clear that probation is preferred.

(D) Not true; this is never mentioned in the passage. The home may be the source of the problem.

9. **(A)**

(A) This is the correct choice. If prostitution is prevalent, it must mean that the law that prohibits it is usually ignored.

(B) Not correct; there is nothing in this quotation to indicate that this is true.

(C) Not correct; the implication of the quotation is that prostitution and other victimless crimes are sometimes ignored by law enforcement officials.

(D) Not correct; the opposite is true according to this quotation.

10. **(D)**

(A) Not correct; the quotation refers to the *theory* of the spanking, not to actual physical punishment.

(B) Not correct; nothing in the quotation supports this implication.

(C) Not correct; self-control is not specifically mentioned or implied in this quotation.

(D) The correct choice; proper discipline will change the attitudes of offenders.

11. **(B)**

(A) Not correct; the quotation does not say that this is so.

(B) The correct choice; the implication is that newspaper readers find robbery stories more interesting.

(C) Not correct; the quotation does not state that crimes against property are completely ignored.

(D) Not correct; the quotation does not deal with the seriousness accorded to specific crimes.

PRACTICE WITH READING COMPREHENSION QUESTIONS

1. "The force reconciling and coordinating all human conflicts and directing people in the harmonious accomplishments of their work is the supervisor. To deal with people successfully, the first one a supervisor must learn to work with is him- or herself." According to the quotation, the most accurate of the following conclusions is

   (A) human conflicts are not the basic lack in harmonious accomplishment

   (B) a supervisor should attempt to reconcile all the different views subordinates may have

   (C) a supervisor who understands him- or herself is in a good position to deal with others successfully

   (D) the reconciling force in human conflicts is the ability to deal with people successfully

2. "Law must be stable and yet it cannot stand still," means most nearly that

   (A) law is a fixed body of subject matter

   (B) law must adapt itself to changing conditions

   (C) law is a poor substitute for justice

   (D) the true administration of justice is the firmest pillar of good government

3. "The treatment to be given the offender cannot alter the fact of the offense; but we can take measures to reduce the chance of similar acts occurring in the future. We should banish the criminal, not in order to exact revenge nor directly to encourage reform, but to deter that person and others from further illegal attacks on society." According to the quotation, prisoners should be punished in order to

   (A) alter the nature of their offenses

   (B) banish them from society

   (C) deter them and others from similar illegal attacks on society

   (D) directly encourage reform

4. "On the other hand, the treatment of prisoners on a basis of direct reform is foredoomed to failure. Neither honest persons nor criminals will tolerate a bald proposition from anyone to alter their characters or habits, least of all if we attempt to gain such a change by a system of coercion." According to this quotation, criminals

   (A) are incorrigible

   (B) are incapable of being coerced

   (C) are not likely to turn into law-abiding citizens

   (D) possess very firm characters

5. "A moment's reflection will show that it is never possible to determine the exact amount of blame to be attached to the individual criminal. How can we ascertain how much is due to inheritance, how much to early environment, how much to other matters over which the offender has had no control whatsoever?" According to this quotation, criminals

   (A) cannot be held to account for their crimes

   (B) cannot be blamed for their crimes

   (C) are variously motivated in committing crimes, and it is senseless to assume that we can know how much blame to attach to a particular violator of the law

   (D) can blame their misdeeds on their early environment

6. "While much thought has been devoted to the question of how to build walls high enough to keep persons temporarily in prison, we have devoted very little attention to the treatment necessary to enable them to come out permanently cured, inclined to be friends rather than enemies of their law-abiding fellow citizens." According to this quotation, much thought has been devoted to the problem of prisons as

   (A) vengeful agencies

   (B) efficient custodial agencies

   (C) efficient sanatoria

   (D) places from which society's friends might issue

7. "There has been a tragic failure on the part of the home, the school, the church, industry, and every other social agency to adjust the incompetent individual to his or her proper sphere and to impart to him or her wholesome principles of proper living. The failure is finally shunted onto the prison in one last desperate effort to make the person over. Theoretically, the church, the school, and the college have a clean page in the mind of the pupil upon which to make their impressions, but the prison school faces the tremendous task of obliterating many erroneous and corrupt notions before it can secure a clean page upon which to write." According to this statement, the prison has as pupils

   (A) those persons with which society's educational institutions have been able to do nothing

   (B) those who have failed in business and the arts

   (C) those who have scoffed at God

   (D) those who have learned nothing from the outside world

8. "Community organizations most often include persons whose behavior is unconventional in relation to generally accepted social definitions, if such persons wield substantial influence with the residents." The inference one can most validly draw from this statement is that

   (A) influential persons are often likely to be unconventional

   (B) the success of a community organization depends largely on the democratic processes employed by it

   (C) a gang leader may sometimes be an acceptable recruit for a community organization

   (D) the unconventional behavior of a local barkeeper may often become acceptable to the community

9. "Essential to the prevention and early treatment of delinquency is the discovery of potential or incipient cases. Finding them is not as difficult as making assistance available and acceptable to them and their families." On the basis of this statement, it is most accurate to state that

   (A) the families of delinquents are largely responsible for their behavior

   (B) "an ounce of prevention is worth more than a pound of cure"

   (C) potential for criminality is readily discernible

   (D) the family of a delinquent may often reject a recommended plan for therapy

10. "The safeguard of democracy is education. The education of youth during a limited period of more or less compulsory attendance at school does not suffice. The educative process is a lifelong one." The statement most consistent with this quotation is:

   (A) The school is not the only institution that can contribute to the education of the population.

   (B) All democratic peoples are educated.

   (C) The entire population should be required to go to school throughout life.

   (D) If compulsory education were not required, the educative process would be more effective.

11. "The state police officer's art consists of applying and enforcing a multitude of laws and ordinances in such degree or proportion and in such manner that the greatest degree of social protection will be secured. The degree of enforcement and method of application will vary with each neighborhood and community." According to this statement

   (A) each neighborhood or community must judge for itself to what extent the law is to be enforced

   (B) a police officer should only enforce those laws that are designed to give the greatest degree of social protection

   (C) the manner and intensity of law enforcement is not necessarily the same in all communities

   (D) all laws and ordinances must be enforced in a community with the same degree of intensity

12. "Police control in the sense of regulating the details of police operations involves such matters as the technical means for organizing the available personnel so that competent police leadership, when secured, can operate effectively. It is concerned not so much with the extent to which popular controls can be trusted to guide and direct the course of police protection, as with the administrative relationships which should exist among the component parts of the police organism." According to this statement, police control is

   (A) solely a matter of proper personnel assignment

   (B) the means employed to guide and direct the course of police protection

   (C) principally concerned with the administrative relationships among units of a police organization

   (D) the sum total of means employed in rendering police protection

13. "As a rule, state police officers, through service and experience, are familiar with the duties and the methods and means required to perform them. Yet, left to themselves, their aggregate effort would disintegrate and the vital work of preserving the peace would never be accomplished." According to this statement, the most accurate of the following conclusions is

   (A) police officers are sufficiently familiar with their duties as to need no supervision

   (B) working together for a common purpose is not efficient without supervision

   (C) police officers are familiar with the methods of performing their duties because of rules

   (D) preserving the peace is so vital that it can never be said to be completed

Answer questions 14 through 16 on the basis of the information given in the following passage.

Criminal science is largely the science of identification. Progress in this field has been marked and sometimes very spectacular because new techniques, instruments, and facts flow continuously from the scientists. But the crime laboratories are understaffed; trade secrets still prevail; and inaccurate conclusions are often the result. Moreover, modern gadgets cannot substitute for the skilled intelligent investigator; he or she must be their master.

14. According to this passage, criminal science

    (A) excludes the field of investigation

    (B) is primarily interested in establishing identity

    (C) is based on the equipment used in crime laboratories

    (D) uses techniques different from those used in other sciences

15. Advances in criminal science have been, according to the passage,

    (A) extremely limited

    (B) slow but steady

    (C) unusually reliable

    (D) outstanding

16. A problem that has not been overcome completely in crime work is, according to the passage,

    (A) unskilled investigators

    (B) the expense of new equipment and techniques

    (C) an insufficient number of personnel in crime laboratories

    (D) inaccurate equipment used in laboratories

17. "The large number of fatal motor vehicle accidents renders necessary the organization of special units in the police department to cope with the technical problems encountered in such investigations." The generalization which can be inferred most directly from this statement is that

    (A) the number of fatal motor vehicle accidents is large

    (B) technical problems require specialists

    (C) many police problems require special handling

    (D) many police officers are specialists

18. "While the safe burglar can ply his or her trade the year round, the loft burglar has more seasonal activities, since only at certain periods of the year is a substantial amount of valuable merchandise stored in lofts." The generalization that this statement best illustrates is that

    (A) nothing is ever completely safe from a thief

    (B) there are safe burglars and loft burglars

    (C) some types of burglary are seasonal

    (D) the safe burglar considers safecracking a trade

Questions 19 through 22 relate to the report of an accident. In Part A you are given the regulations governing filling out the report form. In Part B you are given the completed report, which you will use to answer the questions that follow.

Part A

1. A report form will be filled out for each person injured.

2. Be brief but do not omit any information that can help the department reduce the number of accidents. If necessary, use more than one form.

3. Under Details, enter all important facts not reported elsewhere on the form that may be pertinent to the completeness of the report, such as: the specific traffic violation, if any; whether the injured person was crossing not at the intersection or against the lights; the direction the vehicle was proceeding and if making a right or left turn; attending surgeon; etc. If the officer is an eyewitness, he or she should be able to determine the cause of the accident.

Part B

Injured Person: John C. Witherspoon
Sex: Male   *Age:* 52
Address: 2110 Fairwell Road
Place of Occurrence: 72nd Street and Broadway
Date: 3/12/95
Accident: Yes
Number of Persons Involved: 12
Time: 10 A.M.
Nature of Injury: Right forearm fractured
Struck by: Vehicle 3
Drivers Involved: Vehicle 1: Helmut Baldman, 11 Far Street-Lic. 2831, owner
                                  Vehicle 2: John Dunn, 106 Near Avenue-Lic. 1072, owner
                                  Vehicle 3: Robert Payne, 32 Open Road-Lic. 666, owner
Details: (1) Vehicle 1 came out of 72nd Street just as the lights along 72nd Street were changing to green west. (2) Vehicle 2 proceeding north along Broadway continued across the intersection as the lights in his direction turned red. (3) Vehicle 1 collided with Vehicle 2, turning said vehicle over and throwing it into the path of Vehicle 3, which was going east along 72nd Street. (4) This had manifold results: other vehicles were struck; a hydrant was obliterated; several pedestrians were injured; there was considerable property damage; and the three riders in the cars involved were killed. (5) This was a very tragic accident.

19. Of the following critical evaluations of the report, the most correct is that it is a

    (A) good report; it gives a graphic description of the accident

    (B) bad report; the damage to the car is not given in detail

    (C) bad report; it does not indicate, in detail, the cause of Witherspoons's injury

    (D) good report; it is very brief

20. Of the following, the report indicates most clearly

    (A) the driver at fault

    (B) that Witherspoon was a pedestrian

    (C) the names of all the drivers involved

    (D) that some city property was damaged

21. Of the following, the report indicates least clearly

    (A) the time of the accident

    (B) the direction in which Baldman was driving

    (C) how the accident might have been avoided

    (D) the number of persons involved

22. From the report, as submitted, it is most reasonable to infer that

    (A) Baldman was at fault

    (B) the information is too hazy to determine the guilty person

    (C) Dunn was at fault

    (D) something was wrong with the light system

Answer questions 23 through 26 on the basis of the information given in the following passage.

When a vehicle has been disabled in a tunnel, the officer on patrol in this zone shall press the emergency truck light button. In the fast lane, red lights will go on throughout the tunnel. The yellow zone light will go on at each signal control station throughout the tunnel and will flash the number of the zone in which the stoppage has occurred. A red flashing pilot light will appear only at the signal control station at which the emergency truck button was pressed. The emergency garage will receive an audible and visual signal indicating the signal control station at which the emergency truck button was pressed. The garage officer shall acknowledge receipt of the signal by pressing the acknowledgment button. This will cause the pilot light at the operated signal control station in the tunnel to cease flashing and to remain steady. It is an answer to the officer at the operated signal control station that the emergency truck is responding to the call.

23. According to this passage, when the emergency truck light button is pressed

    (A) amber lights will go on in every lane throughout the tunnel

    (B) emergency signal lights will go on only in the lane in which the disabled vehicle is located

    (C) red lights will go on in the fast lane throughout the tunnel

    (D) pilot lights at all signal control stations will turn amber

24. According to this passage, the number of the zone in which the stoppage has occurred is flashed

    (A) immediately after all the lights in the tunnel turn red

    (B) by the yellow zone light at each signal control station

    (C) by the emergency truck at the point of stoppage

    (D) by the emergency garage

25. According to the passage, an officer near the disabled vehicle will know that the emergency tow truck is coming when

    (A) the pilot light at the operated signal control station appears and flashes red

    (B) an audible signal is heard in the tunnel

    (C) the zone light at the operated signal control station turns red

    (D) the pilot light at the operated signal control station becomes steady

26. Under the system described in the passage, it would be correct to come to the conclusion that

    (A) officers at all signal control stations are expected to acknowledge that they have received the stoppage signal

    (B) officers at all signal control stations will know where the stoppage has occurred

    (C) all traffic in both lanes of that side of the tunnel in which the stoppage has occurred must stop until the emergency truck has arrived

    (D) there are two emergency garages, each able to respond to the stoppage in traffic going in one particular direction

Answer questions 27 through 29 on the basis of the information given in the following passage.

The use of a roadblock is simply an adaptation of the military concept of encirclement to police practices. Successful operation of a roadblock plan depends almost entirely on the amount of advance study and planning given to such operations. A thorough and detailed examination of the roads and terrain under the jurisdiction of a given police agency should be made with the locations of the roadblock pinpointed in advance. The first principle to be borne in mind in the location of each roadblock is the time element. Its location must be at a point beyond which the fugitive could not possibly have traveled in the time elapsed from the commission of the crime to the arrival of the officers at the roadblock.

27. According to the passage

    (A) military operations have made extensive use of roadblocks

    (B) the military concept of encirclement is an adaptation of police use of roadblocks

    (C) the technique of encirclement has been widely used by military forces

    (D) a roadblock is generally more effective than encirclement

28. According to the passage

    (A) advance study and planning are of minor importance in the success of roadblock operations

    (B) a thorough and detailed examination of all roads within a radius of 50 miles should precede the determination of a roadblock location

    (C) consideration of terrain features is important in planning the location of roadblocks

    (D) a roadblock operation can seldom be successfully undertaken by a single police agency

29. According to the passage
    (A) the factor of time is the sole consideration in the location of a roadblock
    (B) the maximum speed possible in the method of escape is of major importance in roadblock location
    (C) the time the officers arrive at the site of a proposed roadblock is of little importance
    (D) a roadblock should be sited as close to the scene of the crime as the terrain will permit

Answer questions 30 through 32 on the basis of the information given in the following passage.

A number of crimes, such as robbery, assault, rape, certain forms of theft, and burglary are high visibility crimes in that it is apparent to all concerned that they are criminal acts prior to or at the time they are committed. In contrast to these, check forgeries, especially those committed by first offenders, have low visibility. There is little in the criminal act or in the interaction between the check passer and the person cashing the check to identify it as a crime. Closely related to this special quality of the forgery crime is the fact that, while it is formally defined and treated as a felonious or "infamous" crime, it is informally held by the legally untrained public to be a relatively harmless form of crime.

30. According to the passage, crimes of "high visibility"
    (A) are immediately recognized as crime by the victims
    (B) take place in public view
    (C) always involve violence or the threat of violence
    (D) are usually committed after dark

31. According to the passage
    (A) the public regards check forgery as a minor crime
    (B) the law regards check forgery as a minor crime
    (C) the law distinguishes between check forgery and other forgery
    (D) it is easier to spot inexperienced check forgers than other criminals

32. As used in this passage, an "infamous" crime is
    (A) a crime attracting great attention from the public
    (B) more serious than a felony
    (C) a felony
    (D) more or less serious than a felony depending upon the surrounding circumstances

Answer questions 33 and 34 on the basis of the information given in the following passage.

The racketeer is primarily concerned with business affairs, legitimate or otherwise, and preferably those which are close to the margin of legitimacy. The racketeer gets the best opportunities from business organizations which meet the need of large sections of the public for goods or services which are defined as illegitimate by the same public, such as prostitution, gambling, illicit drugs, or liquor. In contrast to the thief, the racketeer and the establishments controlled deliver goods and services for the money received.

33. It can be deduced from the passage that suppression of racketeers is difficult because

(A) victims of racketeers are not guilty of violating the law

(B) racketeers are generally engaged in fully legitimate enterprises

(C) many people want services that are not obtainable through legitimate sources

(D) laws prohibiting gambling and prostitution are unenforceable

34. According to the passage, racketeering, unlike theft, involves

(A) objects of value

(B) payment for goods received

(C) organized gangs

(D) unlawful activities

35. In examining the scene of a homicide, one should not only look for the usual, standard traces —fingerprints, footprints, etc.— but should also have eyes open for details which at first glance may not seem to have any connection with the crime." The most logical inference to be drawn from this statement is that

(A) in general, standard traces are not important

(B) sometimes one should not look for footprints

(C) usually only the standard traces are important

(D) one cannot tell in advance what will be important

Answer questions 36 and 37 on the basis of the information given in the following passage.

If a motor vehicle fails to pass inspection, the owner will be given a rejection notice by the inspection station. Repairs must be made within ten days after this notice is issued. It is not necessary to have the required adjustment or repairs made at the station where the inspection occurred. The vehicle may be taken to any other garage. Reinspection after repairs may be made at any official inspection station, not necessarily the same station which made the initial inspection. The registration of any motor vehicle for which an inspection sticker has not been obtained as required, or which is not repaired and inspected within ten days after inspection indicates defects, is subject to suspension. A vehicle cannot be used on public highways while its registration is under suspension.

36. According to the passage, the owner of a car that does not pass inspection must

(A) have repairs made at the same station that rejected the car

(B) take the car to another station and have it reinspected

(C) have repairs made anywhere and then have the car reinspected

(D) not use the car on a public highway until the necessary repairs have been made

37. According to the passage, the one of the following that may be cause for suspension of the registration of a vehicle is that

(A) an inspection sticker was issued before the rejection notice had been in force for ten days

(B) it was not reinspected by the station that rejected it originally

(C) it was not reinspected either by the station that rejected if originally or by the garage that made the repairs

(D) it has not had defective parts repaired within ten days after inspection

38. A statute states: "A person who steals an article worth less than $100 where no aggravating circumstances accompany the act is guilty of petit larceny. If the article is worth $100 or more, it may be larceny second degree." If all you know is that Edward Smith stole an article worth $100, it may be reasonably be said that

   (A) Smith is guilty of petit larceny

   (B) Smith is guilty of larceny second degree

   (C) Smith is guilty of neither petit larceny nor larceny second degree

   (D) precisely what charge will be placed against Smith is uncertain

Answer questions 39 through 41 on the basis of the information given in the following passage.

The City Police Department will accept for investigation no report of a person missing from his residence if such residence is located outside of the city. The person reporting same will be advised to report such fact to the police department of the locality where the missing person lives, which will, if necessary, communicate officially with the City Police Department. However, a report will be accepted of a person who is missing from a temporary residence in the city, but the person making the report will be instructed to make a report also to the police department of the locality where the missing person lives.

39. According to the passage, a report to the City Police Department of a missing person whose permanent residence is outside of the city will

   (A) always be investigated provided that a report is also made to local police authorities

   (B) never be investigated unless requested officially by local police authorities

   (C) be investigated in cases of temporary residence in the city, but a report should always be made to local police authorities

   (D) always be investigated and a report will be made to the local police authorities by the City Police Department

40. Of the following, the most likely reason for the procedure described in the passage is that

   (A) nonresidents are not entitled to free police service from the city

   (B) local police authorities would resent interference in their jurisdiction

   (C) local police authorities sometimes try to unload their problems on the City Police Department

   (D) local authorities may be better able to conduct an investigation

41. Mr. Smith of Oldtown and Mr. Jones of Newtown have an appointment in the city, but Mr. Jones doesn't appear. Mr. Smith, after trying repeatedly to phone Mr. Jones the next day, believes that something has happened to him. According to the passage, Mr. Smith should apply to the police of

   (A) Oldtown

   (B) Newtown

   (C) Newtown and the city

   (D) Oldtown and the city

42. A Police Department rule reads as follows: "A Deputy Commissioner acting as Police Commissioner shall carry out the order of the Police Commissioner, previously given, and such orders shall not, except in cases of extreme emergency, be countermanded." This means most nearly that, except in cases of extreme emergency,

    (A) the orders given by a Deputy Commissioner acting as Police Commissioner may not be revoked

    (B) a Deputy Commissioner acting as Police Commissioner should not revoke orders previously given by the Police Commissioner

    (C) a Deputy Commissioner acting as Police Commissioner is vested with the same authority to issue orders as the Police Commissioner

    (D) only a Deputy Commissioner acting as Police Commissioner may issue orders in the absence of the Police Commissioner

43. "A 'crime' is an act committed or omitted in violation of a public law either forbidding or commanding it." This statement implies most nearly that

    (A) crimes can be omitted

    (B) a forbidding act, if omitted, is a crime

    (C) an act of omission may be criminal

    (D) to commit an act not commanded is criminal

44. "He who by command, counsel, or assistance procures another to commit a crime is, in morals and in law, as culpable as the visible actor himself, for the reason that the criminal act, whichever it may be, is imputable to the person who conceived it and set the forces in motion for its actual accomplishment." Of the following, the most accurate inference from this statement is that

    (A) a criminal act does not have to be committed for a crime to be committed

    (B) acting as counselor for a criminal is a crime

    (C) the mere counseling of a criminal act can never be a crime if no criminal act is committed

    (D) a person acting only as an adviser may be guilty of committing a criminal act

45. "A 'felony' is a crime punishable by death or imprisonment in a state prison, and any other crime is a 'misdemeanor.'" According to this quotation, the decisive distinction between "felony" and "misdemeanor" is the

    (A) degree of criminality

    (B) type of crime

    (C) place of incarceration

    (D) judicial jurisdiction

Answer questions 46 and 47 on the basis of the information given in the following passage.

If the second or third felony is such that, upon a first conviction, the offender would be punished by imprisonment for any term less than his or her natural life, then such person must be sentenced to imprisonment for an indeterminate term, the minimum of which shall be not less than one-half of the longest term prescribed upon a first conviction, and the maximum of which shall be not longer than twice such longest term; provided, however, that the minimum sentence imposed hereunder upon such second or third felony offender shall in no case be less than five years; except that where the maximum punishment for a second or third felony offender hereunder is five years or less, the minimum sentence must be not less than two years.

46. According to this passage, a person who has a second felony conviction shall receive as a sentence for that second felony an indeterminate term

   (A) not less than twice the minimum term prescribed upon a first conviction as a maximum

   (B) not less than one-half the maximum term of the first conviction as a minimum

   (C) not more than twice the minimum term prescribed upon a first conviction as a minimum

   (D) with a maximum of not more than twice the longest term prescribed for a first conviction for this crime

47. According to the passage, if the term for this crime for a first offender is up to three years, the possible indeterminate term for this crime as a second or third felony shall have a

   (A) minimum of not more than two years

   (B) maximum of not more than five years

   (C) minimum of not less than one and one-half years

   (D) maximum of not less than six years

ANSWER KEY - READING COMPREHENSION

1. C	11. C	21. C	31. A	41. B
2. B	12. C	22. B	32. C	42. B
3. C	13. B	23. C	33. C	43. C
4. C	14. B	24. B	34. B	44. D
5. C	15. D	25. D	35. D	45. C
6. B	16. C	26. B	36. C	46. D
7. A	17. B	27. C	37. D	47. C
8. C	18. C	28. C	38. D	
9. D	19. C	29. B	39. C	
10. A	20. C	30. A	40. D	

Observation and Memory

To function effectively, a state police officer must possess a keen memory for details. He or she must be on constant alert for physical characteristics that will help to identify key people, places, or things, thereby leading to the apprehension of a criminal or to the solution of a criminal investigation.

Most people have distinguishing features that are difficult to disguise: the contour of the face; the size, shape, and position of the ears; the shape of the mouth; and the color of the eyes. Any of these may be sufficient for an officer to detect an individual wanted for criminal activities. On the other hand, the color or style of an individual's hair or the first impression of his or her face may change drastically with the addition of a wig, mustache, or beard. Therefore, the police officer must focus attention on those physical features that cannot be changed easily and that might serve as the basis of a positive identification of that person at some time in the future.

Observation is not limited to the act of seeing. In addition, the officer must learn to recognize and recall distinctive features of people, places, and things. An official record in the memorandum book may serve as a refresher for the facts stored in the officer's mental record. The officer should be aware of the people who frequent his or her post, and of the surrounding buildings and stores on that post, so that important details may be brought to bear in a case when necessary. An officer without a keen sense of recall cannot perform his or her duties effectively.

Because state police departments all over the country recognize the importance of a good memory for details and a good sense of recall in the officer's job, examinations for the position frequently contain sections that evaluate these skills. To best sharpen your memory and sense of recall, you must practice using these skills. You need only walk around your neighborhood and observe. Keep your eyes open to everything you see. Later try to recall details of buildings or people that you saw. Remember, your environment is your study aid. Virtually any place you go you can practice observing and recalling details.

POLICE OBSERVATION OF PERSONS, PLACES, AND THINGS

The state police officer must be thoroughly observant at all times. The non-observant officer is soon found out by the criminal element who will take advantage of this deficiency to commit crimes on the officer's post. Good observation is a matter of training and knowledge. A state police officer may have perfect eyesight, yet be blind when it comes to observing matters calling for police action.

Observation and Memory 269

Many dangerous criminals have been arrested due to a state police officer's keen observation. An officer should observe the customary activities on his or her post as well as the people who live in or frequent it so that the officer can quickly spot a stranger or an unusual activity. Some places will call for more observation than others: banks, jewelry stores, taverns, service stations, and any place where crime is likely to occur or where the criminal element may gather.

An essential element in observation is the ability to remember details. Officers should practice observation by giving themselves such tests as describing a man or woman encountered casually or trying to remember details on a billboard. The identification of persons, places, and things depends on accurate observation. Many witnesses testify inaccurately in court because they failed to observe properly at the time of the incident's occurrence. A failure of this kind is *inexcusable* on the part of an officer.

Police Observation Outline

I. DEFINITION

Observation may be defined as

  A. the act, ability, or practice of taking notice

  B. the act of seeing or fixing the mind on anything

  C. the act of drawing a mental picture of what has been seen

II. OBSERVATION BY A STATE POLICE OFFICER

  A. As stated in the definition, observation means first noticing things and second remembering what was noticed. So a police officer should know how to observe if he or she is to be effective in performing police work.

  B. Essentially, observation by a police officer is the control of his or her senses to note and record in his or her mind accurately any occurrence, person, place, thing, or condition that is or may be related to the performance of the officer's duty.

  C. The basis of observation is the *proper* use of the five senses, namely: sight, hearing, smell, taste, and touch.

    1. Sight is used in noting the actions and appearance of persons, places, and things.

    2. Hearing is used in listening to what is said and listening for noises and sounds that may indicate the need for police action.

    3. Smell is used to notice odors, such as gas, liquor, gasoline, dead bodies, etc.

    4. Taste is used in identifying liquids as sweet, salty, sour, etc.

    5. Touch is used in feeling for pulse, temperature, etc.

    NOTE: PSYCHOLOGISTS HAVE ESTIMATED THAT ROUGHLY 85% OF OUR KNOWLEDGE IS OBTAINED THROUGH THE SENSE OF SIGHT, 12% THROUGH THE SENSE OF HEARING, AND THE REMAINING 3% THROUGH THE SENSES OF SMELL, TOUCH, AND TASTE COMBINED. THE RELIABILITY OF ALL SENSE INFORMATION IS CONSIDERED TO BE THE SAME. THE COMBINATION OF SIGHT AND HEARING IS THE MOST USEFUL AND PRODUCTIVE IN OBSERVATION.

  D. The senses are of little value unless they are used and directed by intelligence.

  E. Random reflection is also of little value. We must note consciously all things in relation to our duty. We must refer our observations to our knowledge of laws, places, people, and conditions.

  F. Our senses must be quick to seek out criminal characteristics in those we meet, or lawless possibilities in any situation, and to note that which is unusual.

G. We should be on the alert for emergencies in order to prevent them or to control them properly.

H. We must develop our memory.

I. We must study all situations and conditions closely so as to be able to render an accurate report to higher authority when required.

III. NECESSITY FOR POLICE OBSERVATION

An non-observant state trooper is a poor trooper. Proper police work is greatly dependent on a trooper's power of observation. The following is a list of situations that depend on good observation in police work.

A. **Noting Suspicious Persons.** A state police officer who becomes familiar with the type of people usually on his or her post will quickly notice a stranger, and if he or she knows how criminals act and pays attention to those he or she sees, the officer will note those acting suspiciously.

B. **Preventing Crimes.** Observation of places where lights are ordinarily left burning at night, of when business places usually open and close, and of those who do business on his or her post will prevent many burglaries and robberies.

C. **Saving Lives.** A state police officer noting the odor of poisonous or explosive gases and dangerous conditions will aid in this respect.

D. **Controlling Emergencies.** Noting where the trouble lies is the first step in the proper control of the ordinary emergency.

E. **Securing Evidence.** Many a case is ruined because the police officer overlooked evidence of clues.

F. **Reporting to Superiors.** Proper police administration is greatly dependent on complete and accurate reports. Observation is essential to such completeness.

G. **Recovering Stolen Property.** Stolen cars, particularly, are recovered by the officer who pays attention to license numbers, descriptions, and alarms.

H. **Detecting Criminals.** The police officer who notes something special or unusual about a person, a car, or the modus operandi of a criminal is of great value in locating criminal suspects.

IV. GENERAL OBSERVATIONS BY STATE POLICE OFFICERS

A. Persons

   1. The Individual

      (a) Facial expression

      (b) Complexion

      (c) Scars

      (d) Physique; carriage

      (e) Gait

      (f) Actions

      (g) Manner of dress

      (h) Tone of voice

      (i) Physical deformities; eccentricities

      (j) Occupation

   2. The Group

    (a) Character of the gathering

    (b) Manner of the gathering

    (c) Individual members of the group

    (d) Language of the group; criminal jargon, etc.

    (e) Locale of the gathering

    (f) Time of day or night

B. Places

  1. The Neighborhood

    (a) Social or economic level

    (b) Neighborhood esprit de corps

    (c) Likelihood of, or temptation to, crime, etc.

  2. The Street

    (a) Children

    (b) Obstructions

    (c) Health conditions

  3. The Buildings

    (a) Locations

    (b) Uses

    (c) Occupants; residents; storekeepers; janitors; doormen; etc.

    (d) Licenses

    (e) Signs

C. Things

  1. Vehicles

    (a) Uses

    (b) Location

    (c) Occupants

    (d) Licenses

V. SPECIFIC OBSERVATIONS BY STATE POLICE OFFICERS

A. Persons

  1. With criminal records

  2. On probation or parole

  3. Acting suspiciously

  4. Associating with criminals or suspicious persons

  5. Living in idleness

  6. Hanging about pool parlors, dance halls, cabarets, cellar clubs, etc.

  7. Without any visible means of support

  8. Loitering in hallways, entering or leaving buildings, ringing bells, etc.

  9. Loitering in the vicinity of banks, jewelry stores, railroad and bus stations, near trucks carrying valuable merchandise, etc.

  10. Entering or leaving pawn shops, junk shops, secondhand stores

  11. Showing an inclination to engage patrol officers in conversations, especially in high crime districts at night

B. Places

1. Licensed premises

2. Disorderly houses

3. All-night restaurants, social clubs, discos, nightclubs, etc.

4. Suspicious places and premises where known criminals congregate

5. Premises suspected of housing unlawful practices, such as gambling, vice, prostitution, etc.

6. Business places such as jewelry stores, banks, check cashing stores, loft buildings, garages, hackstands, etc.

C. Things

1. Automobiles, especially those in which the occupants are acting suspiciously

2. Automobiles standing at the curb with the motor running

3. Automobiles stopped in front of banks, financial institutions, etc.

4. Taxicabs and hacks

5. Various classes of business

    (a) Time of opening and closing

    (b) Who opens and who closes such business places

    (c) Location of safes, cash registers, and valuable merchandise

VI. UNDESIRABLE OR DEFECTIVE OBSERVATIONS

A. **Haste.** Combine deliberation with observation. Proceed methodically; omit no details. Remember that patchwork is useless.

B. **Prejudice.** See all things equally. Avoid personal and biased points of view that destroy the real observations.

C. **Absentmindedness.** Avoid daydreaming. No one is on duty while his or her observational faculties—the senses—are off duty.

D. **Carelessness.** Failure to observe and note persons, places, things, and incidents results in fewer arrests, fewer convictions, and an increase in crime.

E. **Exaggeration.** See a thing as it is without enlarging its importance.

F. **Emotion.** The reactions of hope, fear, love, hate, or other strong feelings result in a loss of intelligent thinking, power to observe, and sense of proportion.

VII. QUALITIES OF AN OBSERVANT POLICE OFFICER

A. Faithful in the performance of his or her duties

B. Zealous in his or her work.

C. Unwearying in his or her devotion to the public need and to the civic ideal of which he or she is the personal embodiment

D. Good memory

E. Alertness

F. Knowledge of law, places, persons, etc.

G. Intelligence

H. Suspicion

I. Ambition

J. Attention to details

VIII. RESPONSIBILITY OF A POLICE OFFICER IN THE MATTER OF POLICE OBSERVATION

A. Improve his or her observational faculties by constantly exercising them. Thus, the officer should look at persons, places, and things while patrolling a post, describing them mentally, and fixing their details in his or her mind. On returning back to the same post, the officer should check the accuracy of the observations.

B. Associate his or her observations with some line of police duty. Relevance to police work is the major consideration in the association of a police officer's observations. The main objects of police observation are to save time and effort, solve crimes more efficiently, and prepare effective evidence for presentation in court.

   1. A police officer should learn to associate a certain kind of scar with a certain kind of weapon; a certain kind of gait and mannerism with the drug addict; a vehicle parked outside a jewelry store with the motor running with robbery.

   2. In observing a person whom the police officer suspects of committing crime, the police officer should associate observation of the following general illustrations.

      (a) A guilty person will try to act overly natural, but, in many instances, will make a wrong move that will cause his or her arrest.

      (b) Those who are about to commit a crime usually look about. Sometimes they will walk into hallways and then walk out boldly.

      (c) The reward of careful observations and association of observations is the making of good arrests.

C. A police officer should classify his or her observations. This merely puts the observations into an orderly grouping to aid recall. A police officer who fulfills his or her responsibility in good observation will classify his or her observations into such divisions as health, sanitation, traffic, business, etc.

D. A police officer should review and remember his or her observations. Old impressions are reviewed in the light of new impressions. New impressions are reviewed in the light of old impressions. In this way, the observational faculties are sharpened and the power of retention is perfected. The finest kind of observation is a waste of time if, at the moment of need, the faculty to remember fails.

IX. MAXIMS OF POLICE OBSERVATION

A. Observe sanely and sensibly.

B. Always be suspicious.

C. Do not look for trouble.

D. Look out for trouble.

E. Take nothing for granted.

X. MEMORY AS A PART OF OBSERVATION

As already stated, memory is an essential part of observation. To note a condition and then to forget it is of little use in police work. It is essential, therefore, that police officers train their memories.

Things are best remembered by association with some other thing that we know or have experienced in the past. Thus, when we note something, we should try to associate it with something we already know. Association is easier when what we know is of recent origin or if it was something that made a deep impression on us.

XI. MISTAKES IN OBSERVATION

A. **Memory.** Much of what we see or hear is frequently supplied by our memory. Thus, if we read a printed page, we often don't notice a misprint because we suppose the words are spelled correctly.

B. **Imagination.** Imagination of what we see is often regarded as an observation. Thus, children left in a dark room often "see" things that don't exist except in the imagination.

C. **Illusion.** The eye is often deceived. Thus, if we look at a stick partly under water, it seems to be bent although it actually isn't.

D. **Rapidity of Action.** If something occurs rapidly, we often fail to notice all details and often supply these details from past experiences.

E. **Emotional Stress.** Under stress of emotion, excitement, etc., we often see things that never happened. This has been proven time and again by questioning witnesses on stated situations.

F. **Prejudice.** What we see is often colored by what we want to see or expect to see. If we want our side to win, we see only the good features and often disparage those of the other side.

XII. TESTING RELIABILITY OF OBSERVATION

We can test the reliability of an observation by referring to:

A. Circumstances at the time

B. Whether the observation was carelessly or deliberately and calmly made

C. State of mind of the observer

D. Type of mind of the observer

E. Eyesight, etc., of the observer

F. Time between observation and recording it

G. Subject matter observed

H. Whether fact regarded as having been observed is consistent with known facts and physical laws

XIII. HOW TO DESCRIBE PERSONS AND PROPERTY WANTED

A. Importance

1. A description of persons or property wanted by a police department is of little or no value unless it is *distinctive*. Remember that such descriptions must be relied upon by other police officers for recognition and identification of the wanted person or property.

2. When a criminal flees after the commission of a crime, his or her chance of escape will be greatly reduced by an accurate description immediately broadcast to all police officers in that area through a general alarm or all points bulletin (APB).

3. Therefore, the original police investigator must be certain to obtain distinctive descriptions since many other officers must work from such descriptions.

4. The data for obtaining descriptions is particularly important for detectives, and it is equally applicable to members of the uniformed branch of a police department. Review the following lists for important points to cover in your description.

B. Description of Persons Wanted, such as an Escaped Criminal or Missing Person

1. Sex

2. Color

3. National Origin

4. Occupation

5. Age

6. Height

7. Weight

8. Build (stout or very stout, medium, slim; stooped or square shoulders)

9. Complexion (florid, sallow, pale, fair, dark)

10. Hair (color, thick or thin, bald or partly bald, curly, kinky, wavy, how cut or parted)

11. Eyes and Eyebrows (color, eyes bulgy or small, eyebrows bushy or meeting, any peculiarities)

12. Nose (small or large, pug, hooked or straight)

13. Whiskers (color, Vandyke, straight, rounded, goatee, chin whiskers, side whiskers)

14. Mustache (color, short, stubby, long, pointed ends, turned-up ends, Kaiser style)

15. Chin (small, large, square, dimpled, double)

16. Face (long, round, square, peg-top, fat, thin)

17. Neck (long, short, thick, thin)

18. Lips (thick, thin)

19. Mouth (large, small; drooping or upturned at corners)

20. Ears (small, large; close to or sticking out from head)

21. Forehead (high, low, sloping, bulging, straight, wrinkled)

22. Distinctive Marks (scars, moles, missing fingers or teeth, gold teeth, tattoos, lameness, bow legs, pigeon toes, knock knees, cauliflower ears, pockmarked)

23. Peculiarities (twitching of features, rapid or slow gait, eyeglasses, cane, stuttering, gruff or effeminate voice)

24. Clothes (hat and shoes—color and style; suit—color, cut, maker's name; shirt and collar—style and color, make; tie—style and color; neat or careless dresser)

25. Jewelry (kind, where worn)

26. Where likely to be found (residence, former residences, places frequented or hangouts, where employed, addresses of relatives)

27. Personal Associates (friends who might know of movements of wanted person or with whom wanted person would be most likely to communicate)

28. Habits (heavy drinker or smoker, drug user, gambler, frequenter of theaters, dance halls, taverns, race tracks, or casinos)

29. Personal possessions (licenses, union cards, club memberships, credit cards, social security card, etc.

C. Property Wanted

1. Watches (kind of metal; description of case, movement and numbers; type—pocket or wrist; initials; inscriptions; value; man's or woman's)

2. Rings (kind of metal; man's or woman's; setting; kind and number of stones; weight; maker's name; initials or other marks; value)

3. Chains (kind of metal; length; weight; kind of link or style; value)

4. Earrings or Studs (kind of metal; style; screw-backed or pierced; size and number of stones; value)

5. Miscellaneous Jewelry (kind of article; kind of metal or material; kind and number of stones; design; initials; inscriptions; maker's name; value)

6. Antiques and Works of Art (kind of article; material; design; size; shape; carved, engraved, inlaid; age; value)

7. Handbags, Suitcases, etc. (kind of article; material; size; color; shape; maker's name; contents; initials; peculiar marks; value)

8. Clothing (kind of article; material; style; color; shape; maker's name; labels; marks; value)

9. Furs (kind of article; kind of fur; size color; value)

10. Animals (kind; size; color; distinctive markings; age; sex)

11. Trucks and Wagons (type; shape; color; distinctive marks; size; contents)

12. Motorcycles (make; year of model; number of cylinders; manufacturer's number; make of saddle; make and condition of tires; position of speedometer; horn, front and rear lights; distinctive marks; license number)

13. Bicycles (make; color; type; number; kind of brake and saddle; number of speeds)

14. Typewriters (kind; serial and model numbers)

15. Automobiles (license number; make and year; kind of body and description of appearance; motor number; changes or repairs; exterior injuries; kind of wheels; size, make, and condition of tires; what precautions were taken to prevent theft of car: doors locked, alarm, etc.)

16. Table Silverware (kind of article; solid silver or plated; heavy or lightweight; maker's name; design, such as plain, beaded, flower, formal, animal; initials, inscriptions, or monograms; value)

17. Miscellaneous Gold and Silver Goods (kind of article; kind of material; plated or solid; size; maker's name; design; number of pieces, if a set; initials, inscriptions, or monograms; plain, chased, etched, or engraved; open or solid pattern; value)

18. Television Sets, Stereo Equipment, Video Recorders, Cameras, Computers, etc. (serial number; make; model; size; other identifying markings; value)

D. Description of Escaping Automobiles

1. License number

2. Make and model of car

3. Number of passengers and their descriptions

4. Direction taken

5. Kind of body

6. Color

7. Size

8. Shape and location of ventilators of hood

9. Shape of mudguards

10. Type, shape, and location of lights

11. Tail light position

12. Hub caps

13. Type of wheels

14. Damage such as broken lights, hub cap missing, dents, etc.

15. Rear view—Note the presence of anything such as a tire carrier, tool box, gas tank, baggage rack, bumper, etc.

OBSERVATION QUIZ 1

This exercise measures your ability to observe and recognize the basic differences and similarities in the faces of people. Many alleged criminals being sought by the police disguise their facial features to make it difficult for the police to apprehend them. Aside from surgery, there are many things that the wanted person can do to make recognition difficult. The addition and removal of beards and mustaches, or even change in hair color or hair style, are relatively easy to accomplish. Tinted contact lenses, now very common, can alter the color of eyes. However, there are some features that an individual cannot change easily. These are the features a police officer should concentrate on when attempting to identify a wanted person: the size, shape, and position of the ears; the shape of the jaw. The shape of the nose and the jaw are difficult to change without surgery. The police officer should also recognize that the wanted male with a distinctive jaw would likely try to disguise that feature by growing a beard.

Directions: Answer the following ten questions by selecting the face, labeled (A), (B), (C), or (D), which is most likely to be the same as that of the suspect on the left. You are to assume that no surgery has taken place since the sketch of the suspect was made. Only observation and recognition are factors in this exercise. Do not try to memorize features of these faces. Circle the letter of the face you choose. Explanations follow the last question.

1.   A   B   C   D

2.   A   B   C   D

3.   A   B   C   D

4.   A   B   C   D

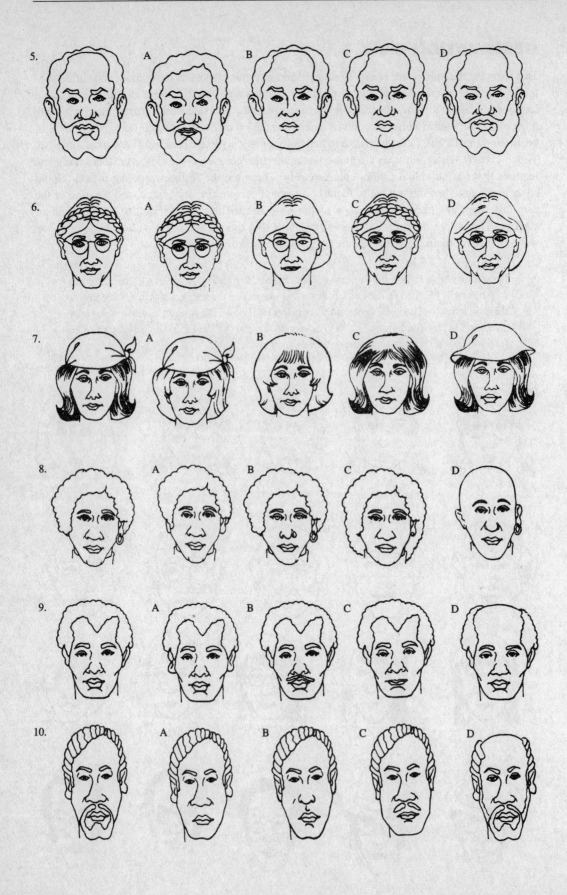

ANSWER KEY

1. D	3. C	5. C	7. B	9. B
2. B	4. D	6. D	8. A	10. A

EXPLANATORY ANSWERS

1. **(D)** Choice (A) has different nose; (B) and (C) have different chins.
2. **(B)** Choice (A) has a longer face; (C) has a fuller face with different chin; (D) has a different nose.
3. **(C)** Choice (A) has a longer face; (B) has dark eyes; (D) has much fuller lips.
4. **(D)** Choice (A) has thinner lips; (B) has a different nose; (C) has different ears.
5. **(C)** Choice (A) has a different mouth; (B) has a different nose; (D) has different eyes.
6. **(D)** Choice (A) has a different chin; (B) has a different mouth; (C) has different eyes.
7. **(B)** Choice (A) has different eyes; (C) has a different nose; (D) has a different mouth.
8. **(A)** Choice (B) has different eyes and nose; (C) has a wider face at the jaw line; (D) has a different nose and chin. It would appear that the original face has larger eyes than any of the choices. Be aware that makeup can create illusions in the original face as well as in the choices.
9. **(B)** Choice (A) has different ears; (C) has a different mouth; (D) has less prominent nostrils. The difference in hairline could be wearing a wig, but judging from his hairstyle that is unlikely.
10. **(A)** Choice (B) has a different nose; (C) has different ears; (D) has different eyes and, again the original's hairline suggests that it is natural, not a wig.

OBSERVATION QUIZ 2

Directions: Answer the following questions on the basis of the following sketches. The first face on top is a sketch of an alleged criminal based on witnesses' descriptions at the crime scene. One of the four sketches below that face is the way the suspect might look after changing his or her appearance. Assume that NO surgery has been done on the suspect's face. Circle the letter of the face you choose.

1.

(A)

(C)

(B)

(D)

2.

(A)

(C)

(B)

(D)

3.

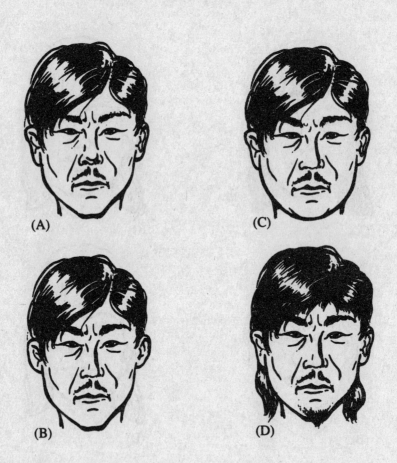

(A)

(C)

(B)

(D)

4.

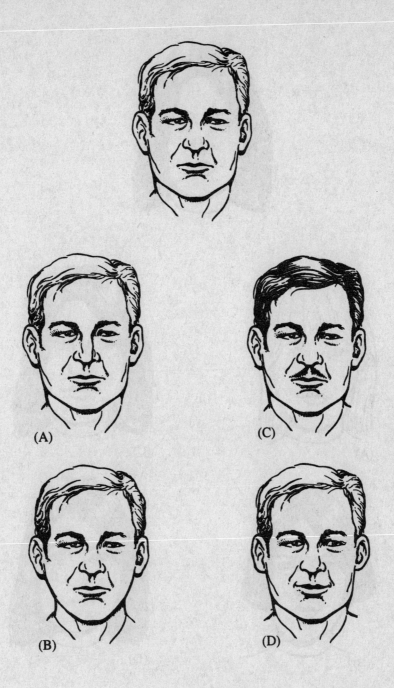

(A)   (C)

(B)   (D)

5.

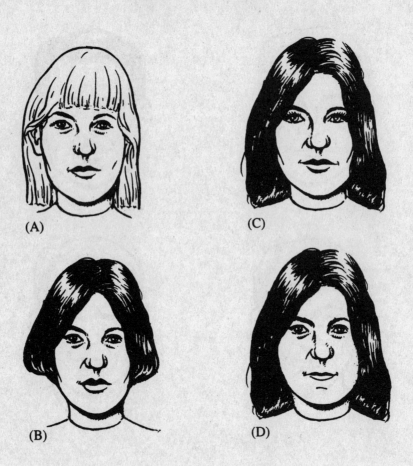

(A)

(C)

(B)

(D)

ANSWER KEY

1. B   2. B   3. D   4. C   5. B

EXPLANATORY ANSWERS

1. **(B)** The suspect in choice (A) has larger eyes; the suspect in choice (C) has different ears; the suspect in choice (D) has a fuller face.

2. **(B)** The suspect in choice (A) has a smaller nose; the suspect in choice (C) has a fuller face and fuller lips; the suspect in choice (D) has lighter eyes and thinner lips.

3. **(D)** The suspect in choice (A) has a different nose; the suspect in choice (B) has different ears; the suspect in choice (C) has an entirely different head and face shape.

4. **(C)** The suspect in choice (A) has a much finer nose; the suspect in choice (B) has a narrower jaw structure; the suspect in choice (D) has different ears.

5. **(B)** The suspect in choice (A) has a smaller nose; the suspect in choice (C) has lighter eyes and a wider mouth; the suspect in choice (D) has a fuller face and thinner lips.

MEMORY QUIZ 1

MEMORY BOOKLET

Directions: You will be given 10 minutes to study the six "Wanted Posters" below and to try to remember as many details as you can. You may not take any notes during this time.

WANTED FOR ASSAULT

Name: John Markham
Age: 27
Height: 5'11"
Weight: 215 lbs.
Race: Black
Hair color: black
Eye color: brown
Complexion: dark
Identifying marks: eagle tattoo on
    back of right hand; very hard
    of hearing
Suspect is a former boxer.
    He favors brass knuckles as his
    weapon.

WANTED FOR RAPE

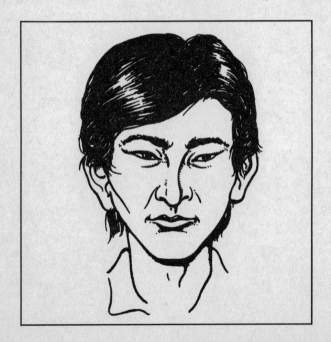

Name: Arthur Lee
Age: 19
Height: 5'7"
Weight: 180 lbs.
Race: Asian
Hair color: black
Eye color: brown
Complexion: medium
Identifying marks: none
Suspect carries a pearl handled
    knife with an eight-inch
    curved blade. He tends to
    attack victims in subway
    passageways.

WANTED FOR ARMED ROBBERY

Name: Antonio Gomez
Age: 31
Height: 5'6"
Weight: 160 lbs.
Race: Hispanic
Hair color: brown
Eye color: brown
Complexion: medium
Identifying marks: missing last
    finger of right hand; tattoo on
    back says "Mother"; tattoo on
    left biceps says "Linda";
    tattoo on right biceps says
    "Carmen"
Suspect was seen leaving the
    scene in a stolen yellow 1987
    Corvette. He carries a gun
    and must be considered
    dangerous.

WANTED FOR CAR THEFT

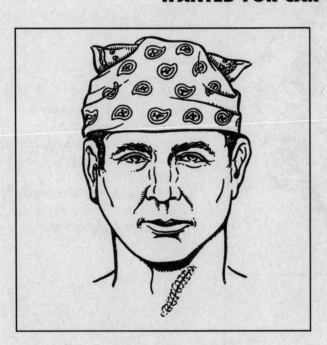

Name: Robert Miller
Age: 24
Height: 6'3"
Weight: 230 lbs.
Race: White
Hair color: brown
Eye color: blue
Complexion: light
Identifying marks: tracheotomy
    scar at base of neck; tattoo of
    dragon on right upper arm
Suspect chain smokes unfiltered
    cigarettes. He always wears a
    red head scarf.

WANTED FOR MURDER

Name: Janet Walker
Age: 39
Height: 5'10"
Weight: 148 lbs.
Race: Black
Hair color: black
Eye color: black
Complexion: dark
Identifying marks: large hairy
    mole on upper left thigh;
    stutters badly
Suspect has frequently been
    arrested for prostitution. She
    often wears multiple ear and
    nose rings.

WANTED FOR ARSON

Name: Margaret Pickford
Age: 42
Height: 5'2"
Weight: 103 lbs.
Race: White
Hair color: red
Eye color: green
Complexion: light
Identifying marks: known heroin
    addict with track marks on
    forearms; walks with decided
    limp because left leg is
    shorter than right
Suspect has a child in foster care
    in Astoria. She usually carries
    two large shopping bags.

MEMORY QUESTIONS

Directions: Answer the following questions on the basis of the information given on the "Wanted Posters" that you just studied. Circle the letter of the answer you choose.

1. Which of the following suspects may have committed a crime in order to support a drug habit?

(A)

(C)

(B)

(D)

2. Which one of the following is missing a finger? The suspect wanted for
   (A) rape
   (B) assault
   (C) murder
   (D) armed robbery

3. Which of the suspects is most likely to be found in the subway?
   (A) John Markham
   (B) Margaret Pickford
   (C) Arthur Lee
   (D) Robert Miller

4. Which of these suspects has a dragon tattoo?

(A)

(C)

(B)

(D)

5. Which is an identifying mark of this suspect?

(A) Deafness

(B) A large mole

(C) A tattoo that reads "Mother"

(D) Needle tracks

6. Which of the following is considered to be the most dangerous?

(A)

(C)

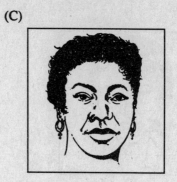

(B)

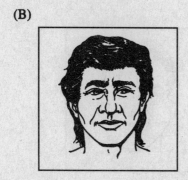

(D)

7. Which of these suspects is known to be a parent?

(A) The suspect who stutters

(B) The former boxer

(C) The smoker

(D) The suspect who limps

8. Which of these suspects escaped the scene of the crime in a stolen car?

(A)

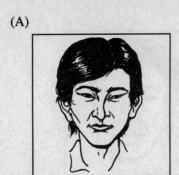

(C)

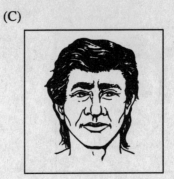

(B)

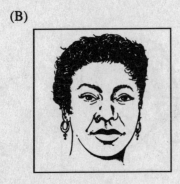

(D)

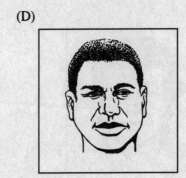

9. Which of these suspects would have the hardest time running from the police?

(A) The heroin addict

(B) The suspect who is nearly deaf

(C) The suspect who wears lots of jewelry

(D) The suspect with brass knuckles in his pocket

10. Which of these suspects is wanted for rape?

(A)

(C)

(B)

(D)

ANSWER KEY

1. B	3. C	5. B	7. D	9. A
2. D	4. A	6. B	8. C	10. C

EXPLANATORY ANSWERS

1. **(B)** Margaret Pickford is a known heroin addict.

2. **(D)** Antonio Gomez is wanted for armed robbery. He is missing the last finger of his right hand.

3. **(C)** Arthur Lee often attacks his victims in subway passageways.

4. **(A)** Robert Miller has a tattoo of a dragon on his right upper arm.

5. **(B)** Janet Walker has a large hairy mole on her upper left thigh.

6. **(B)** Antonio Gomez carries a gun. Arthur Lee carries a wicked looking knife, but Lee is not offered among the choices.

7. **(D)** Margaret Pickford, who walks with a limp because her left leg is shorter than her right, has a child in foster care so obviously is a parent.

8. **(C)** Antonio Gomez escaped from the scene of a recent armed robbery in a stolen yellow 1987 Corvette.

9. **(A)** Margaret Pickford, who is a drug addict, has a severe limp caused by one leg's being shorter than the other and would have a hard time running from police.

10. **(C)** Arthur Lee is wanted for rape.

MEMORY QUIZ 2

Directions: You will have ten minutes to read and study the following description of a police action. Then you must answer 15 questions based on this incident without referring back to the description.

Police Officers Brown and Reid are on patrol in a radio car on a Saturday afternoon in the fall. They receive a radio message that a burglary is in progress on the fifth floor of a seven-floor building on the corner of 7th Street and Main. They immediately proceed to that location to investigate and take appropriate action.

The police officers are familiar with the location, and they know that the Fine Jewelry Company occupies the entire fifth floor of the building. They are also aware that the owner, who is not in the office on weekends, often leaves large amounts of gold in his office safe. The officers, upon arrival at the scene, lock their radio car and proceed to look for the building superintendent in order to get into the building. The superintendent states that he has not seen or heard anything unusual, although he admits that he did leave the premises for approximately one hour to have lunch. The officers start for the fifth floor, using the main elevator. As they reach that floor and open the door, they hear noises followed by the sound of the freight elevator door in the rear of the building closing and the elevator descending. They quickly run through the open door of the Fine Jewelry Company and observe that the office safe is open and empty. The officers then proceed to the rear of the building and use the rear staircase to reach the ground floor. They open the rear door and go out onto the street where they observe four individuals running up the street, crossing at the corner. At that point, the police officers get a clear view of the suspects. There are three males and one female. One of the males appears to be white, one is obviously Hispanic, and the other male is black. The female is white.

The white male is bearded. He is dressed in blue jeans, white sneakers, and a red and blue jacket. He is carrying a white duffel bag on his shoulder. The Hispanic male limps slightly and has a large dark mustache. He is wearing brown pants, a green shirt, and brown shoes. He is carrying a blue duffel bag on his shoulder. The black male is clean-shaven, wearing black pants, a white shirt, a green cap, and black shoes. He is carrying what appears to be a tool box. The white female is carrying a sawed-off shotgun, has long brown hair, and is wearing white jeans, a blue blouse, and blue sneakers. She has a red kerchief around her neck.

The officers chase the suspects for two blocks without being able to catch them. At that point, the suspects separate. The white and black males quickly get into a black 1983 Chevrolet station wagon with Connecticut license plates with letters AWK on them and drive away. The Hispanic male and the white female get away in an old light blue Dodge van. The van has a prominent CB antenna on top and large yellow streaks running along the doors on both sides. There is a large dent on the right rear fender and the van bears New Jersey license plates, which the officers are unable to read.

The station wagon turns left and enters the expressway headed towards Connecticut. The van makes a right turn and proceeds in the direction of the tunnel headed for New Jersey.

The officers quickly return to their radio car to report what has happened.

Do not refer back to the passage while answering these questions. Circle the letter of your choice.

1. The officers were able to read the following letters from the license plates on the station wagon:

   (A) WAX

   (B) EWK

   (C) AUK

   (D) AWK

2. The van used by the suspects had a dented

   (A) left front fender

   (B) right front fender

   (C) right rear fender

   (D) left rear fender

3. The officers observed that the van was headed in the direction of

   (A) Long Island

   (B) Pennsylvania

   (C) New Jersey

   (D) Connecticut

4. The best description of the female suspect's hair is

   (A) short and light in color

   (B) long and light in color

   (C) short and dark in color

   (D) long and dark in color

5. The suspect who was wearing a white shirt is the

   (A) white male

   (B) Hispanic male

   (C) black male

   (D) white female

6. The suspect who wore white jeans is the

   (A) white male

   (B) Hispanic male

   (C) black male

   (D) white female

7. The Hispanic male suspect carried a duffel bag of what color?

   (A) Yellow

   (B) Red

   (C) Blue

   (D) Brown

8. Of the following, the best description of the shoes worn by the Hispanic suspect is
   (A) white sneakers
   (B) black shoes
   (C) black boots
   (D) brown shoes

9. The suspect who was carrying the white duffel bag was the
   (A) white female
   (B) black male
   (C) Hispanic male
   (D) white male

10. The suspect who was carrying the shotgun was the
    (A) white female
    (B) black male
    (C) Hispanic male
    (D) white male

11. The green cap was worn by the
    (A) white female
    (B) black male
    (C) Hispanic male
    (D) white male

12. The suspect who limped when he or she ran was the
    (A) white female
    (B) black male
    (C) Hispanic male
    (D) white male

13. Of the following, the best description of the station wagon used by the suspects is
    (A) 1983 black Chevrolet station wagon
    (B) 1981 blue Ford
    (C) 1981 green Dodge
    (D) 1986 red Ford

14. The best description of the suspects who used the station wagon to depart is
    (A) a black male and a white female
    (B) a black male and a white male
    (C) a white female and a Hispanic male
    (D) a black male and a Hispanic male

15. The van's license plates were from which of the following states?

(A) New York

(B) Delaware

(C) New Jersey

(D) Connecticut

ANSWER KEY

1. D	4. D	7. C	10. A	13. A
2. C	5. C	8. D	11. B	14. B
3. C	6. D	9. D	12. C	15. C

EXPLANATORY ANSWERS

If you answered any of these questions incorrectly, the fault may lie either in the care with which you read the description or with your memory of the facts. For ease in locating the source of your errors, we refer you to the source of the information in the passage.

1. **(D)** Fourth paragraph, third sentence.
2. **(C)** Fourth paragraph, last sentence.
3. **(C)** Fifth paragraph, second sentence.
4. **(D)** Third paragraph, next-to-last sentence.
5. **(C)** Third paragraph, seventh sentence.
6. **(D)** Third paragraph, next-to-last sentence.
7. **(C)** Third paragraph, sixth sentence.
8. **(D)** Third paragraph, fifth sentence.
9. **(D)** Third paragraph, third sentence.
10. **(A)** Third paragraph, next-to-last sentence.
11. **(B)** Third paragraph, seventh sentence.
12. **(C)** Third paragraph, fourth sentence.
13. **(A)** Fourth paragraph, third sentence.
14. **(B)** Fourth paragraph, third sentence.
15. **(C)** Fourth paragraph, third sentence.

Police Judgment Quizzer

ABOUT THE POLICE JUDGMENT QUIZZER

Early police officer examinations were a strange mixture of questions covering municipal government, municipal geography, spelling, grammar, first aid, everything, in fact, that every person should know something about, but very little specific to measuring the ability of future police officers to do their job well. As testing methods matured and examiners gained experience in mass testing, they determined that the best measure of a good police officer is a measure of his or her judgment in actual police situations. So the emphasis shifted from factual to actual exams. "Let the questions supply the facts," the examiners reasoned, "and let the aspiring police officers display their judgment in choosing the correct answers."

What Would You Do If . . .

This is the essential form of the practical question on police officer exams. Assume you are a police officer. Here is a given situation. How would you respond to it? This is a very subtle and efficient method of testing. Questions are often based on actual patrol situations. What would you do if you saw a woman walking down the street dressed only in a sheet and leading a doe on a leash? Arrest her? On what charge? Take the doe to an animal shelter? Take the woman to a doctor? Ask her for her phone number? It actually happened. What would you do?

Test-Taking Strategy for Practical Judgment Questions

Police applicants are placed in a peculiar position by practical judgment questions in that the correct answers for these questions are influenced by actual police department procedures. As an applicant taking the exam, you are not expected to know the police department's policies or procedures. Yet test-makers often assume that police departmental policies or procedures are just common sense. To do really well on practical judgment questions, you need something more than common sense. You need a good understanding of ordinary police department policies and procedures as they apply to routine patrol situations. This is the reason why close relatives of police officers tend to earn high scores on the police officer exam. Their familiarity with "police language" and "police thinking" stands them in good stead when they must choose the correct answers to police practical judgment questions.

This chapter will familiarize you with many of the "common sense" ideas that underlie police practical judgment questions. The chapter will serve as "your brother the police officer," teaching you to think like a patrol officer. By the time you have finished studying this material, you will be thinking like a patrol officer. You will then be prepared to score high on your police officer exam.

The Police Role

To start with, you must understand the role of a police officer. This role varies according to size, location, and philosophy of the police department. State police find that their role encompasses major problems like traffic pileups and serious accidents, as well as the more routine problems of stranded motorists. Small-town police find that they have a broad role in maintaining public safety and assuring law and order. Big-city police tend to have a more narrow role because in big cities other agencies take on primary responsibility for certain tasks: medics handle health situations beyond emergency first-aid; traffic department personnel deal with many traffic situations; social workers handle many crises concerning the elderly, children, and the mentally ill. Part of your preparation for your own exam should be acquiring some familiarity with the ordinary role of police officers in the department to which you are applying.

With this information in mind, you must follow one basic rule when answering police practical judgment questions—fulfill the police role and only the police role. This means:

1. Be professional. Avoid emotional responses, show of bias, or incurring any kind of indebtedness to persons on your beat.

2. Avoid all roles other than the police role, e.g., parent, physician, tradesman, private security, etc. Sometimes you may find it hard to draw the line, such as that between emergency first-aid and the role of the medic. In an emergency where time is pressing, the police officer must provide assistance to people to the full extent of his or her competence. Where more time is available, leave doubtful roles to others.

3. Fulfill the police role of assisting endangered people twenty-four hours a day. Be prepared to assist in keeping the peace at any time and to take the initiative in urgent situations. Fulfilling the police role does not necessarily mean making arrests when there is no great need to do so. In practical judgment questions, think of the police role as one of keeping the peace rather than one of making arrests, especially in the off-duty situation.

4. Avoid even the slightest appearance of corruption. Maintain police integrity. Avoid all partiality. Do not accept gifts or favors. Do not refer business to any particular businessman, company, or professional person.

Police Priorities

A *hierarchy* is an arrangement of things according to their importance. Something near the top of a hierarchy is more important than something near the bottom of the hierarchy. Basically it is an arrangement of things or activities according to their priorities.

There are five basic functions in police work. These have a definite hierarchical order. If an officer finds him- or herself in a situation in which several of these functions must be done, the officer should consider the hierarchical order, or order of priorities, and act in accordance with the position of each function in that order.

1. *Assist endangered people.* Essentially this means assisting:
   a. seriously injured persons.
   b. physically endangered persons (e.g., victims of a crime in progress, drowning persons, etc.).

2. *Keep the peace.* Calm any major disorder. Prevent tumult, aggression, or destruction of property.

3. *Enforce the law.* Where no actual harm to persons or property is threatened, peace-keeping and maintaining order may be adequate. Where there is unlawful injury or loss, arrest may be necessary in addition to the restoring of order.

4. *Assist people who are not immediately endangered but who need help.* This means assisting:

   a. physically or mentally needy persons: children, the elderly, the handicapped, the homeless, and persons who appear to be sick, mentally ill, or intoxicated.

   b. crime victims, lost persons, and stranded persons.

5. *Maintain order on the beat.* This involves:

   a. Investigating suspicious persons or circumstances. Something is suspicious if it is *unusual* for the time or the place or the persons involved.

   b. Regulating the use of streets and sidewalks for safety and for the efficient flow of traffic.

   c. Knowing the beat. You must be familiar with the physical features of the beat, you must be aware of routine events, and you must develop positive contacts with the people on the beat.

   d. Making recommendations that will improve safety or flow of traffic in the area. Remember to stay "professional" by recommending only activities, not particular products or businesses.

The Principle of Use of Minimum Necessary Force

Many police practical judgment questions concern the possible use of force. Police officers are empowered to use force, even deadly force, under certain circumstances. In general, common sense should rule judgments about the use of force. There are some basic principles that are part of "common sense."

Police officer should always handle problems with the *minimum amount of force necessary* to resolve the problem. Never use more force than the problem deserves. Obviously, a police officer should not shoot somebody for failing to show identification, even if the person is being unreasonably stubborn. A police officer's action should not cause greater harm than the problem the officer is trying to resolve. In other words, a problem should not be handled in such a way as to create an even bigger problem.

When a police officer is evaluating the gravity of a situation to determine how much force is necessary (or when a candidate is making this choice in an examination), the officer must consider the physical setting, the actual actions and the apparent intentions of the people involved, and the intent of the law. Differences in physical settings require differences in policies and regulations. Big-city police departments, for example, practically never permit police officers to fire warning shots, to shoot at moving vehicles, or to shoot at people on public streets. It is assumed that such shooting would endanger innocent bystanders. On the other hand, state police departments often do allow warning shots, shooting at moving vehicles, and even shooting at people on the road because they assume a highway setting without any innocent bystanders in the line of fire.

The Value Hierarchy

Occasionally a police officer has to make a quick decision in a situation that involves value conflicts. For example, it may be necessary to chose between risking injury to a hostage or letting a dangerous criminal escape. Such a decision involves a value judgment. An officer makes the decision based on the order of priorities.

If a police department's hierarchy of values is spelled out clearly, officers are assisted in making rapid and proper judgments. Police exam candidates can rely on the same list of priorities. The list below is the value hierarchy that has been the basis for practical judgment questions on police officer exams for many years. In order of priority:

1. Protection of life and limb.
2. Obeying orders in an emergency situation.
3. Protection of property.
4. Obeying orders in a non-emergency situation.
5. Maintaining the assigned role.
6. Efficiency in getting the job done.
7. Avoiding blame or earning praise or respect.

Use the hierarchy of values in making decisions. If a situation presents a conflict of values, always choose the value that is highest on the list. Here are two examples:

Example 1. You are assigned to stay in a particular spot during an emergency situation, but by leaving that spot you will save a life. You are justified in shooting to save a life (1) rather than obeying orders (2). The understanding is, of course, that leaving your spot will not result in other lives being lost. "Protecting life and limb" is your number one priority, the highest value in the police hierarchy of values.

Example 2. You are assigned to watch a prisoner, and a fellow officer is assigned to write up the arrest report. Stay in your own role even if you are more skilled than the other officer at writing up arrest reports. The conflict is between carrying out an assigned duty (5) and getting a job done efficiently (6). Choose the highest priority.

One more: You are patrolling alone at night, and you come across a business that has been burglarized with the front door smashed in. At this hour you are expected to be making a routine check of illegal parking on a certain street. The police department might be criticized by residents if the illegal parking is not acted on, but the store is likely to be further burglarized if you leave this spot. Stay where you are and protect the property (3) rather than carrying out your assigned illegal parking patrol (5) or concerning yourself with criticism of the department (7). Always choose the highest value.

Please note that no value is given to the officer's personal gains or benefits or reputation. Personal consideration is *never* a good reason for doing anything so far as a civil service exam question is concerned.

As the hierarchy of values suggests, the best reason for any action is the protection of life and limb. If safety is a real issue in the fact pattern of the question, then safety is the number one priority in choosing the answer. Sometimes there is no real issue of safety. In such a case, the next value assumes the greatest importance. If there is an emergency situation and you have been given specific orders, your priority is to carry out those orders. If not, the next priority is the protection of property. Property includes public property and police department property as well as private property. If there are no threats to property, you are expected to carry out routine, non-emergency orders and to fulfill your assigned duties. Doing what you were told to do and carrying out your routine assignments as a police officer take priority over efficiency. A police force is a highly organized bureaucracy. The organization will function best as a whole if each person does just his or her own assigned job.

Read each question carefully. Is there really something in the question situation to indicate that there is an issue of life and limb at stake? Would a proposed answer based on efficiency really be possible and efficient? Be realistic. Unless told otherwise, assume that the officer is an ordinary police officer and not a sharpshooter or a trained firefighter.

When all other reasoning fails you, answer to the Chief. In other words, the Chief of Police is testing you for your job. If you are faced with a difficult choice in making a decision, imagine that the question is being asked you personally by the Chief of Police. Give the answer the Chief would want you to give.

Answering the Questions

This quizzer contains questions that have actually appeared on examinations for entry-level law enforcement positions conducted over a considerable number of years. The questions have been carefully screened for current relevancy.

Answering these questions will accomplish much in preparing you to do your best on the examination. Ideally, you can consider yourself well prepared if on the day of the examination you are thinking like a police officer. This quizzer will help you get in that frame of mind. Most of the questions found here concern incidents that a police officer may encounter on a daily basis.

The position of police officer is unique in that, although it is an entry-level position, it involves a great deal of responsibility and requires the ability to make reliable on-the-spot decisions. Therefore, accurate judgment is perhaps the most important qualification of the police officer. In order to make accurate police decisions, the officer must thoroughly understand the duties of the position and the police officer's role in society.

By the time you finish the Police Judgment Quizzer, you no doubt will be thinking like a police officer, and you thus will be well on your way towards earning that high examination score.

Choose from among the four suggested answers the *best* answer to each question. Circle the letter of your answer choice. Following the answer key is a full explanation of the police reasoning behind each correct answer choice.

1. An off-duty police officer was seated in a restaurant when two men entered, drew guns, and robbed the cashier. The officer made no attempt to prevent the robbery or apprehend the criminals. Later he justified his conduct by stating that an officer, when off duty, is a private citizen with the same duties and rights of all private citizens. The officer's conduct was

   (A) wrong; a police officer must act to prevent crimes and apprehend criminals at all times

   (B) right; the police officer was out of uniform at the time of the robbery

   (C) wrong; he should have obtained the necessary information and descriptions after the robbers left

   (D) right; it would have been foolhardy for him to intervene when outnumbered by armed robbers

2. While you are on traffic duty, a middle-aged man crossing the street cries out with pain, presses his hand to his chest, and stands perfectly still. You suspect that he may have suffered a heart attack. You should

   (A) help him cross the street quickly in order to prevent his being hit by moving traffic

   (B) permit him to lie down flat in the street while your divert traffic.

   (C) ask him for the name of his doctor so that you can summon him

   (D) request a cab to take him to the nearest hospital for immediate treatment

3. Assume that you have been assigned to a traffic post at a busy intersection. A car bearing out-of-state license plates is about to turn into a one-way street going in the opposite direction. You should blow your whistle and stop the car. You should then

   (A) hand out a summons to the driver in order to make an example of him, since out-of-town drivers notoriously disregard our traffic regulations

   (B) pay no attention to him and let him continue in the proper direction

   (C) ask him to pull over to the curb and advise him to get a copy of the latest New York City traffic regulations

   (D) call his attention to the fact that he was violating a traffic regulation and permit him to continue in the proper direction

4. You have been assigned to a patrol post in the park during the winter months. You hear the cries of a boy who has fallen through the ice. The first thing you should do is to

   (A) rush to the nearest telephone and call an ambulance

   (B) call upon a passerby to summon additional police officers

   (C) rush to the spot from which the cries came and try to save the boy

   (D) rush to the spot from which the cries came and question the boy concerning his identity so that you can summon his parents

5. While you are patrolling your post, you find a flashlight and a screwdriver lying near a closed bar and grill. You also notice some jimmy marks on the door. You should

   (A) continue patrolling your post after noting in your memorandum book what you have seen

   (B) arrest any persons standing in the vicinity

   (C) determine whether the bar has been robbed

   (D) telephone the owner of the bar and grill to relate what you have seen outside the door

6. While patrolling a post late Saturday night, a police officer notices a well-dressed man break a car window with a rock, open the front door, and enter the car. He is followed into the car by a female companion. Of the following, the most essential action for the officer to take is to

   (A) point a gun at the car, enter the car, and order the man to drive to the station house to explain his actions

   (B) approach the car and ask the man why it was necessary to break the car window

   (C) take down the license number of the car and note the description of both the man and the woman in the event that the car is later reported as stolen

   (D) request proof of ownership of the car from the man

7. Assume that a police officer is assigned to duty in a radio patrol car. The situation in which it would be *least* advisable for the officer to use the siren to help clear traffic when answering a call is when a report has come in that

   (A) a man is involved in an argument with a cleaning store proprietor

   (B) a man is holding up a liquor store

   (C) two cars have crashed, resulting in loss of life

   (D) two gangs of juveniles are engaged in a street fight

8. Police officers are instructed to pay particular attention to anyone apparently making repairs to an auto parked in the street. The most important reason for this rule is that

(A) the person making the repairs may be stealing the auto

(B) the person making the repairs may be obstructing traffic

(C) working on autos is prohibited on certain streets

(D) many people injure themselves while working on autos

9. Inspections of critical points on a post are purposely made at irregular intervals to

(A) permit leaving the post when arrests are necessary

(B) make it difficult for wrongdoers to anticipate the inspections

(C) allow for delays due to unusual occurrences at other points

(D) simplify the scheduling of lunch reliefs and rest periods

10. Suppose that, in the course of your duties, you are called to the scene of a disturbance in which some seven or eight people are involved. Of the following, the action most likely to end the disturbance quickly and effectively is for you to

(A) divide the disorderly group immediately into three approximately equal sections

(B) take the nearest person promptly into custody and remove that person from the scene

(C) announce your authority and call for order in a firm and decisive manner

(D) question a bystander in detail about the reasons for the disorder

11. A newly appointed officer of a uniformed force may *least* reasonably expect an immediate supervising officer to

(A) help him or her avoid errors

(B) give him or her specific instructions

(C) check on the progress he or she is making

(D) make all necessary decisions for him or her

12. In lecturing on the law of arrest, an instructor remarked: "To go beyond is as bad as to fall short." The one of the following that most nearly expresses the same thing is

(A) never undertake the impossible

(B) extremes are not desirable

(C) look before you leap

(D) too much success is dangerous

13. In addressing a class, an instructor remarked: "Carelessness and failure are twins." The one of the following that most nearly expresses the same thing is

(A) negligence seldom accompanies success

(B) incomplete work is careless work

(C) conscientious work is never attended by failure

(D) a conscientious person never makes mistakes

14. The primary function of a police department is
    (A) the prevention of crime
    (B) the efficiency and discipline of its members
    (C) to preserve property values
    (D) to minimize conflicts

15. Law enforcement officials receive badges with numbers on them so that
    (A) their personalities may be submerged
    (B) they may be more easily identified
    (C) they may be spied upon
    (D) their movements may be kept under constant control

16. The best attitude for an officer to take is to
    (A) be constantly on the alert
    (B) be hostile
    (C) vary watchfulness with the apparent necessity for it
    (D) regard tact as the most effective weapon for handling any degree of disorder

17. An officer receives instructions from his supervisor that he does not fully understand. For the officer to ask for a further explanation would be
    (A) good; chiefly because his supervisor will be impressed with his interest in his work
    (B) poor; chiefly because the supervisor's time will be needlessly wasted
    (C) good; chiefly because proper performance depends on full understanding of the work to be done
    (D) poor; chiefly because officers should be able to think for themselves

18. Which of the following statements concerning the behavior of law enforcement officers is most accurate?
    (A) A show of confident assurance on the part of a law enforcement officer will make it possible to cover a shortage of knowledge in any given duty.
    (B) In ordinary cases, when a newly appointed officer does not know what to do, it is always better to do too much than to do too little.
    (C) It is not advisable that officers recommend the employment of certain attorneys for individuals taken into custody.
    (D) A prisoner who is morose and refuses to talk will need less watching by an officer than one who is suicidal.

19. The one of the following which is the most probable reason for the considerably increasing proportion of serious crimes committed by women is
    (A) that the proportion of women in the population is increasing
    (B) the increasing number of crime gangs in operation
    (C) the success of women in achieving social equality with men
    (D) the increasing number of crime stories in the movies and on television

20. It frequently happens that a major crime of an unusual nature is followed almost immediately by an epidemic of several crimes, in widely scattered locations, with elements similar to the first crime. Of the following, the most likely explanation for this situation is that

   (A) the same criminal is likely to commit the same type of crime

   (B) a gang of criminals will operate in several areas simultaneously

   (C) newspaper publicity on a major crime is apt to influence other would-be criminals

   (D) the same causes which are responsible for the first crime are also responsible for the others

21. "A member of the department shall not indulge in intoxicants while in uniform. A member of the department, not required to wear a uniform, and a uniformed member, while out of uniform, shall not indulge in intoxicants to an extent unfitting him or her for duty." It follows that a

   (A) member off duty, not in uniform, may drink intoxicants to any degree desired

   (B) member on duty, not in uniform, may drink intoxicants

   (C) member on duty, in uniform, may drink intoxicants

   (D) uniformed member, in civilian clothes, may not drink intoxicants

22. The reason police officers have greater authority than private citizens in making arrests is

   (A) to protect citizens against needless arrest

   (B) to ensure a fair trial

   (C) that they have greater knowledge of the law

   (D) that they are in better physical shape

23. A police officer stationed along the route of a parade has been ordered not to allow cars to cross the route while the parade is in progress. An ambulance driver on an emergency run attempts to drive an ambulance across the route while the parade is passing. Under these circumstances, the officer should

   (A) ask the driver to wait while the officer calls headquarters and obtains a decision

   (B) stop the parade long enough to permit the ambulance to cross the street

   (C) direct the ambulance driver to the shortest detour available, which will add at least ten minutes to the run

   (D) hold up the ambulance in accordance with the order

24. Which of the following is the most accurate statement concerning the proper attitude of a police officer towards persons in his or her custody?

   (A) Ignore any serious problems of those in custody, if they have no bearing on the charges preferred.

   (B) Do not inform the person who has been arrested of the reason for the arrest.

   (C) Do not permit a person in custody to give vent to feelings at any time.

   (D) Watch a brooding or silent person more carefully than one who loudly threatens suicide.

25. When approaching a suspect to make an arrest, it is *least* important for the police officer to guard against the possibility that the suspect may

    (A) be diseased

    (B) have a gun

    (C) use physical force

    (D) run away

26. "In any uniformed service, strict discipline is essential." Of the following, the best justification for requiring that subordinates follow the orders of superior officers without delay is that

    (A) not all orders can be carried out quickly

    (B) it is more important that an order be obeyed accurately than promptly

    (C) prompt obedience makes for efficient action in emergencies

    (D) some superior officers are too strict

27. In submitting a report of an unusual arrest or other unusual occurrence, the first paragraph of the report should contain

    (A) a brief outline of what occurred

    (B) your conclusions and recommendations

    (C) the authority and reason for the investigation of the arrest or occurrence

    (D) complete and accurate answers to the questions who? what? where? when? why? and how?

28. A police officer in civilian clothes appearing as a witness in a court must wear his or her shield over the left breast. This procedure

    (A) helps the officer in reporting for duty promptly if called

    (B) impresses the judge

    (C) identifies the witness as a police officer

    (D) preserves order

29. According to the police manual, when circumstances permit, not more than one prisoner shall be confined in a cell. Of the following, the most important reason for this regulation is to

    (A) ensure reasonable privacy for the prisoners

    (B) minimize the development of troublesome situations

    (C) protect the civil rights of the prisoners

    (D) separate the hardened from the less hardened criminals

30. A motorist who has been stopped by an officer for speeding acts rudely. He hints about his personal connections with high officials in the state government and demands the officer's name and shield number. The officer should

    (A) ask the motorist why he wants the information and give it only if the answer is satisfactory

    (B) give both name and shield number without comment

    (C) ignore the request since both name and shield number will appear on the summons the officer will issue

    (D) give name and shield number but increase the charges against the motorist

31. "Driver 1 claimed that the collision occurred because, as he approached the intersection, Driver 2 started to make a left turn suddenly and at a high speed, even though the light had been red for 15 to 20 seconds." Suppose that you have been assigned to make a report on this accident. The position of the vehicles after the accident is indicated in the diagram below. The point in each case indicates the front of the vehicle. On the basis of this diagram, the best reason for concluding that Driver 1's statement is false is that

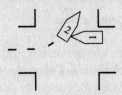

   (A) Driver 2's car is beyond the center of the intersection
   (B) Driver 2's car is making the turn on the proper side of the road
   (C) Driver 1's car is beyond the sidewalk line
   (D) Driver 1's car is on the right-hand side of the road

32. While patrolling a bridge approach road alone in a radio car, you are signaled to stop by a private car traveling in the opposite direction. The driver tells you that he was robbed by two men in a sedan ahead of him. Your car cannot cross the concrete safety-strip to get into the other lane. Of the following, the best course of action for you to take is to
   (A) tell the driver you cannot cross to his lane and ask him to report the matter
   (B) leave your car where it is, cross over to the private car, and use it to pursue the suspects
   (C) notify headquarters over your radio
   (D) make a U-turn in your car and chase the suspect vehicle on the wrong side of the parkway

33. It is suggested that an officer should keep all persons away from the area of an accident until an investigation has been completed. This suggested procedure is
   (A) good; witnesses will be more likely to agree on a single story
   (B) bad; such action blocks traffic flow and causes congestion
   (C) good; objects of possible use as evidence will be protected from damage or loss
   (D) bad; the flow of normal traffic provides an opportunity for an investigator to determine the cause of the accident

34. Before permitting automobiles involved in an accident to depart, a police officer should take certain measures. Of the following, it is *least* important that the officer make certain that
   (A) both drivers are properly licensed
   (B) the automobiles are in safe operating condition
   (C) the drivers have exchanged names and license numbers
   (D) he or she obtains the names and addresses of drivers and witnesses

35. A radio motor patrol team arrives on the scene a few minutes after a pedestrian has been killed by a hit-and-run driver. After obtaining a description of the car, the first action the officer should take it to

    (A) radio a description of the fleeing car to precinct headquarters

    (B) try to overtake the fleeing car

    (C) obtain complete statements from everyone at the scene

    (D) inspect the site of the accident for clues

36. It has been claimed that a person who commits a crime sometimes has an unconscious wish to be punished, which is caused by strong unconscious feelings of guilt. Of the following actions by a criminal, the one which may be partly due to an unconscious desire for punishment is

    (A) claiming that he or she doesn't know anything about the crime when questioned by the police

    (B) running away from the state where the crime was committed

    (C) revisiting the place where the crime was committed

    (D) taking care not to leave any clues at the scene of the crime

37. Which of the following statements about fingerprints is *least* accurate?

    (A) The value of fingerprints left at the scene of the crime does not vary with the distinctness of the fingerprint impressions.

    (B) It is of value to fingerprint a person with an abnormal number of fingers.

    (C) Fingerprints of different persons have never been found to be alike.

    (D) The prime value of fingerprints lies in their effectiveness in identifying people.

38. According to a police manual, the delivery for laboratory examination of any article required as evidence must be made by the member of the force finding or coming into the possession of such evidence. Of the following, the most likely reason for this procedure is that it

    (A) assists in the establishment of the authenticity of the evidence

    (B) encourages a more careful search of the crime scene for all physical evidence that may be related to the crime

    (C) ensures that the evidence will be properly marked or tagged for future identification

    (D) prevents the undue delay that might result from a delivery through official channels

39. You are watching a great number of people leave a ball game. Of the persons who are described below, the one whom it would be easiest to spot would be

    (A) female; age 15; height 5'6"; weight 140 lbs.; long straight black hair

    (B) male; age 50; height 5'8"; weight 150 lbs.; missing toe on right foot

    (C) male; age 60; height 5'7"; weight 170 lbs.; all false teeth

    (D) male; age 25; height 6'3"; weight 220 lbs.; pockmarked

40. You are preparing a description of a woman to be broadcast. Of the following characteristics, the one which would be of most value to an officer driving a squad car is

    (A) wanted for murder

    (B) age 45 years

(C) height 6'1"

(D) smokes very heavily

41. Assume that on a hot summer day you are stationed on the grass at the south bank of a busy parkway looking at southbound traffic for a light blue 1974 Ford two door sedan. If traffic is very heavy, which of the following additional pieces of information would be most helpful to you in identifying the car?

(A) All chrome is missing from the left side of the car.

(B) There is a bullet hole in the left front window.

(C) The paint on the right side of the car is somewhat faded.

(D) The front bumper is missing.

42. You are watching a great number of people leave a sports arena after a boxing match. Of the characteristics listed below, the one which would be of greatest value to you in spotting a man wanted by the department is

(A) height: 5'3"; weight: 200 lbs.

(B) eyes: brown; hair: black, wavy; complexion: sallow

(C) that he frequents bars and grills and customarily associates with females

(D) scars: thin $1/2$" scar on left upper lip; tattoos: on right forearm—"Pinto"

43. "Social Security cards are not acceptable proof of identification for police purposes." Of the following, the most important reason for this rule is that the Social Security card

(A) is easily obtained

(B) states on its face "for Social Security purposes—not for identification"

(C) is frequently lost

(D) does not contain a photograph, description, or fingerprints of the person

44. Stationed at a busy intersection, you are given the description of a vehicle that has been stolen. Of the following characteristics, the one which will permit you to eliminate most easily a large number of vehicles is

(A) no spare tire

(B) make—Buick, two-door sedan, 1986

(C) color—black

(D) tires—750 x 16, white-walled

45. "The four witnesses to the bank robbery, including the bank president and the cashier, were left together for one hour in the president's office at the bank before they were questioned." This kind of procedure is

(A) desirable and considerate as there is no point in treating respectable citizens as criminals

(B) unwise as it permits undue pressure to be brought upon some of the witnesses

(C) unwise as it permits an exchange of actual and imagined details that may result in invalid testimony

(D) wise as it keeps the witnesses all in one place

46. Suppose that you are questioning witnesses to a hit-and-run accident. Of the following, the information that will probably be *least* valuable for the purpose of sending out an alarm for the hit-and-run automobile is the

    (A) direction which the automobile took after the accident

    (B) number of occupants in the automobile at the time of the accident

    (C) speed at which the automobile was moving when it struck the victim

    (D) part of the automobile that struck the victim of the accident

47. The marks left on a bullet by a gun barrel are different from those left by any other gun barrel. This fact is most useful in directly identifying the

    (A) direction from which a shot was fired

    (B) person who fired a particular gun

    (C) gun from which a bullet was fired

    (D) bullet that caused a fatal wound

48. Uniformed officers are constantly urged to consider every revolver loaded until proven otherwise. Of the following, the best justification for this recommendation is that

    (A) no time is lost when use of the revolver is required

    (B) there are many accidents involving apparently empty revolvers

    (C) less danger is involved when facing armed criminals

    (D) ammunition deteriorates unless replaced periodically.

49. A police officer should fire a pistol

    (A) only as a last resort

    (B) at no time

    (C) primarily to inspire fear

    (D) to impress upon citizens the need for respect

50. Assume that you are driving a police car, equipped with a two-way radio, along an isolated section of the parkway at 3 A.M. You note that the headlights of a car pulled to the side of the road are blinking rapidly. When you stop to investigate, the driver of the car informs you that he was just forced to the side of the road by two men in a green station wagon, who robbed him of a large amount of cash and jewelry at gunpoint and then sped away. Your first consideration in this situation should be to

    (A) drive rapidly along the parkway in the direction taken by the criminals in an effort to apprehend them before they escape

    (B) question the driver carefully, looking for inconsistencies indicating that he made up the whole story

    (C) obtain a complete listing and identification of all materials lost

    (D) notify your superior to have the parkway exits watched for a car answering the description of the getaway car

51. When the bodies of two women were found stabbed in an inner room of an apartment, it was first believed that it was a case of mutual homicide. Of the following clues found at the scene, the one that indicates that it was more likely a case of murder by a third party is the fact that
    (A) the door to the apartment was found locked
    (B) there were bloodstains on the outer door of the apartment
    (C) there was a switchblade knife in each body
    (D) no money could be found in the room where the bodies were

52. "The questioning of witnesses is often much less truth-revealing than are physical clues found at the scene of the crime." Of the following, the chief justification for this statement is that
    (A) most witnesses rarely tell the truth
    (B) physical clues are always present if examination is thorough
    (C) questioning of witnesses must be supported by other evidence
    (D) the memory of witnesses is often unreliable

53. Jones, who is suspected of having committed a crime of homicide at 8:30 P.M. in the building where he lives, claims that he could not have committed the act because he worked overtime until 8:00 P.M. In order to prove that Jones actually could not have committed the act in question, it is most important to know
    (A) how long it takes to get from Jones's building to Jones's place of work
    (B) if there are any witnesses to that fact that Jones worked overtime
    (C) Jones's reputation in the community
    (D) what kind of work Jones does

54. In a recent case of suicide, the body was found slumped in a chair and no revolver, knife, or razor was found in the room. Of the following, the most reasonable hypothesis from the data given is that
    (A) the person had taken some poison
    (B) the person had hanged himself
    (C) the person had died as a result of a heart attack
    (D) the murderer had taken the weapon

55. Suppose that a seven-year-old boy was kidnapped as he was returning home from a playground at dusk. The following day, his parents received an anonymous letter that told them the child was well and designated a close friend of the family, who was known to be very fond of the boy, as an intermediary to arrange payment of a ransom. On the basis of these data only, we may most reasonably assume that
    (A) the friend kidnapped the boy
    (B) the friend was probably an accessory in the kidnapping
    (C) further investigation is necessary to determine the identity of the kidnapper
    (D) the boy is dead

56. A representative group of young criminals in a certain state were found to be normal in intelligence, but 86 percent were behind from one to six grades in school. The best inference from these data is that

(A) lack of intelligence is highly correlated with delinquency

(B) criminals should be removed from the school system

(C) educational maladjustments are closely associated with delinquency

(D) the usual rate at which criminals progress educationally represents the limit of their learning powers

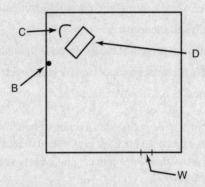

57. Assume that you are investigating a case of reported suicide. You find the deceased sitting in a chair, sprawled over his desk, a revolver still clutched in his right hand. In your examination of the room, you find that the window is partly open. Only one bullet has been fired from the revolver. The bullet has lodged in the wall. Assume that the diagram above is a scale drawing of the scene. D indicates the desk, C indicates the chair, W indicates the window, and B indicates the bullet. Of the following, which indicates most strongly that the deceased did not commit suicide?

(A) the distance between the desk and the bullet hole

(B) the relative position of the bullet hole and the chair

(C) the fact that the window was partly open

(D) the relative position of the desk and the window

58. The proprietor of a tavern summons a police officer and turns over a loaded revolver that was found in one of the tavern's booths. The *least* appropriate action for the officer to take is to

(A) unload the gun and place it in an inside pocket

(B) determine exactly when the revolver was found

(C) obtain the names or descriptions of the persons who occupied the booth before the revolver was found

(D) question the proprietor very closely concerning the matter

59. Assume that you have stopped a 1988 Dodge four-door sedan, which you suspect is a car reported as stolen the day before. The items of information that would be most useful in determining whether or not this is the stolen car is that

    (A) the stolen car's license number was QA2356; this car's license number is U21375

    (B) the stolen car's engine number was AB6231; this car's engine number is CS2315

    (C) the windshield of the stolen car was not cracked; this car's windshield is cracked

    (D) the stolen car had whitewall tires; this car does not have whitewall tires

60. In some states, statutes forbid the payment of ransom to kidnappers. Such statutes are

    (A) actually in violation of the due process of law clause of the federal constitution

    (B) necessary to encourage kidnappers to return the kidnapped person unharmed

    (C) harmful because kidnapping is encouraged by such legislation

    (D) examples of laws that protect society although sometimes working hardships on individuals

ANSWER KEY

1. A	11. D	21. B	31. A	41. D	51. B
2. A	12. B	22. C	32. C	42. A	52. D
3. D	13. A	23. B	33. C	43. D	53. A
4. C	14. A	24. D	34. C	44. B	54. A
5. C	15. B	25. A	35. A	45. C	55. C
6. D	16. A	26. C	36. C	46. C	56. C
7. A	17. C	27. A	37. A	47. C	57. B
8. A	18. C	28. C	38. A	48. B	58. A
9. B	19. C	29. B	39. D	49. A	59. B
10. C	20. C	30. B	40. C	50. D	60. D

EXPLANATORY ANSWERS

1. **(A)** A police officer is always a police officer, even when not officially on duty. Off-duty status does not relieve a police officer from fulfilling the police role.

2. **(A)** The first thing to do is to protect the man's life by escorting him out of danger. Securing medical assistance should follow.

3. **(D)** Obviously, going the wrong way on a one-way street creates a dangerous situation for many people. By stopping the driver, you have averted the danger. The out-of-towner has not actually committed a violation, he was just about to. It would be wise to point out to him exactly how one-way streets are marked in your town.

4. **(C)** Drowning occurs very quickly. Try to rescue the boy.

5. **(C)** Anything unusual should be investigated as soon as possible. The first thing to do is to determine whether or not a burglary has occurred. Then the premises should be secured and the owner notified. If the premises were not entered, they should be kept under surveillance in case the burglar returns.

6. **(D)** You can assume that these people are up to no good. The quickest way to find this out is to ask for registration papers, for proof of ownership. If the keys were simply locked inside the car, the owner should readily clear up your suspicion. If ownership cannot be proved, arrest is indicated.

7. **(A)** An argument in a cleaning store is not an emergency situation. There is no need to disrupt traffic nor to create alarm. On the other hand, the situation could lead to blows so the officer should stop in to try to calm the tempers.

8. **(A)** The owner may indeed be caring for his or her car, in which case the owner can prove ownership. An open hood can also be a sign of car theft by means of jump start or of battery theft in progress.

9. **(B)** A pattern of regular inspections gives fair notice to prospective wrongdoers as to when no one will be looking.

10. **(C)** Seven or eight people do not constitute an unruly crowd. The appearance of a person of authority demanding order should end the disturbance.

11. **(D)** A newly appointed officer assumes some responsibility immediately. The supervising officer will give guidance but will not make all decisions.

12. **(B)** Common sense. Extremes are not desirable. You must respect the rights of the innocent even as you make sure to arrest the guilty.

13. **(A)** The careless person is not likely to succeed; the negligent person will probably fail.

14. **(A)** You have four choices. Of these, crime prevention is the primary function of a police department.

15. **(B)** Police badges serve as identification of the police officers.

16. **(A)** The police officer must be alert at all times.

17. **(C)** The officer must understand what he or she is to do in order to do it. Watch out for distracting answers like that offered by choice (A). Self-interest is never the reason for doing anything when taking a civil service exam.

18. **(C)** Remember not to step out of the police officer's role. The police officer must never recommend individuals, not even a choice of individuals. The most the police officer may do is recommend that the individual contact the local bar association or consult directories in a library.

19. **(C)** Criminal behavior is not exempt from the struggle for equality.

20. **(C)** This phenomenon is called "copycat crime." It is an unfortunate but unavoidable consequence of a free press.

21. **(B)** This question requires careful reading and interpreting rather than judgment. A member on duty but not in uniform may drink intoxicants but not to an extent to make him or her unfit for duty. Judgment enters into the situation in that the officer must judge for him- or herself at what point to stop drinking.

22. **(C)** Police officers are trained in the law and in the law of arrest. They are better able to judge when arrest is called for.

23. **(B)** The police officer's first priority is to save lives. An ambulance on an emergency run is on a mission to save a life. Lifesaving supersedes all other orders.

24. **(D)** If you do not really know the answer to this question, you can reach it by a process of elimination. (A) is incorrect because a medical problem cannot be ignored; (B) is incorrect because the person must be informed of the reason for arrest; (C) is incorrect because the person is certainly allowed to speak and to express feelings. **(D)** is your best choice. While all suicide threats must be taken seriously, the person newly taken into custody may well be blustering. Suicide in custody is a serious problem. The silent, brooding, distressed prisoner must be carefully watched.

25. **(A)** Even in this age of AIDS, the officer must be *least* concerned with diseases the suspect may carry. The officer must be more concerned with the possibility that the suspect will use a gun or physical force to resist arrest or that he or she will try to flee.

26. **(C)** Your superiors have the advantage of years of training and experience. Their judgment is quicker, and they must be obeyed without question at the site of an emergency.

27. **(A)** An introductory statement describing the occurrence establishes the framework on which to hang details and conclusions.

28. **(C)** The police badge is an identifying emblem. The police officer who serves as a witness must be identified as such.

29. **(B)** Pure common sense. Overcrowding leads to friction. Furthermore, prisoners in constant close proximity have more opportunity to plan trouble together.

30. **(B)** It is true that the officer's name and shield number will appear on the summons, but there is no harm in giving these to the motorist. Professional behavior requires that the summons be given without further discussion.

31. **(A)** You do not need to have had training in investigation of traffic accidents to recognize from the diagram that car 2 is too far beyond the center of the intersection to have been attempting a left turn. Driver 1 is trying to cover himself with a false statement about Driver 2.

32. **(C)** You have a radio. Use it. The alleged robbers should be pursued promptly and safely.

33. **(C)** Access to the area of an accident should be limited to those who are attending to the injured. Beyond lifesaving the first priority is to preserve evidence. Inconvenience to the public is a later consideration.

34. **(C)** The police role at the scene of a property-damage accident is to be certain that both drivers are licensed drivers and are authorized to drive the vehicles, that the automobiles are safe to operate on the public roadway, that information has been obtained for police files as to those involved in the accident and witnesses. It is not the role of the police officer to be concerned with the parties' arrangements to collect damages from one another.

35. **(A)** A hit-and-run driver must be pursued and apprehended as quickly as possible. The efficient way to intercept the hit-and-run car is to radio a description of the car to precinct headquarters for instant broadcast to patrol cars in the vicinity.

36. **(C)** The person with an unconscious wish to be punished, also known as a "death wish," will draw attention to him- or herself with respect to the crime. Revisiting the crime scene is a common means of doing this. The other choices represent efforts to avoid detection and punishment.

37. **(A)** Read carefully. *The least accurate* format of the question makes is tricky to answer. Choices (B), (C) and (D) make correct, positive statements. Choice **(A)** makes a wrong statement. The value of fingerprints left at the scene of the crime *does* vary with the distinctness of the fingerprint impressions. Clearer fingerprints are more valuable.

38. **(A)** In general, the fewer people who handle a piece of evidence, the fewer things can go wrong. Personal delivery of the evidence makes for less hearsay. Choice (C) is incorrect because of the strong word "ensures." Evidence can still be mismarked even with personal delivery and initially correct information.

39. **(D)** Descriptions (B) and (C) are of no use whatsoever. Watching people leave a ball game, you have no way of knowing who is missing a toe nor who has false teeth. Choice (A) describes a very typical young girl. Choice **(D)** is a big man who stands out in a crowd, and his pockmarked face is further visible identification.

40. **(C)** Common sense. How many 6'1" women do you see roaming the streets?

41. **(D)** As the car is coming towards you, the most useful information is that the front bumper is missing. A bullet hole would be too small to see in a moving car on a busy highway.

42. **(A)** A 5'3" man weighing 200 lbs. is obese. He should be relatively easy to spot if you are alerted to watch for him. All these identification judgment questions are meant to test your judgment as to what you would report if other officers were to search on the basis of your descriptions.

43. **(D)** A Social Security card is not acceptable proof of identification for any purpose because it does not identify. The Social Security card contains no picture nor descriptive text of any sort.

44. **(B)** Common sense. There are a great number of black cars. Spare tire or lack thereof and tire size are ridiculous characteristics by which to attempt to identify a vehicle in a busy intersection. Make, body style, and year give you something definite to go by.

45. **(C)** You want the personal recollection of each individual witness, not the consensus of a committee.

46. **(C)** The speed at which an automobile was traveling when it hit a victim may affect the extent of damage to the vehicle, but it is the *least* valuable information from among the choices. The direction in which the automobile fled can direct the chase; the number of occupants helps with identification; the part of the automobile that struck the victim may be distinctively damaged.

47. **(C)** Markings on a bullet left by a gun barrel serve the same purpose as fingerprints. Since they are unique, they effectively identify the gun from which the bullet was fired.

48. **(B)** Common sense. Read the newspapers for confirmation.

49. **(A)** Of course, there are police regulations concerning the firing of guns. Common sense dictates that the officer has a pistol to use if necessary, but that there must be a very good reason to use that gun.

50. **(D)** You can't catch the robbers yourself; they have already gone too far. On the other hand, you must not allow them to exit the parkway while you are questioning the victim. Radio to have the exits monitored. A limited access parkway offers possibilities for interception of thieves that are absent on city streets.

51. **(B)** The blood on the door bears investigation. It was likely left by the murderer at exit.

52. **(D)** Unfortunately, observation is often incomplete and memory may fill in the gaps or even distort the facts.

53. **(A)** The first question to be raised is the amount of time taken to travel from Jones' place of work to his home. If it is determined that it does indeed take longer than one half hour, then Jones must supply proof that he really was working at 8 P.M. If the distance can be covered in less than a half hour, whether or not Jones was really working at 8 P.M. is irrelevant.

54. **(A)** Read carefully. The question describes a suicide, thereby eliminating choices (C) and (D). A body slumped in a chair is not consistent with hanging.

55. **(C)** With these facts, the only certainty is that further investigation is warranted on an urgent basis.

56. **(C)** A person who is normal in intelligence but is below grade level in school is educationally maladjusted. The fact that 86 percent of delinquents appear to be normally intelligent but below grade level points to a close association of educational maladjustment with delinquency. With this information, we can describe a correlation but not a causal relationship. The data do not indicate that educational maladjustment causes delinquency nor that delinquency leads to educational maladjustment, only that they are related.

57. **(B)** For the deceased to have committed suicide with the bullet lodged as indicated, the shot would have had to come from a revolver in his left hand. The revolver is in his right hand.

58. **(A)** This is unintelligent handling of evidence. Fingerprints and ballistics evidence may be destroyed. It would be wise to close off the booth to the public so as to safeguard possible clues such as match covers, bits of paper with notes on them, and fingerprints on drinking glasses.

59. **(B)** Comparison of engine numbers is usually the determining factor in establishing whether or not a car is indeed the stolen one in question. Engine numbers are changed only with great difficulty; it is most unlikely that this would be accomplished in one day. This 1988 Dodge is probably not the car that was reported stolen. License plates and tires are easily changed and cannot serve as positive identification of stolen cars. A stolen car can easily acquire a cracked windshield.

60. **(D)** This is a situation in which individual interests must be subverted for the common good. The individual family wants its kidnapped member back at any price. However, allowing kidnappers to profit from kidnapping encourages other kidnappers. The principle is the same as the principle of not negotiating with terrorists. Wrongdoers must not achieve their goals through their wrongdoing. Hopefully, prospective kidnappers who know that they will fail in their attempt to collect ransom will be discouraged from kidnapping.

Compass Direction Quiz

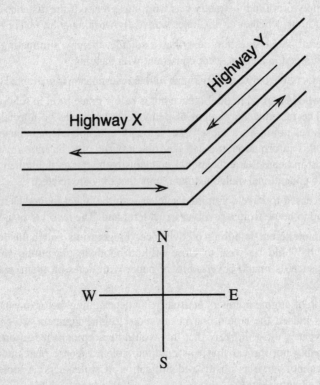

1. Highway Y comes down to join Highway X at the direction of

   (A) southwest

   (B) northeast

   (C) southeast

   (D) east

2. A vehicle traveling on Highway Y and entering Highway X would then be traveling

   (A) northeast

   (B) east

   (C) southwest

   (D) west

3. A vehicle traveling east on Highway X would enter Highway Y and then be traveling

(A) southwest

(B) northeast

(C) southeast

(D) east

4. Highway X comes in to join Highway Y while traffic is moving in the direction of

(A) north

(B) south

(C) northeast

(D) west

5. A motorist traveling southwest on Highway Y would have to make the following turn to continue his trip:

(A) right lane east on Highway Y

(B) left lane east on Highway Y

(C) right lane west on Highway X

(D) left lane south on Highway X

6. Highway X and Highway Y are said to have a junction at

(A) an acute angle

(B) an obtuse angle

(C) a right angle

(D) a direct intersection

7. Although a car traveling east on Highway X would enter Highway Y for continuous travel, its direction would change

(A) toward the left and north

(B) toward the left and west

(C) toward the left and northeast

(D) toward the right and south

8. Motorists traveling east on Highway X must enter Highway Y and then

(A) travel northwest on Highway Y

(B) travel northeast on Highway Y

(C) move east on Highway X

(D) none of the above

9. The one of the following vehicle movements that would not be permitted at the junction of Highways X and Y would be

   (A) a left turn from Highway X to Y

   (B) a U-turn at the junction

   (C) a right turn from Highway Y to X

   (D) a left turn from Highway X into a lane traveling in the same direction

10. Assume that a cautionary yellow light is in place at each traffic lane. The purpose of the light would be to prevent

    (A) speeding cars from crossing traffic lanes and continuing into opposite directional traffic

    (B) slow-moving cars from continuing their pace as they turn from Highways Y to X

    (C) normal-moving cars from continuing at their current speed

    (D) slow-moving cars from continuing their pace as they turn from Highways X to Y

ANSWER KEY—COMPASS DIRECTIONS

1. A	3. B	5. C	7. C	9. B
2. D	4. C	6. B	8. B	10. A